Clara Gottler

Sent to Earth

Sent to Earth

God and the Return of Ancient Disasters

by

Michael H. Brown

PUBLISHING COMPANY
P.O. Box 220 • Goleta, CA 93116
(800) 647-9882 • (805) 692-0043 • Fax: (805) 967-5843

Acknowledgments

There are many I could thank. Thanks first off to my wife Lisa for her tireless help in editing and her tireless devotion. I would also like to thank those many hundreds I have interviewed over the past ten years, too numerous to list, but all sent my heartfelt gratitude. I would like to thank my publisher, Robert Schaefer, for courageously taking on this project, and my agent for her skills and integrity.

©2000 Queenship Publishing – All Rights Reserved

Library of Congress Number 00-135495

Published by:
 Queenship Publishing
 P.O. Box 220
 Goleta, CA 93116
 (800) 647-9882 • (805) 692-0043 • Fax: (805) 967-5843

Printed in the United States of America

ISBN: 1-57918-147-3

Contents

Chapter 1
The Beginning of Calamities 1

Chapter 2
The Evil of This World 11

Chapter 3
Rain of Fire 19

Chapter 4
A Storm of Quakes 23

Chapter 5
Cycles of Admonishment 27

Chapter 6
Sons of the Gods 29

Chapter 7
Theater of Horrors 33

Chapter 8
The Sun Darkened 39

Chapter 9
A Fire on the Moon 43

Chapter 10
Blacker Than Death 49

Chapter 11
Secrets on a Mountain 53

Chapter 12
"I am terrified of these prodigies" 65

Chapter 13
"A time of darkness" 69

Chapter 14
"The seasons will be altered" 73

Chapter 15
Wondrous Times 81

Chapter 16
A Thousand Devils 87

Chapter 17
The Earth Rumbling 89

Chapter 18
A Flaming Sword 93

Chapter 19
The Hour of Persecution 99

Chapter 20
The Dark Horseman 105

Chapter 21
A Horror in Paradise 109

Chapter 22
The Great Sign 115

Chapter 23
"Tsunami!" 119

Chapter 24
Something Underneath 123

Chapter 25
"There were tornadoes all over the place" 129

Chapter 26
"Fire will fall" 135

Chapter 27
   The Warnings 143

Chapter 28
   "They have no idea what awaits them" 149

Chapter 29
   Edge of Catastrophe 157

Chapter 30
   An Hour of Fire 165

Chapter 31
   "Behold, I will destroy them with the earth" . . . 169

Chapter 32
   Valkyries on a Rampage 177

Chapter 33
   Threats Close and Distant 183

Chapter 34
   The Warning in L.A. 187

Chapter 35
   The Ocean Afire 191

Chapter 36
   A Haunted Countryside 195

Chapter 37
   Signs in Asia. 201

Chapter 38
   A Change in Landscape 207

Chapter 39
   The Storm Next Time 213

Chapter 40
   Kings of the World 219

Chapter 41
   A Remarkable Horror 225

Chapter 42
   Ground Zero 229

Chapter 43
   A Supervolcano? 237

Chapter 44
   Tragedy in Waiting 247

Chapter 45
   The Superquake 261

Chapter 46
   The Last Secrets 267

Chapter 47
   Superwave 277

Chapter 48
   A Sinister Disease? 283

Chapter 49
   "Evil Star" 287

Chapter 50
   Floods, a Flash, Darkness 295

Chapter 51
   "Return to My embrace" 301

Notes 311

About the Author 321

"And the sanctuary of God in heaven opened. Then came flashes of lightning and peals of thunder. And darkness came over the whole land, and the earth trembled. Something like a huge mountain all in flames was cast into the sea. And, behold, the plague was begun (Revelation 11:19 and 8:8, *Luke* 23:44, *Matthew* 27:51, *Numbers* 16:46).

For Christ

CHAPTER 1

The Beginning of Calamities

It was some while back, in the 1980s, that I became aware of an undercurrent across many religious denominations, a deep sense that earth was about to undergo a period of turmoil similar to times in the past. God was not happy with the course of human progress, many felt, and was about to send disasters to earth. It was not necessarily "apocalyptic" (although that was always a possibility) but rather a period of chastisement similar to what happened at the time of Sodom and Gomorrah or Nineveh.

I didn't know what to think of such claims, but I had the same feeling that God was about to break down societal evil, and through the years, as I spoke with more and more people, I became increasingly convinced that God was beginning to do just that: that He was slowly unfolding events. Nature was beginning to rise. Events were already beginning to occur. God was not happy with the constructs of mankind and was ready to break it down as He often had: through events in nature.

It has been my premise in the course of writing a series of books over the past decade that we are in a very special time. It's an exciting time, but also a dangerous time. We have strayed, and God is about to put us to the test. It's a spiritual issue, and though it has the backdrop of natural disasters, this is an unabashedly spiritual book. In the past few years we have seen tangible signs that something strange is going on, that events, especially in nature, are building up, that something or somethings, plural, are about to break loose. We see such indications on the news every night, and it is also pronounced by our prophets. In the past 150 years there have been some fascinating private revelations, at least three of which are truly major and indicate that we are nearing what I can only describe as cataclysms. While false predictions have numbed us to such warnings, the real ones bear great warnings and as you will see, they are borne out by what has been happening in the world.

Something is about to occur.

This intuition is even felt in the secular world. In Tokyo is a futuristic emergency center with long sleek chairs that face several huge screens and tall metallic walls. Here top officials will meet when the catastrophic earthquake — all but inevitable — finally comes. In California it's a facility filled with computers, satellite feedback, and seismographs. It too waits. The odds of a huge quake in the next thirty years are 67 percent. In Miami the government has built a new weather center with ten-foot steel reinforced walls. Like other southern cities Miami is overdue for a massive, once-in-a-lifetime hurricane.

Chastisement. Disasters. The world has been in a period of relative quiet, but by most indications that calm is ending. A time that has seen only standard natural events is drawing to a close. We have only to turn on the television each day to know this. There are blizzards. There are quakes. There are floods in Venezuela. Storms sweep across the United States. Record wildfires blaze. Since 1989 seven of the top ten disasters in U.S. history have occurred and in that time the country has incurred 38 weather-related disasters in which damages reached or exceeded $1 billion.

Of the nation's greatest-ever calamities, only three — the great Chicago fire, the famous Galveston flood, and the San Francisco quake of 1906 — have *not* taken place during the last two decades.

The Beginning of Calamities

There are always disasters but what we have seen worldwide has been tremendous. In 1999 winds from a system of low pressure ripped through France, the gale also buffeting Spain and Germany, what the national meteorological office in Offenbach called "the worst hurricane Germany has ever had," three days of devastating storms that howled through the Alps where it turned to snow and triggered avalanches. In Rome slabs were torn off a roof designed by Michelangelo while in France there was damage to the Cathedral of Notre Dame. A few years before the government in Canada declared that its people had suffered "some of the most extreme and destructive weather ever to hit the country, the stuff of a Hollywood catastrophe film — 'weather bombs' in Vancouver Island, hailers on the prairies, deluges of biblical proportion," while in Vietnam the first-ever hailstorm sparked rumors of doomsday. In Ontario an ice storm dumped the equivalent weight of 77,000 Titanics.

There are always natural events but they are forming a baffling cluster. In 1999 1,225 tornadoes struck the U.S. at the same time that quakes rocked ancient Mesopotamian sites — granting it a biblical flavor.

"Then suddenly, in an instant, you shall be visited by the Lord of hosts, with thunder, earthquake, and great noise, whirlwind, storm, and the flame of consuming fire," says the Old Testament (*Isaiah* 29:6) and indeed flames whipped by the dry winds of El Niño have destroyed millions of acres in Asia, Mexico, and the Amazon. One witness described it as a "stinking wind" that reeked of sulfur and was "a gust of dark ill omen."

During the summer of 2000 a wall of flame — often threatening nuclear sites — swept across the American West, as God often speaks through fire.

Actuaries report that large-scale natural disasters are three times more common than in the 1960s and with $90 billion in damage 1998 was the most calamitous on record.

"Comparing the figures for the 1960s and the last ten years, the number of great natural catastrophes has risen by a factor of three, with economic losses — after being adjusted for inflation — rising by a factor of nine and insured losses by a factor of no less than fifteen," reports Munich Re Group, one of the world's largest insurers.

The National Oceanic and Atmospheric Administration (NOAA) tells us that the situation has grown "critical" and warns us to prepare for "an abrupt change in climate." There have never been more hurricanes, and the weather seems but a backdrop. Experts are worried about everything from the collapse of ice sheets in the Antarctic to a new stage — a ratcheting up — of epidemics. "Expect the unexpected," Dr. Joseph E. McDade, deputy director of the CDC's National Center for Infectious Diseases, told me, and the same is said by seismologists: There were double the average number of earthquake deaths around the world in 1999 at the same time as outbreaks of malaria, West Nile fever, and flesh-eating bacteria.

Why is this happening? Why is there turmoil in the world? Why disaster?

As I said, this is a spiritual book, and the premise is that anytime evil accumulates, anytime there is idolatry, anytime the culture turns materialistic, self-indulgent, and immoral — anytime children kill children — there is a price to pay, and that price is often exacted by nature. When a society turns to crudity and cold-heartedness, when it defies God's love, when it rejects Him, it fashions its own ruin.

Such is the case today. We are in serious times and are entering ones that will be yet more serious because our culture has reverted to old paganism. It has created new divinities. It is centered on man. It is focused on worldliness. And as you will see, that has *always* led to devastation. As you will see, sins similar to those in our day brought huge events in the Bronze Age, the Classical Period, and the Middle Ages. Throughout history God has sent large and small events to awaken man. Sometimes the events are isolated. A large disaster may arrive in an otherwise normal period. Other times He sends them — He allows them to occur — in larger clusters. This is what we face: a large upheaval, a truly tumultuous series of events, the return of disasters that occurred in ancient eras and are of a scale larger than any we know.

That's what prophecy tells us, and our officials don't know quite why, but they too sense it. The past is prologue and in the past have been gargantuan episodes — volcanoes, landslides, and even cosmic events — that are returning for spiritual reasons.

It is not science fiction. The scenario taking shape is that of disasters intensifying in all regions. They come and grow and precipitate larger events and eventually there will be a show-stopper. Some scoff at this as "Chicken Little," but history is filled with events much larger than the vast majority of us realize, events that cluster, events that change the world. Archaeologists are finding tantalizing evidence that disasters periodically tend to congregate, and the signs of just such a convergence are around us. There is change in wind patterns. There is change in rainfall. There is a swerving of temperatures.

It's as if nature is rising up and it is my premise — my message — that due to spiritual forces more, much more, is coming. We are seeing the precursors. We are watching the build-up. Small events are becoming larger.

That's not to scare you. It is not to intimidate you. It is not a time for fear but of reparation. Only through God, only through conversion — a lifting of our spiritual blinders — will we avert huge problems, and that is the message of this book: come back to God before it is too late. Yes, it is the old refrain of Jonah; it is the refrain of John the Baptist, on whose feast day one of the revelations we will study occurred. And it is supported by fact. A recent study for the National Science Foundation raises the prospect of a disaster that could cost $250 billion in one city alone; others say half a trillion. "The increasing number and severity of natural disasters in the past decade demands that action be taken to reduce the threat that disasters impose upon the economic stability, economic future, and safety of the citizens of the United States," says the Federal Emergency Management Agency, which has seen the number of major disaster declarations increase from 31 in 462 counties in 1989 to 75 in 1,537 counties in 1996. Some of the counties were declared more than once, but the point is made: there is a step-up. There is a growing siege. We were given certain moral choices in the 1990s, and we failed. We chose a reckless path. We let evil reach new heights. And the signs were swift. In 1999 19 disasters were declared for hurricanes alone, eclipsing the previous record of 11. In all there were 55 major declarations and 37 states needed emergency aid.

The stage is set. God has tapped us on the shoulder. In His mercy He always warns, but soon He will more than tap us on the shoulder. All major religions see signs of the times and the Vatican has recently studied "secret" prophecies that delineate disasters. These secrets are the backdrop of this book. They started at a place called LaSalette in France, and they have proceeded through the famous secrets of Fatima, Portugal, to Medjugorje in former Yugoslavia. They are from the Virgin Mary, who in serving as an emissary of Christ, warns, as He did (*Luke* 21 or *Matthew* 24), that evil has its consequences — both here and in eternity. I make no apologies for relying on her. She works for Jesus. She is His envoy. From the cross she was proclaimed as our Mother (*John* 19:27) and now in true maternal fashion (despite the attempts by Satan to smear her) she comes to warn us, to help us, to call us back to her Son. I well understand the concern that her apparitions could be demonic or that she is "idolized," but having discerned the matter closely for many years and having traveled to each of the sites where secrets were issued (in some cases a number of times, and in many countries), I agree with the great Pentecostal leader, David du Plessis, a non-Catholic who journeyed to Medjugorje and declared it a work of the Holy Spirit. The fruit of these sites has been astounding (millions brought back to Jesus), and in the decades since they have happened, secrets like those of Fatima have never exhibited the least hint of evil, delusion, or fraud. And they are pertinent to the notion of chastisement. When the third secret of Fatima was released on June 26, 2000, it revealed the image — a drastic image — of an angel about to strike earth with a flaming sword!

This is what I am talking about: chastisement from heaven, purification that is sent to earth by God. While in the case of Fatima the flames were drowned by the light coming from the Blessed Mother, the indications from others are that we're not out of the woods — not by a long shot. At Medjugorje we are told that the world is out of balance, that a spiritual darkness reigns, that it is the hour of the power of darkness — the hour in which Satan acts with greatest force. If we do not confront that evil, if we don't purge it ourselves, God, in His mercy — in His wisdom — will do it for us. *"People will tear their hair,"* said Mary. *"Brothers will plead with brothers, they will curse their past lives lived without God."*

I'm a Catholic and I do not intend to hide, that but I write for all denominations. I write for Baptists, Methodists, Episcopalians, Jews, Lutherans, nondemoninationalists, and any faith that accepts God. I write for the agnostic and nonbeliever knowing we are all God's children. I believe in Christ and I have no doubt that He is alive and warning us as He warned us back in His time on earth. "There will be great earthquakes, plagues, and famines in various places," He had said; He said the sea would roar; He said the sky would grow dark. And that's what we face: a slew of events that may be punctuated by one of unprecedented — and, yes, terrifying — moment.

God has always spoken through nature. He thundered against the Philistines (*1 Samuel* 7:10). He answered Moses through a storm (*Exodus* 19:16). He went forth in a quake (*Judges* 5:4). We know about Noah. When there is wickedness — when there is greed, unbelief, and selfishness, when there is hardness of heart — God sends events to cleanse us.

My warning is that He is beginning to do so again. I hope there is repentance and that the events you will see building in this book do not reach the feared crescendo, but my message for years and now more urgent has been that we are passing a dangerous threshold and that disasters — greatly enhanced disasters, disasters as you have not seen — are coming. Ancient chastisement is about to return. For more than a century we have embarked on a course that negates religion — negates God — and we will suffer for it. We have dehumanized each other, we have built an artificial reality — we're even ready to clone! — and we will see the result.

Evil leads to destruction.

Evil is the word "live" spelled backwards.

Throughout history humans have been lured by the temptations of the world and the result has been "swift disaster" (*2 Peter* 2:1-3).

Catastrophe awaits a godless earth.

Unfortunately, many have stopped paying attention to such warnings. They became discouraged in 2000 when apocalypse did not ring in the new millennium or because the predictions of other seers fell to naught. Let me assure you that God does not care about the human calendar. He works in His own time. We do not have times and dates. But we do have the indications that we or our children will see massive global commotion. We're not to obsess on the negative but neither are we to ignore it. It is a time of darkness and so the situation is extremely precarious. We are headed in the wrong direction. It's that simple. The evils to which we will soon be witness because of our hardheartedness and disobedience will multiply. We have already been warned. We are now approaching the last admonitions. While we are not to fear, we must know what we are up against and call others to prayer, to conversion, to disseminating the warning. *"Pray, and do it with fervor,"* says Medjugorje (11/83). *"Include the whole world in your prayer. You must redouble your efforts. Day after day, increase your fervor* (11/83). *I have come to call the world to conversion for the last time* (5/82). *I have come here as Queen of Peace to tell the world that peace is necessary for the salvation of the world. You cannot imagine what is going to happen nor what the Eternal Father will send to earth* (6/83). *That is why you must be converted. Through fasting and prayer, one can stop wars, one can suspend the laws of nature* (7/82). *Advance against Satan by means of prayer* (8/85). *Pray, dear children, so that God's plan may be accomplished and all the works of Satan be changed in favor of the glory of God* (2/85). *Tell the faithful that I need their prayers, and prayers from all the people. God has chosen each one of you in order to use you in a great plan for the salvation of mankind* (1/87). *Raise your hands and yearn for Jesus. The most important thing is to ask for the gift of the Holy Spirit* (10/84). *When the Holy Spirit comes, peace will be established. When that occurs, everything changes around you* (10/84)."

Without those prayers, without a reverting back to God, we face destruction. It is that simple. Is that a controversial notion? It will rankle many who are "scientific." They have come to view earth only in terms of what can be seen or "proven" statistically and while I have plenty of statistics, in the end we must rely on the Spirit. There is still time but it is short. That should not scare us; it should not make us paranoid; it should call us to action — those who have fallen into lethargy because the world has not ended as false seers proclaimed or who were not in tune to begin with. No matter what field of science I have investigated, I have come away with the conviction that events are overdue. It is only by the grace of God that we have not been hit already. But nature is stirring. There is tremendous change in our climate — irises bloom in Vermont in December — and the weather has turned erratic. There are always famines, disease, and earthquakes, but what we face is extraordinary. We are in a special time and we and our children will see special events. I can't help it if some will lump me with the "apocalyptical." There are apocalyptical elements. However, I'm not talking about the end of the world; I don't pretend to have a date for the Second Coming. I know only that we're in a time of peril and I'm not going to hold back. I'm going to give it to you straight from the shoulder. We are in a beginning of calamities. We have sin as there was not sin in the days of Noah. And now as in ancient times God will send events to exile the great deceiver. Something is coming. Something is building. Never have the children of God delighted in sin as now, and now as in ancient times, as in periods throughout the past, God will send events, large events, events that have not been seen, to stop it, to purge it — to send His adversary into exile.

Chapter 2
The Evil of This World

What has happened in the past? What might we approach?

There have been any number of times in history when God has sent chastisement to earth. Let me take you first to one of the most mysterious. It was what they call the Early Bronze Age, and it occurred around 2300 B.C. (give or take a few centuries). We know it as the exotic time of pyramids.

To visualize this time we can imagine the market gardens and the groves of date palms and the fig trees that stretched as far as the eye could see. People lived in mud-brick homes that faced small courtyards. It was a heady time during which man in the Fertile Crescent had developed the first trade, agriculture, and writing. I call this the Mesopotamian Era because the first sophisticated people the world had known are thought to have originated in Mesopotamia (the heart of current-day Iraq).

In Asia Minor — the center of present-day Turkey — was Anatolia, the powerful kingdom of the ancient Hittites. In Mesopotamia, between the Euphrates and Tigris Rivers, were the kingdoms of Akkad and Sumer. This is where Babylon was located. In the Mediterranean were islands with advanced peoples like the Minoans.

I don't intend on getting into detail but it's important to know that it was the onset of commerce. In many ways, it was like our own time, a heady, materialistic time. There were inventions and innovations and more material wealth than ever. There were silver, ivory, and gold. Food was abundant. In fact, like our era, it was a time of excess. We only need to look at the tombs to know this. If one were to add the value of what was buried with many of the pharaohs, it would be beyond the reach of most modern billionaires. Sarcophagi were pounded from gold. There were gold statuettes and jeweled headdresses; there were the beads, anklets, and earrings. I remember the astonishment I felt at the sheer volume of precious metal when I visited King Tut's tomb in Cairo.

This was Satan's trap, materialism, and there was also sex. In Mesopotamia, Egypt, and the Near East, that too was rampant. I don't pretend to understand all the mysteries of sex, but God ordained it between wife and husband and this was violated badly in Egypt, where there were concubines, prostitutes, and incest. While it is said that the average person condemned such behavior, so widespread was corruption that harlots even plied their trade *in the temples*. There was rape, bestiality. There was homosexuality. There was necrophilia: rumors that embalmers used the dead. Egyptians placed phallic symbols in the temple of Hathor, a love goddess, and there were lewd celebrations during the worship of Bastet, a cat-goddess. "Some of the women make a noise with rattles, others play pipes all the way, while the rest of the women, and the men, sing and clap their hands," wrote an ancient historian named Herodotus. "As they journey by river to Bubastis whenever they come near any town they bring their boat near the bank; then some of the women of the town do as I have said, while some shout mocking of the women of the town, others dance, and others stand up and expose their persons. This they do whenever they come beside any riverside town. But when they have reached Bubastis, they make a festival with great sacrifices, and more wine is drunk at this feast than in the whole year beside."

We see immediately the great danger of occultism. Aside from materialism and lust, those in Egypt and across Mesopotamia — from Iraq up to Turkey, and around the Mediterranean — had put other gods before the one true Lord. They were communicating with evil. They were repeating the mistake in the Garden. Across the region were demonic images: statues of creatures that were half animal and half human, bodies of men but the heads of rams or hawks or jackals. There were gods of the water. There were gods of the stars. Isis. Horus. There were gods of the air. There was the symbol of the snake, which is a classic depiction, of course, of a demon.

Magicians roamed the land and cast spells and conducted incantations.

There was rampant idolatry (what we would today call witchcraft), and it was thought to bring good earthly fortune. It was like the New Age; it involved crystals. There was the energy of darkness, and it was real, testified to by the number of those who have come in contact with Tut's tomb and met mysterious ends. (One was a famous explorer named Lord Carnarvon, and others included two archaeologists who died within 24 hours of entry.)

It was a culture beholden to sorcery. At Ur was a great staged tower with an altar dedicated to a "moon-god" and throughout the Mesopotamian region were symbols of magic: ankhs, sphinxes, and the "sun sign" — a bent cross that later became known as the swastika.

While the gods seemed quaint to modern scientists, who have no time for "superstition," such images represented evil spirits, and idolatry — the worship of them — was what the Bible called an "abomination" (*Isaiah* 66:3). "Behold the Lord rideth upon a swift cloud, and shall come into Egypt: and the idols of Egypt shall be moved at His presence, and the heart of Egypt shall melt in the midst of it," warned *Isaiah* 19:1 at a later time, having obviously learned something from this period.

And then there were Sodom and Gomorrah. They may have existed at this same time, and the wickedness there, of course, was epic. There were sodomy, adultery, greed, and callousness. Visitors were robbed. Money was hoarded. "Look at the guilt of your sister Sodom," says *Ezekiel* 16:49-50. "She and her daughters were proud, sated with food, complacent in their prosperity, and they gave no help to the poor and needy. Rather, they became haughty."

And as a result the two cities, thought to have existed at the southern end of the Dead Sea, were destroyed. It was not a lone event. Across the breadth of Mesopotamia, Egypt, and the Near East came what I call the Great Mesopotamian Chastisement. I can't prove to you that all the events were linked, but in this same general part of the Bronze Age came a remarkable series of events that broke down the societies and washed away the evil. Around 2300 B.C. something happened to Egypt, Syria, Iraq, Palestine, Turkey, and Crete. Something truly momentous. There was a dramatic change. There was a tremendous alteration of the weather. There were what appeared to be widespread, unrelenting disasters. There was general upheaval in the climate. In Egypt and Mesopotamia — in the land of Baal and Ra and Isis — an excruciating, interminable, and possibly unprecedented drought set in, so dry that cropland was destroyed, rivers were dried, and settlements across this part of the world abandoned. There was a "drastic reduction of normal winter rainfall and an increase in erratic, torrential heavy rainstorms," according to Dr. Harvey Weiss of Yale, who told me the drought may have lasted for 300 years. This was shown from ancient samples of dust not only in old land deposits but at the bottom of the Gulf of Oman.

People fled what are known as the Habur and Assyrian plains, and the Old World collapsed. The world's first urban civilizations — the Old Kingdom in Egypt, the Akkadian Empire in Mesopotamia, the early societies in

Greece, Turkey, and Israel — all fell at once. There was drought at one time or one place while at other points were storms, tidal surges, and floods. There were references to a time when dust blotted out the sun. There was famine (as shown in art from the pyramid at Unas). Disease raged. As Weiss wrote, "Seasonal rains became scarce, and withering storms replaced them. The winds cut through northern wheat fields and blanketed them in dust. They emptied out towns and villages, sending people stumbling south with pastoral nomads, to seek forage along rivers and streams. For more than a hundred years the desertification continued, disrupting societies from southwestern Europe to central Asia. Egypt's Old Kingdom, the towns of Palestine, and the great cities of the Indus Valley also were among the casualties."

There was substantial evidence, in short, for abrupt widespread catastrophes. "In Mesopotamia, vast areas of land appear to have been devastated, inundated, or totally burned," said a British historian named Benjamin J. Peiser, and indeed ancient texts described walls "burnt up" and Egypt "an empty waste."

Dunes formed along the Nile as water vanished.

According to the descriptions of an ancient scribe named Ankhtifi, "The sky was in storm clouds and the land in the wind."

Rivers changed and sea levels fluctuated.

While the area near the Dead Sea and Sodom and Gomorrah was described at one time as "well-watered" and "like the Lord's own garden" (*Genesis* 13:10), it became the desert we know today.

From east to west, from north to south, the climate changed. Although focused in the Mideast, it was a global event. Lakes throughout Europe, China, and Africa shriveled up. Indians in South America changed their way of life, while islanders began to move about the Pacific. There were mass migrations. Canada dried up while hurricanes wailed along the coasts of Florida. Although in this case the change was to a cooler, not a warmer, environment, the upheaval was similar. "The cooler temperatures altered the northern Westerlies flow from a strong to a weak pattern with large north-south flows, thereby drastically changing weather conditions over most of the earth's surface," wrote one expert on this period, Moe M. Mandelkehr, who said temperatures dropped between one and five degrees.

That caused one area to dry while it rained in others. Along with the wind, sea currents shifted.

There were sudden environmental disruptions and while it's hard to specify dates, there's a consensus that around this time something spectacular, something mysterious, happened. If it had only to do with weather, it would be easier to explain. But it appears there may also have been tremors: massive earthquakes. At site after site was evidence of walls that had crumbled, foundations that had been dislocated, and fires that with the change in weather had destroyed all advanced cultures of the time. Among them was Troy, where in the words of an archaeologist named Carl Blegen "the catastrophe struck suddenly, without warning, giving the inhabitants little or no time to collect and save their most treasured belongings before they fled. All the houses exposed were still found to contain fire-scarred wreckage of their furnishings, equipment, and stores of supplies. Almost every building yielded scattered bits of gold ornaments and jewelry, no doubt hastily abandoned in panic."

This enormous destruction extended from one end of the plain to the other, while elsewhere in the world, coastal land lifted or fell.

There was also evidence of comets, asteroids, and other forms of space debris. If Sodom was destroyed by brimstone that fell at this time, such debris is one possible hypothesis, and whether there is any plausibility to that, something seems to have arrived from the sky at this time.

In northern Syria scientists found a strange layer of dust (fine spherules of silica and calcite, black carbonate, and packed crystals) in the same area where the drought occurred, and while one of the chief scientists involved, Marie-Agnes Courty, initially thought the soot was from a volcano, she has come to believe that it was the result of an "extra-terrestrial projectile."

There was a fallout of melted particles and it was followed by the dust of the great dry period as well as wildfires and rain. Whether such a strike occurred and if so whether it was behind the climatic change (or just part of the overall chastisement) may never be known, but a run of calamities there was and it was centered on lands where paganism and all forms of immorality were rampant. In Ireland were floods that submerged oaks whose rings revealed a period of extraordinarily low growth — hinting again that the time of quakes had also been a time of climatic upheaval.

"The earliest of the four extreme tree-ring events takes place at a time which must be very close to the beginning of the Bronze Age," wrote another archaeologist, Michael Baillie of Queens College in Northern Ireland. "It shows up as an extremely narrow band of rings, beginning in 2354 B.C. and reaching lowest growth — the narrowest rings — at 2345 B.C. It is apparent that trees in Lancashire (near Belfast) also show reduced growth at the same time, reinforcing the view that this is a widespread event. While the event was very apparent in the ring width patterns, it was a surprise to discover a highly unusual growth defect in one of the samples from trees which grew in the fenlands just to the south of Lough Neagh. The sample shows a change in the character of growth, from normal ring porous to diffuse porous — an anomaly which lasts for about a decade and which could be consistent with the tree being inundated. So, there is clear evidence for an environmental event affecting oak growth generally and trees near Lough Neagh specifically."

Baillie quoted an ancient history known as the Anno Mundi section of the Irish Annals that pointed to a time during the 24th century B.C. when, according to the annals, "nine thousand ... died in one week. Ireland was thirty years waste." It was a disaster of such reach that some have wondered if it was part of the biblical Flood.

CHAPTER 3

Rain of Fire

We don't know a lot about what occurred in the centuries that followed, but eventually men regrouped and the development of civilization proceeded. I have no idea if there were other sporadic events. I know only that there was a pattern over time. Evil occurred, and it was followed by destruction. There were times when God sent events to cities, and other times regions. On occasion they were global. They were sent when they were needed to where they were needed and at the root was alienation: a distancing from God through unbelief, immorality, and idolatry, which was treacherous because it was a direct infringement on the Lord. There was only to be one God and there were to be no other gods before Him (*Jeremiah* 10:10, *Exodus* 20:3). He was the Father Almighty, the mighty One, the everlasting Counselor (*Isaiah* 9:6). There was to be no Baal. There was to be no idol of any kind (including money). A curse followed those who worshipped idols and judgment was executed on the disobedient (*Deuteronomy* 11:28, *Numbers 33:4*). The Lord was love but He would not put up with the masquerade of demons.

"Here, then, I have today set before you life and prosperity, death and doom," said the Lord in *Deuteronomy* 30:15-18. "If you obey the commandments of the Lord, your God, which I enjoin on you today, loving Him, and walking in His ways, and keeping His commandments, statutes, and decrees, you will live and grow numerous, and the Lord, your God, will bless you in the land you are entering to occupy. If, however, you turn away your hearts and will not listen, but are led astray and adore and serve other gods, I tell you now that you will certainly perish."

In Egypt He sent plagues for every false god. When there was worship of the Nile as a god of all gods, He caused it to flood or dried it up. When there was worship of a toad goddess, He sent a plague of frogs (*Exodus* 8:1). When the vegetation was worshipped — when it too was given a god — the Lord sent locusts to chew it up (*Exodus* 10:3). When there was worship of animals he struck down livestock (*Exodus* 9:3).

The Lord sent curses, confusion, and rebuke. He sent sudden ruin. He plagued men with disease, struck them with wasting illness, with fever and inflammation, "with scorching heat and drought, with blight" (*Deuteronomy* 28:20-24).

He sent fire. He rained it down. For an example of this we go to the Aegean island of Thera. It was there south of Greece, near Crete, that a civilization as advanced as the Egyptians flourished around 1600 B.C. and adopted the mystery religions of Mesopotamia. They were called Minoans (after King Minos) and so advanced that some believe they were the origin for the Atlantis myth (there were palaces, frescoes, and running water). While that was fine, there was again an eruption of sensuality and idolatry. Art from this period depicted an alluring "snake goddess." Women exposed their breasts and wore flounced skirts. Worst of all, the Minoans, who may have descended from Ancient Egyptians, indulged in the great evil of human sacrifice (to a bull-headed creature called a minotaur).

This was about five centuries after the conclusion of Mesopotamian chastisements, and the resurgence of sorcery meant the resurgence of disaster. While most of the power was at a palace called Knossos on Crete, there was also the stronghold on Thera, and it was here that a volcanic explosion at least forty times the power of Mount St. Helens occurred. Villages on the island were steeped with up to 150 feet of ash, and according to one scholar, there was a darkness so total "that not even lamplight could penetrate it" — a darkness that affected land within 130 miles and lasted up to three days.

Thera was blown into five bits and towns on neighboring islands were terrorized. Ash rained. Rock vaporized. Knossos. Zakros. In Cyprus there was a foot of ash, and on Crete the great palace of Zakros fell despite a distance of 70 miles. "Stone slabs were slammed horizontally across the ground in a manner originally attributed to an earthquake, but all the stones seem to have toppled in the same direction as if pushed over by a great wind," wrote one expert, Charles Pellegrino. "Like Herculaneum, Zakros perished so quickly that people did not have time to flee with household objects. All the implements of Minoan life were left behind: gold rings, razors, tweezers, and rare perfumes. At the same time, Phaistos, second in size only to Knossos, was utterly carbonized on the southeast coast."

Many believe that when the crater collapsed, as seawater was sucked in, as it then rebounded, there was also a great tidal wave. We don't have specifics. Scientists don't agree on how significant the wave was. It may have been hundreds of feet. We know only that there was fantastic ruin and that another advanced civilization (the first in Europe) vanished.

SENT TO EARTH

CHAPTER 4

A Storm of Quakes

There was only ruin when a society left the grace of God and society after society did just that. There were other chastisements. They were too many to recount. There was chastisement in Israel. There was destruction in Babylon. There were invasions. There were more plagues on the Egyptians (when they not only kept to their idolatry but tried to make the Israelites do the same) God made His strictures clear. People were to help each other, to love their neighbors, to tell the truth, to keep the sabbath holy, to honor parents. There were the Ten Commandments and besides idolatry they warned about stealing, adultery, and murder.

Above all men were to love God. They were to serve Him. They were sent to do His battle and when they went instead to the side of the enemy — when souls were in danger of damnation — heaven reacted. There were local, regional, and global repercussions. Another major chastisement appears to have occurred five centuries after Thera. There were extreme temperatures, exceptional rain, and floods. There was a *violent* increase in the volume of rivers. On the Hungarian Plain a vast area of low-lying land went under water. "From many other sources of information it is obvious that these events were sudden and occurred worldwide," said two Swedish researchers, Lars

Franzen and Thomas B. Larsson, who studied this period and found deposits indicating a severe flooding catastrophe around 1000 B.C. In one 50-year period, from 1225 B.C. to 1175 B.C., at least 47 cities around the Mediterranean fell to earthquakes, with substantial destruction in Greece and Turkey. In Israel, where Solomon bowed before strange gods (and where children were sacrificed to a god called Molech), huge marble pillars were knocked on their sides and men buried beneath them. Some believe it may even have been one massive quake of earth-rattling proportion. "There were truly major events," said Amos Nur, a geophysicist at Stanford University. "Whether it's a global storm or a regional storm needs to be sorted out."

So severe were the tremors that Nur and others believe they may have led to the collapse of east Mediterranean civilizations. As many times as temples were rebuilt to serve demon gods, as often as man disobeyed the clear rules set down in the Ten Commandments, which were given in this epoch, so did the constructs collapse into belches of dust. Dozens of structures appear to have collapsed simultaneously. There were signs of quakes in Midea, Kynos, and Pergamum (which was to be cited in *Revelation* 2:13 as "the very place where Satan's throne is erected").

An earthquake storm had unzipped the seams of continental boundaries, and if it didn't completely destroy the cities (these cities where Apollo and Poseidon were venerated, where they had inherited the ancient Minoan gods, that existed around the time of Jericho), it left them vulnerable to invasion. At Phylakopi a shrine complex was destroyed around 1120 B.C. in an event that may also have been responsible for the final destruction of a major temple at Ayia Irini. "During these generations the changes that came about are little short of fantastic," wrote scholar V. R. Desborough in *The Greek Dark Ages*. "The craftsmen and artists seem to have vanished almost without trace: there is little new stone construction of any sort, far less any massive edifices; the metal workers techniques revert to primitive, and the potter, except in the early stages, loses his purpose and inspiration; and the art of writing is forgotten. But the outstanding feature is that by the end of the twelfth century the population appears to have dwindled to about one-tenth of what it had been little over a century before. This is no normal decline, and the circumstances and events obviously have a considerable bearing on the nature of the subsequent Dark Ages, and must be in part at least a cause of its existence."

CHAPTER 5

Cycles of Admonishment

There was thus a pattern: Every so often mankind was hit by a medley of disasters, and these episodes were often accompanied or heralded by a change in climate.

The weather, as in current times, formed the background.

It was a sign, an omen. When it got hotter or cooler, storms came and so did drought and flood, which were accompanied by earthquakes, tidal waves, and possibly asteroids. (Again during the 1000 B.C. event, there were strange glassy spherules as if from melted sand).

There was also pestilence. Besides those of ancient Egypt, plagues rose throughout history and caused tremendous effects. Of all chastisements, this may have taken the most lives. One came at the height of Greece's "golden age" and killed a quarter of Athens.

It was not just the intersection of cycles. While there were times when one caused another, when for instance bad weather led to plague, the way events flowed often indicated the supernatural. It was Einstein who said that "God does not play with dice," and indeed the past had pulsed with His intervention. This was what most scientists did not factor in. This was the missing scientific component. There were storms that came as a matter of course — yes — but there were also times when they were part of

27

a spiritual dynamic. God controlled the weather — used it — like He controlled everything. It was throughout the Bible. It was in *Genesis, Exodus,* and *Psalms*. It was in *Deuteronomy*. Rare was the book it *wasn't* in. It was in the New Testament. Lightning was His sign (*Matthew* 24:27); it came from His throne (*Revelation* 4:5); and while much arrived as cycles that were "natural," He controlled nature! Disasters rearranged societies. They swept away evil. It was Jesus Who defined the essence of chastisement when He prophesied quakes and pestilence, when He said there would be roaring seas, that the sun would be darkened, that the moon would lose its glow, that stars would fall. "When you see the abominable and destructive thing which the prophet Daniel foretold standing on holy ground," said Christ, "those in Judea must flee to the mountains" (*Matthew* 24:7-29).

Although He was alluding to apocalyptical times (the time of His return), Christ outlined a pattern when He described wars and rumors of wars, persecution, nation rising against nation, along with roaring seas, strange signs in the skies (including stars that would fall), the moon losing its glow, the sun darkened, and events like those I have just mentioned: "famine and pestilence and earthquakes in many places" (*Matthew* 24:1-7 and *Luke* 21:10-12).

After His death were the admonitions of Paul and the disciples. Sin, they said, would lead to fire. There would be "wrath and fury to those who selfishly disobey the truth and obey wickedness" (*Romans* 2:9). Israel as a nation was constantly warned, and we all know there were prophecies in *Revelation*.

In the end, it was precisely this pattern of events that brought down the Roman Empire.

CHAPTER 6

Sons of the Gods

Earthquakes. Signs in the sky. Nation against nation. That was what spelled the end of the Romans, who of course ruled Palestine and much of the known world. Its fall can be seen as beginning with the death of Jesus. First in the years following the Crucifixion, then in a constant spattering of events through the next several centuries, with a background of constant carnage — a grinding down by barbarian invaders — Rome, a truly wicked empire, was destroyed. I don't know if this should be categorized as one huge tribulation or a number over the years, but it was a direct response to the evil of this era.

Let's take a look at it for a moment: the evil of Rome.

In His famous prophecy in *Matthew* 24, Christ had spoken of the *"abomination of desolation"* standing in the *"holy place."* He said that would foretell the great trial. And it was nearly fulfilled by the ruler of the time, Caligula, who tried to have a bust of himself installed in the Temple of Jerusalem (an action that helped initiate war with the Jews).

This indicated the first great sin of Rome: idolatry. The Romans took the worship of pagan deities to its ultimate and adopted, glorified, and added to the pantheon of Egyptian, Babylonian, and Minoan-Greek gods. In cities like Pompeii there was a temple on every corner, a god for every eventuality of life, and ardent devotion: throughout

Rome men and women spent much time, often several visits a day, in the temples, praying or writing gods devotional letters. In addition to common idols such as Saturn and Hercules (which like the Egyptian gods controlled various forces of nature, standing behind the earth, moon, and sun), there were secret groups that included what was known as a "Cybeline" cult and the development of witchcraft. Enemies were destroyed through *pharmakeia* (the use of poison or drugs), often to the accompaniment of incantations, and blood sacrifices were a daily occurrence. Food was dedicated to idols (a practice we see today in modern India), and there was self-idolatry of the most blatant kind: Emperors even dressed as gods, and in the case of Caligula, impersonated Apollo as he stood on high platforms uttering revelations. Choirs had to sing actual praise to him, and the spirits took hold: Caligula was known to fall into tremendous convulsive states that seemed like possession, had fierce demonic energy, and at night experienced terrifying visions. There were similar signs of demonism with other emperors. When Augustus Caesar's mother was pregnant she was said to have been visited by a serpent in the temple of Apollo (which she took to mean that her child would be the son of that "god"), and emperors like Domitian lived by astrology.

As societies advanced, as the people grew wealthy, as they incorporated and expanded upon the ingenuity of previous people, such as the Minoans, so too was there a refinement of wickedness. It was a fantastic time and the evil was tangible. With the occult was also perversity. Rome was filled with lust, at least at the top. There were sex slaves. There was incest. One emperor used infants. Rooms in the palace were decorated with pornographic scenes and women were hired to romp in the imperial woods as nymphs. Caligula opened a palace brothel where Roman matrons, their daughters, and freeborn youths could be hired for money. He delighted in stealing the wives of others, and also had homosexual flings. A fertility god was honored with huge phallic symbols that were paraded through cities and crowned by a matron. In some cases a penis-shaped idol was set on the very gates of a city. *Hic habitat delicitas* — "happiness dwells here," was the motto, and those who thought otherwise were cast off. In Pompeii prostitutes advertised with public graffiti, which was etched into walls across the city, and in Herculaneum a statue portrayed the god Pan copulating with a goat — so scandalous that for centuries museum curators kept it concealed. It was a society that was "guilt-free, lusty, unfaithful, and deceitful," in the words of one historian. Venus the love goddess was manifest in the bars where men lusted and brawled and played dice, in the quarters of ill repute, in dark corners. "We find crude remarks about amorous prowess, the names and nicknames of pimps and procuresses, prostitutes (both boys and girls), and colorful illustrations in the half-light of cells depicting the techniques of experienced whores," wrote historian Robert Etienne. Unwanted pregnancies were ended with abortion, which was often administered through *pharmakeia* (linking it to witchcraft, which would later consider it a sacrament), although yet more prevalent was infanticide: babies who were left in the wilderness, where wolves or the elements got to them.

  This extravagance of lust was joined by gluttony. We all know how preoccupied the Romans were with food. So ravenous was one emperor that after eating a meal he would have a feather stuck down his throat so he could retch and make room for more.

  The lust for food was joined by a lust for blood. Life was cheap in Rome. People suspected of disloyalty were executed or driven to suicide. A supervisor of games and beast-fights was flogged with chains for days on end, and was not put to death until Caligula was offended by the smell of gangrene in his brain. On one occasion, when there weren't enough condemned criminals to fight the tigers and lions in the arena, the emperor ordered spectators dragged from the stands. He followed the incestuous practices of pharaohs, forcing his favorite sister to live with him. It was said that when she became pregnant he couldn't wait for their god-like child and disemboweled her to pluck the unborn baby from the womb.

There were abuses of every kind. If a slave committed theft his hands might be chopped off and hung around his neck, and there was the account of a father who was ordered to dine at the royal palace after the execution of his son, sitting as Caligula joked and ridiculed him. Many were executed or made to fight grisly battles in an arena known as Circus Maximus. There was also persecution — almost inconceivable persecution — of early Christians. Throughout the empire they were ordered to worship at the feet of idols, and when they refused, when they declined to sacrifice to gods, were put on racks and stretched until their limbs were ripped out of joint or were beheaded (as was John the Baptist in Palestine) or eviscerated, their insides pulled out while they were still alive. Martyrs were forced to walk long ways with nails through their feet or screamed as their skin was peeled or their limbs chopped, severed, and spread around their writhing torsos. On at least one occasion Caligula ordered the bowels of a victim stacked in a heap before him. Christians at the time of Nero were smeared with pitch and burned like torches.

CHAPTER 7

Theater of Horrors

That was the evil of Rome (a more flagrant if not necessarily more pervasive wickedness than what is approached in the current world), and it led to centuries of tribulation. As I said, I'm not quite sure whether to consider what happened from about 60 A.D. to 540 A.D. one huge long-running event, a truly unrelenting punishment, or several episodes strung together. They all led to a common end, the destruction of Rome, and there had been a wave of forebodings — what an ancient historian named Flavius Josephus called "premonitory signs" that led to "calamities of their own choosing," what I will call the Roman Chastisement.

Throughout early Roman times nature had acted up; the Nile had flooded as Vespasian entered Egypt to conquer it, and there had been an earthquake in Tiberius's last days; changes in government "were foreshadowed by lightning bolts, earthquakes, floods, strange births of or behavior by animals," wrote an historian named Howard Clark Kee; and the same occurred at the onset of the chastisement. Christ had said there would be quakes and on February 5 in 62 A.D. a tremor rocked Pompeii. It was the first of many and so powerful that it shook the distant city where Nero, who featured himself a singer, was performing. Abysses opened — one so huge that a large flock of sheep was lost in it. "Magnificent country villas were so badly damaged as to be beyond repair," noted another historian, Marcel Brion. "In the city itself, public buildings had been damaged worse than private houses, which were constructed of lighter materials. The temples had particularly suffered: the one dedicated to Isis, almost wholly destroyed; the Temple of Jupiter, where the columns had crashed to the ground, dragging down the gilded roof with its glittering acroteria; the Temple of Venus Pompeiana...."

And this was only the onset. It was a prefigurement. As in other events, disaster unfolded in stages. But the beginning was rapid. Just two years after the quake, Rome caught fire (the conflagration Nero was said to have watched as he sang to the accompaniment of a lyre), and it was a full-scale disaster, specifically targeting Rome's evil areas. "It began in the Circus, where it adjoins the Palatine and Caelian hills," wrote the historian Tacitus. "Breaking out in shops selling inflammable goods, and fanned by the wind, the conflagration instantly grew and swept the whole length of the Circus. There were no walled mansions or temples or any other obstructions which could arrest it."

Sweeping the low parts of the city, the fire then climbed the hills and returned to the lower ground. "When people looked back, menacing flames sprang up before them or outflanked them," said Tacitus. "The flames could not be prevented from overwhelming the whole of the Palatine, including Nero's palace."

For six days and seven nights the fire consumed all in its path, and when it was over, seventy percent of the city was in ruins. That was followed by war. Soon after an unusual appearance of Halley's Comet, which hung like a sword over Israel, Rome attacked Jerusalem, surrounded the city (in an eerie fulfillment of what Christ had foreseen), and destroyed the Temple such that not one stone was left on another.

Tens of thousands were killed; nation rose against nation; the forces of nature were in a fury. Floods struck in the very vicinity where the apostle Peter was crucified (now the site of the Vatican, which rests on his ossified rock-like bones), and a severe food shortage led to famine. That was in 69 A.D. It was a year that saw four different emperors, palace uprisings, and civil war. Another fire erupted and destroyed the Temple of Jupiter. "No one could have supposed that the great triple shrine on the hill towards which the company moved would in this year sink into ashes and rubble, a symbol no longer of Rome's eternity but of its seemingly imminent extinction," wrote Kenneth Wellesley. "That Italy should be twice invaded by Roman armies, that its cities and capital should be taken by storm, that three successive emperors should die by assassination, suicide or lynching, and that the whole empire, from Wales to Assouan and from the Caucasus to Morocco, should be convulsed and disarrayed."

The distress in the land and the wrath against this people would be great, Christ had said; on the earth, nations would be in anguish, distraught at the roaring sea (*Luke* 21:23-25). "Immediately after the stress of that period, the sun will be darkened, the moon will not shed her light, the stars will fall from the sky, and the hosts of heaven will be shaken loose," Jesus was quoted as saying (*Matthew* 24:29), and while I'm not saying this totally fulfilled the specific prophecy, it was like a formula. It was exactly what was to happen next. In 79 A.D. Mount Vesuvius erupted near Pompeii and for several days — three terrifying days — that wayward city and its vicinity (including Herculaneum) suffered through quakes, soot, and darkness. Sheets of fire leapt in the volcano and terror gripped a people who "debated whether to stay indoors or take their chance in the open, for the buildings were now shaking with violent shocks, and seemed to be swaying to and fro as if they were torn from their foundations. Outside, on the other hand, there was the danger of falling pumice stones. As a protection against falling objects they put pillows on their heads tied down with cloths. Elsewhere there was daylight by this time, but they were still in darkness, blacker and denser than any ordinary night, which they relieved by lighting torches and various kinds of lamps. Then the flames and smell of sulfur which heralded the approaching fire drove the others to take flight. For several days we had experienced earth shocks, which hardly alarmed us as they are frequent in Campania but that night they became so violent that it seemed the world was not only being shaken, but turned upside down," wrote Pliny the Younger. "The sea appeared to have shrunk, as if withdrawn by the tremors of the earth. In any event, the shore had widened and many sea creatures were beached on the sand. In the other direction loomed a horrible black cloud ripped by sudden bursts of fire, writhing snakelike and revealing sudden flashes larger than lightning. And now came the ashes, but at first sparsely. I turned around. Behind us, an ominous thick smoke, spreading over the earth like a flood, followed us. 'Let's go into the fields while we can still see the way,' I told my mother — for I was afraid that we might be crushed by the mob on the road in the midst of the darkness. We had scarcely agreed when we were enveloped in night — not a moonless night or one dimmed by cloud, but the darkness of a sealed room without lights. To be heard were only the shrill cries of women, the wailing of children, the shouting of men."

By the end Pompeii was covered by twenty feet of ash, its residents entombed. An entire city had been destroyed. We have seen photographs of the corpses, of the remains, captured the way they were at the last moment — lying in a fetal position, trying to cover their faces, a look of horror, or running for their lives, the corpses of young women who tore off their garments to run more swiftly and families huddled together and the owners of what was known as the House of Faun "who, too much attached to the things of this world, lost time which might have saved their lives in emptying jewel coffers, their caskets of gold and their sideboard full of silver dishes," in the words of Brion, who like others reported that there seemed to have been a small clandestine group of Christians in Herculaneum because there was the shape of a cross in one doomed room and in Pompeii, someone who was repulsed by the decadence had scratched the words "Sodoma, Gomora" (as if in prophecy) on a blackened wall.

SENT TO EARTH

CHAPTER 8

The Sun Darkened

It was the beginning of the end. For the next several centuries Rome and its territories were ravaged by a constant series of catastrophes. There was a change in climate, severe outbreaks of plague (which came wave after wave), and attacks by barbarians — throngs of shaggy-haired horsemen who terrorized the empire.

They were from the Germanic regions, known as Goths, Avars, and Huns, and they too were pagan. I know I have been graphic but I have to give you the full picture. As they invaded the empire, as they plundered and burned towns, as they raped women, or cannibalized the elderly, and hung captives from trees, they did so, often, as part of their own ritual. Their god was named Woden — the "furious one" or "mad one," the god of war, to be heard in the howling of a storm — and they were so savage that many thought them to be offspring of the devil. It was said the Huns roasted pregnant women, devoured the fetuses, and howled as they broke through city walls, and they attacked from northern Europe to what is now Italy, taking over entire regions and leaving the empire — the kingdom of Rome — in shambles.

"They were a faceless mass, terrible and subhuman," wrote historian Otto J. Maenchen-Helfen, and on one fateful day in 378 A.D. they annihilated two-thirds of the Roman army. It was something out of an Old Testament prophecy (see *Ezekiel* 38:9); Rome was tormented as she had tormented others. There was political turmoil and it went hand in hand with natural disturbances. Promoted by unusually wet weather, bacteria spread from Africa to Europe. Entire towns fell prey, and as in Mesopotamian times, the chastisement was breaking down idols everywhere; there were disorders around the world. Drought attacked China, the land of the dragon (where nature spirits formed part of the religion), and there were floods: At Shandong the water rose so high that toads croaked from the trees. The chastisement, grinding on for centuries, tearing at the final fabric of the Roman Empire and other pagan lands, peaked from 530 A.D. to 570 A.D. Large shooting stars were seen in China and in 532 those in the Mediterranean reported a great meteor shower. At the same time, quakes rocked the imperial city of Constantinople and 250,000 died when a tremor and the blaze it caused — a scorching, fire-raining blaze — leveled Antioch. In Rome "the sun gave forth its light without brightness like the moon" from 535 to 536 A.D., according to a scribe named Procopius. From Sweden to Chile something occurred that all but stopped tree growth, and there were savage storms. In Britain hundreds died in an awful storm in 548 A.D. and hail like "pullet's eggs" (a chicken's) fell in Scotland two years later. So severe were the winters that birds and other wildlife allowed themselves to be taken by hand. It snowed in southern Europe. It snowed in Mesopotamia. It snowed in summer in China. The southern part of what is now the U.S. was battered by storms worse than any on the modern ledger, storms that according to one researcher, Dr. Kam-biu Liu of Louisiana State University, who has studied sand from ancient ocean surges, amounted to megahurricanes. The other extreme of drought hit out west and affected Indians who as in China practiced shamanism, honored nature gods, and made beguiling mystical use of the sun sign or swastika. Drought ravaged the Moche, Nasca, and Mayans of South America (causing the collapse of Teotihuacan, where they had built a massive pyramid known as the Temple of the Sun), while huge El Niños —

storms from warm Pacific waters — blasted Peru, sweeping villages away and altering the shoreline.

Scientists aren't sure why it happened but it caused chaos and spelled the end not only of Rome but of Persia, Arabia, Arianism, the great Mayan city of Tikal, and the Nasca Indians. Paganism had been crushed. Some speculate that a massive volcano erupted in Indonesia, while others said the climate changed when the earth swept through the "dust veil" of a comet. From 536 to 543 trees in the western part of America stopped growing and yellow dust fell in Asia. There were also extreme vegetal effects in Scandinavia (where the swastika was used as "Thor's hammer"), and massive flooding in Korea.

A string of chastisements that had begun with the calamities of the first century was driven to a roaring peak when as one expert, David Keys, noted "mankind was hit by one of the greatest natural disasters ever to occur. It blotted out much of the light and heat of the sun for eighteen months, and the climate of the entire planet began to spin out of control. The result, direct or indirect, was climatic chaos, famine, migration, war, and massive political change on virtually every continent."

SENT TO EARTH

CHAPTER 9

A Fire on the Moon

So grim was the situation that in Rome Pope Gregory the Great led a procession through the diseased, plundered streets, carrying a miraculous image of the Virgin (who by this time had been appearing at times of distress, during fires and storms as well as plagues). The Roman Empire was through, and so was the chastisement. As they approached what is now Castel Sant'Angelo, Gregory saw an angel on top of the mausoleum putting away what looked like a bloody sword.

For centuries after the great Roman Event, Europe changed. There had been a reduction to poverty and simplicity. People turned to Christ. They realized that the world was but a passing place. They sought penance, not riches. So austere was the mood that adultery might draw a seven-year fast on bread and water as penance. It was the end of ancient times, and the onset of the Middle Ages. Throughout Europe paganism was replaced by the teachings of Jesus and idolatrous images were replaced by Christian portraits. Cathedrals were built and banners emblazoned with the cross waved from castles. Much of this was at the behest of Mary, who had first manifested in an appearance to the apostle James and had since come countless times, imploring Europeans to follow Jesus, healing mutes, cripples, and other sick, and requesting the construction of chapels, shrines, churches, monasteries, and cathedrals. She appeared in Portugal near a place called

Fatima (long before the famous apparitions), and also in Spain at a swampy area known as Guadalupe (which would later link to a site in Mexico).

For centuries Christianity took root in Europe. The way of Jesus was considered the true way. Kings were beholden. But as time wore on, as the beginning of the Middle Ages gave way to the middle part of the medieval period, and then to the High Middle Ages, mankind began to revert back to old mistakes, as was its tendency. Once more, as it advanced, it distanced itself from God. Once more, there was self-idolatry. As trade routes were established and commerce began, there was the lure of money, and as it swept from nobles to peasants, from France to England, men became enchanted by their own ingenuity. Fueled by commerce, there was a surge in architecture, art, medical books, universities. Gunpowder was invented, as was modern astronomical observation. There were gold, jewels, and spices. There was silk. Bankers swarmed to cities like Vienna. Fashion arrived, along with the first vanity mirrors. These were in high demand, for in these times of nearly overwhelming wealth it seemed everyone had ornate clothes. "There was so much pride amongst the common people in vying with one another in dress and ornaments that it was scarce possible to distinguish the poor from the rich, the servant from the master, or a priest from other men," said chronicler Henry Knighton.

It was the time most like our own, a peak of materialism after centuries of a spiritual mood. Although the Church forbade the lending of money at high interest (and considered it a sin for merchants to sell a product at too large a profit, which was defined as anything beyond the cost, time, and labor of the merchant), usury and profiteering were rife; goods were sold (and money lent) at whatever the market bore. "In the name of God and profit," was the motto of one merchant, and while many got wealthy, the line between rich and poor grew stark, which quickly soured the mood.

There was fraud. There was drunkenness. There was lechery. Familiar speech became rude, lewd, and finally obscene. Since it was popular belief that the size of a man's feet was linked to the size of his organ, men wore long pointy shoes called *poulaines,* stuffing the points with sawdust. Theft, robbery, and rape became huge problems.

While in the words of historian Thomas Bokenkotter the popes in the 1300s were "without exception worthy and religious men, even austere in certain cases," and while it was the Church, not the state, that cared for the indigent, that tended to the crippled, that adopted the orphans, that led the blind, while it was the Church that distributed the Bible, that sought to defend the Holy Land from the attacks of infidels, that gave men visions of heaven, of angels, of a world beyond the mire of a medieval village (where the stench of sewage was a constituent of the air), and while it had done a phenomenal job at eradicating idols, it was also a Church that succumbed to the sensuality of the times, that listened too closely to bankers, that like the rest of society became worldly. The papacy moved from Rome to Avignon, France, where a massive papal palace was constructed and filled with luxurious furnishings (though too few religious paintings). A crowd of courtiers — knights, squires, and chamberlains — filled the spacious rooms. The palace's lavishness was the talk of Europe, and to pay for it the popes began to levy taxes on bishops, abbots, and pastors. There was also the selling of dispensations, absolutions, indulgences, and Church positions (which in time led to the Protestant Reformation). Bishops paid the curia for their appointments, and for a fee priests were allowed to have mistresses!

Outside, in the rest of society, the descent into evil — into the old errors of the Egyptians and Romans, of the Minoans, of the Greeks — was swift. Stone masons founded secret societies based on old Mesopotamian religions, and there were templars, a cult of men accused of committing sodomy with each other, worshipping Satan in the form of a cat, and urinating on the cross (which if true would be a lineage for satanism).

They were based in Paris, the seat of rationalism, where it was said the Goddess of Wisdom had found a new roost, and there was witchcraft. Gods of nature were back, and so were the potions of *pharmakeia*. Secret rituals took place at woodland sanctuaries, or were conducted at the occult British site of Stonehenge. Nor was Europe alone. The ancient mysteries had taken firm root in India (where mantras were formed from demonic names, blood was drunk, and there were too many gods to count), while China continued along the road of the dragon. As paganism resurged, Christianity came under new attack. Every Christmas was a burlesque called the "Feast of Fools" in which the Church was ridiculed in mock ceremonies that saw dice thrown on the altar, censers swung with the smoke of burning shoes, and men pull carts of manure, which they flung at bystanders while others, nude, committed lewd acts.

It was a jolly good time followed by wine and beer and the problems continued in Avignon, which was "full of pride, avarice, self-indulgence, and corruption," according to Saint Bridget of Sweden, who could have been describing the entire society. And as it descended, as it approached the depravity of Rome, as godlessness and materialism, as coarseness and occultism, took root, so came what would turn out to be the last and greatest known chastisement. It was an event that started in a way strikingly similar to what is currently transpiring. By 1000 A.D. the climate had shifted into a state of global warming, and it had begun in the Arctic. Glaciers were dwindling. Northmen colonized Greenland. Corn was grown as far north as Norway. The warming lasted for several centuries and then took a sudden reverse into a cooler climate with severe effects. As was the case whenever climate gyrated, there were droughts, floods, and storms. One of the warmest periods had crashed and taken sodden crops with it. Hunger spread. In Europe whole districts of corn lapsed into marsh. Across the continent an endless rain pelted the landscape and as if on cue there were perturbations in the sky: as there had been signs of meteors in 2300 B.C., 1000 B.C., and at the end of the Roman era, so now were there astronomical disturbances — the "falling stars," the shifting heavens that Christ had mentioned. In New Zealand the natives reported fire falling from the sky, in America an object allegedly fell in the Bald Mountains (at the Tennessee-North Carolina border), and in England a monk named Gervase of Canterbury reported that in 1178 "on the Sunday before the Feast of St. John the Baptist after sunset when the moon had first become visible a marvelous phenomenon was witnessed by some five or more men who were sitting there facing the moon. Now there was a bright new moon, and as usual in that phase its horns were tilted toward the east; and suddenly the upper horn split in two. From the midpoint of the division a flaming torch sprang up, spewing out, over a considerable distance, fire, hot coals, and sparks. Meanwhile the body of the moon which was below writhed, as it were, in anxiety, and, to put it in the words of those who reported it to me and saw in with their own eyes, the moon throbbed like a wounded snake."

It sounded like they had seen asteroids hitting the lunar surface, while on earth there were wholesale migrations. Whether from heightened El Niño activity, tidal waves that may have resulted from meteors, or some mysterious shift, Indians in South America seemed to be avoiding the coasts and islanders were moving all over the Pacific. A pall had descended on the planet. Crops crashed and starving peasants roamed the countryside. (In Rhineland troops were posted at the gallows when peasants began cannibalizing corpses.) As the weather continued to change, prophets rose with hysterical prophecies (the antichrist, the end of the world).

From China came word of bizarre events.

"The mountain Tsincheou disappeared and enormous clefts appeared in the earth," recounted writer George Deaux. "Near King-sai, it was said, the mountains of Ki-ming-chan utterly fell in and in their place appeared suddenly a lake more than a hundred leagues in circumference."

There was "subterranean thunder" in Canton and a flood along the Yellow River that a climatologist named H. H. Lamb described as "one of the greatest weather disasters ever known, alleged to have taken seven million lives in the great river valleys of China, and destroying not only the human settlements and their sewage arrangements but also the habitats of wildlife." As in Europe famine resulted and in true apocalyptical fashion there were vast swarms of locusts — insects that destroyed crops and deepened the shortage of crops.

In a province "hard by Greater India" were "horrors and unheard of tempests" for a span of three days, according to a Flemish missionary who reported to Church authorities that "sheets of fire fell upon the earth, mingled with hailstones of marvelous size; which slew almost all, from the greatest to the least." In Europe, earthquakes shook Greece, washed it with tidal waves, collapsed highland in Cyprus, and did the same in Naples, Pisa, Padua, Bologna, and Venice. Tremors rumbled all the way into Germany. As Knighton wrote, "many cities in Corinth and Achaia were overturned, and the earth swallowed them. Castles and fortresses were broken, laid low, and swallowed up. Mountains in Cyprus were leveled into one, so that the flow of the rivers was impeded, and many cities were submerged and villages destroyed. Similarly, when a friar was preaching at Naples, the whole city was destroyed by an earthquake. Suddenly, the earth was opened up, as if a stone had been thrown into water, and everyone died along with the preaching friar."

At St. Mark's Basilica in Venice the bells had been set to ringing.

CHAPTER 10

Blacker Than Death

Then came true disaster.
As rats fled the droughts and floods, they carried with them fleas full of a bacteria that caused bubonic plague.

Victims coughed blood and died in days, sometimes hours; it was said that you had lunch with relatives and dinner with ancestors. Black swellings erupted and oozed pus that caused a foulness, the victims vomiting blood. Everything about it was revolting, the stricken more the object of loathing than pity. It was written that "all the matter which exuded from their bodies let off an unbearable stench, sweat, excrement, spittle, breath, so fetid as to be overpowering, urine turbid, thick, black or red...."

Countless fell in China and then India. No one knew precise figures, but estimates for China ranged from 13 to 35 million; by the end of the 14th century (with additional causes) the population would drop from 135 million to 90 million. Millions more died in India, where they were stacked like cordwood. Kurds fled to the mountains and fish died through mysterious cause, their stench adding to the idea that the disease was carried by an ill wind. Storms with astounding lightning sparked massive fires that were followed by disease — a disease that swept across the Near East rapidly, horrifyingly, through mere contact with victims or the deadly aerosol of a sneeze. In Crimea dead were numbered in the tens of thousands and it was said that in

Caramania and Caesarea none were left as survivors. India was depopulated. So was the Middle East. "Tartary, Mesopotamia, Syria, Armenia were covered with dead bodies," wrote Abbot Francis Aidan Gasquet while in Acre, in Jerusalem, and along the Nile, mosques filled with corpses or the dead were piled at roadside — so high that bandits hid behind them.

A third to a *half* in Arab nations died, and at the same time, Europe, still shaken by weird storms, and by the tremors, saw plague enter its ports, and now we come to the height of tragedy — of the events the prophets, the seers, had seemed to sense. It was what one writer called "a crescendo of calamity." In southern Europe the three hubs were Sicily, Venice, and Genoa, while to the north plague entered Pisa and moved rapidly to Rome and Tuscany. In Florence — home to artistic splendors, home to the new pride of man — between 45 and 75 percent died in a single year, and in Venice, which kept excellent records, there was a toll of 60 percent in 18 months. Doctors caught it and died before some of their patients. Grand palaces were abandoned. It jumped with fleas. It passed with rodent droppings. It was even said to spread with contaminated jewelry. "It is impossible for the human tongue to recount the awful truth," recalled a man named Agnolo di Tura of Siena. "Indeed, one who did not see such horribleness can be called blessed. The victims died almost immediately. They would swell beneath the armpits and in the groin, and fall over while talking. Father abandoned child, wife husband, one brother another; for this illness seemed to strike through breath and sight."

At least 33 percent of Italy succumbed and it was the common practice of neighbors, wrote another observer, Giovanni Boccaccio, "to drag the corpses out of the houses with their own hands, aided, perhaps, by a porter, if a porter was to be had, and to lay them round in front of the doors, where any one that made the round might have seen, especially in the morning, more of them than he could count; afterwards they would have biers brought up or, in default, planks whereon they laid them. Nor was it only once or twice that one and the same bier carried two or three corpses at once; but quite a considerable number of such cases occurred, one bier sufficing for husband and wife, two or three brothers, father and son.... Nay, the evil went yet further, for not merely by speech or association with the sick was the malady communicated to the healthy with consequent peril of common death, but any that touched the clothes of the sick or aught else that had been touched or used by them, seemed thereby to contract the disease."

As the disease made its way through Europe, strange phenomena accompanied it. Meteors were seen (known as "black comets"), and there were reports of strange columns of fire. These were witnessed in Florence and Avignon — above the papal palace! A ball of flame was also seen over Paris, and there were phantoms — demons that in places like Messina were said to transform into frightening "dogs."

More horrid, however, was the disease itself, which moved rapidly west and north, striking Avignon. The death rate there was fifty percent. Hundreds who worked at the papal palace were turned into corpses, Pope Clement VI fled, and such was the shortage of priests that laymen had to give last rites. In Vienna the evil came as a hovering light that was exorcised by a bishop.

Spain fell under assault. Five million died in France. Throughout Europe cadavers were left in the front of homes like refuse and even scavenging animals wouldn't touch them. In England in one field 5,000 lay dead and within two years half of the 17,500 monks, nuns, and friars in that nation's monasteries were no longer counted among the living. At Cambridge 16 of 40 resident scholars succumbed, and the Archbishop of Canterbury fell victim in 1348, his successor died the following August, and *his* successor died three months after that. An astonishing 66 percent of clergy in Buckinghamshire were killed, and by 1350 the death toll was at least 35 percent in London. It was relentless. It was sinister. At sea, ghost ships wandered. It was as if the whole world had been placed "within the grasp of the Evil One," noted a friar in Kilkenny, Ireland, who wondered just before his own death if "any child of Adam may escape this pestilence."

It was a good question; never before (at least not since Noah) had there been a trauma like this; on three continents the very existence of *homo sapiens* was threatened. Men and women, driven to despair, wandered as if mad across the breadth of Europe. According to the *Neuburg Chronicle*, "cattle were left to stray unattended in the fields for no one had any inclination to concern themselves about the future. The wolves, which came down from the mountains to attack the sheep, acted in a way which had never been heard before. As if alarmed by some invisible warning they turned and fled back into the wilderness." In Frankfurt-am-Main two thousand people perished in seventy-two days.

It was estimated that half of Hamburg died, and seventy percent of Bremen. There was also famine — so acute that peasants ate grass. The weather was still astir and bridges were washed away by floods, but the plague was at center stage: such was the stench that peasants carried flowers or fragrant herbs — a pocketful of posey (which was to inspire the rhyme) — to blunt it. "God for the sins of men has struck the world with this great punishment of sudden death," proclaimed King Magnus II of Sweden. "By it most of our countrymen are dead."

CHAPTER 11

Secrets on a Mountain

About 24 million Europeans — a third of the continent — had perished. This was between 1347 and 1351 — a period of less than five years. From that time to the beginning of the current series, there were sporadic events and a sustained drop in temperatures, but no great episode. Nature, having exacted its price, having once more knocked man down to size, seemed to quiet itself. A period of cold, what we know as the "Little Ice Age," predominated from the time of the bubonic plague to the French Revolution. As had happened after the Roman event, man returned to God. This was seen with explorers who, coming from countries that had been savaged by the Black Death, put Christian names on territories in the New World — El Salvador, Guadeloupe (different spelling); indeed, the Mississippi was originally known by explorers as the River of the Immaculate Conception, and the Chesapeake as the Bay of Saint Mary. When it came time to form the new nation, Christian men put it squarely under the banner of God. And in Mexico, millions of Indians turned from paganism (including blood sacrifice and use of the swastika, which remained a symbol of occult power) to Christianity after the Virgin Mary appeared to a humble Aztec named Juan Diego.

This piety began to end in the 1800s, and here we get to the nitty-gritty; here we arrive in our own time; for it was in the 1800s that evil, having dissipated or at least appeased the justice of God for five centuries, was returning, and bringing a special time. As in the Middle Ages, there was a return, in the 1800s, to rationalism. This meant explaining away everything in terms of natural (as opposed to spiritual) forces, the worship of nature once more, if in a new way, and relying more on the human brain than God. The Goddess of Reason was rising again. Man began to worship his own intellect. There was "progress." The sciences began to take over the scene. And, once more, there was irreverence. But this time it went beyond the Feast of Fools; this time it was more like the Roman persecutions. Unbelievers had assumed power, and they desecrated churches, destroyed shrines, melted down chalices, killed priests, and brutalized nuns and anyone else who, by life or word, proclaimed Christ in France. It made the mock Masses of the Middle Ages look tame. And just as startling was what humans sought to do to the earth itself. Armed with a new array of inventions — including chemistry, which reconfigured elements — man set up the establishment of a new reality. He was going to redefine life on earth. If Christ had indicated that life was a series of sufferings and tests, telling those who followed Him to take up their crosses each day, mankind was now going to exert the bulk of its energy, in nearly fanatical manner, to circumventing any such suffering, and to bring the gods of nature into full rein. It went beyond subduing the earth; with chemistry, the new alchemy, men set about a re-creation. In great earnest, mankind urged itself into a massive overhaul of the actual physical environment. And it scoffed at belief: science was granting men new conveniences and power, and science operated (or so men believed) on an entirely physical basis, with no need for the spirit. In fact, religion was a roadblock.

This was the real thing, Satan showing his shameful clever face, and it represented a challenge to God's authority as nothing since Roman paganism, and perhaps beyond. A new world would be constructed — *without* Him. An artificial world. And it precipitated a special response from heaven: Where, for 18 centuries, the Virgin had been sent with short messages, with the mission of converting villages, and building churches (albeit with situations like Guadalupe on a massive scale), now she was coming with longer missives — and warnings.

This was now a more urgent mission. As we have seen, there had been at least six major chastisements. They had occurred on average every five centuries. Now there was another, the beginning of the current cycle. Across France, nuns were receiving prophecies of tremendous coming events — and great peril. In 1830 Mary warned of an evil time when she appeared to a novitiate nun in the heart of Paris — in the very seat of rationalism itself — in what became famous as the Miraculous Medal apparitions, and there were other prophecies. Something was afoot, and it was beginning to show itself in the climate: the cool period was ending, and in fact, according to records I saw at an ancient observatory in Armagh, Ireland (handwritten parchment logs), there was now a remarkable shift back to the kind of warming last seen before the plague. In 1846 mean temperatures suddenly jumped to 50.9 degrees Fahrenheit, an increase of two and a half degrees.

That same year, on September 19, on a mountaintop near Grenoble, France, just above the hamlet of LaSalette, two children, Melanie Calvat, 14, and Maximin Giraud, 11, were tending to several grazing cows. It was a Saturday afternoon and following a nap they had ambled to an overlook, a ravine, to see where their animals, owned by local farmers, had wandered. Spotting the livestock and returning to where they had left their knapsacks, Melanie suddenly noticed a bright light, a strange circular luminosity, and pointed it out to Maximin, who was equally stunned.

It was in the ravine, a light that whirled, turned on itself, and grew stronger. They were about to flee when they noticed the circle opening. Soon they could make out a form inside. There was the shape of a woman seated with her head down and her face in her hands, weeping. As they stared they could make out her head, hands, and elbows. Soon the figure stood, crossed her arms across her breast, and approached along a brook. There was an immediate feeling of "something inconceivably fantastic," Melanie later told countless inquisitors. The woman had a face of magnetic beauty and her voice exuded peace. She began to address the astonished youngsters. *"Come to me, my children. Do not be afraid. I am here to tell you something of the greatest importance.*

"For a long time I have suffered for you. If I do not want my Son to abandon you, I am forced to pray to him myself without ceasing. You pay no heed. However much you would do, you could never recompense the pain I have taken for you.

"I have given you six days for work; I have reserved the seventh day for myself and no one will grant it to me. It is this which weighs down the hand of my Son. Those who drive the carts cannot swear without introducing the name of my Son. It is these two things that weigh down the hand of my Son."

Clearly this was a reference to Jesus and a warning of local chastisement. Since the first century, when she appeared to James at Zaragoza, Mary had been coming to help specific localities, and so it was now. It was like the apparitions of Elijah and Moses to Jesus (*Matthew* 17:3). That too had been on a mountain; that too had involved light. Now she was a messenger. Now she was returning. A change in climate, the onset of what appeared to be another series of events (it had been five centuries since the last), bore, as in other cases, a spiritual element. Throughout the eruptions of plague Mary had appeared to tell villagers they would be spared if they honored her Son and now, centuries later, she was issuing another warning.

"If the harvest is spoiled, it is your fault. I warned you last year about the potatoes, but you have not heeded it. On the contrary, when you found the potatoes had spoiled

you swore and you introduced the name of my Son. They will continue this year so that by Christmas there will be none left.

"If you have wheat, it is not good to sow it. All that you will sow, the beasts will eat," she said, *"and that which remains the beasts will not dare to eat. In the upcoming year it will fall into dust.*

"A great famine will come. Before the famine comes, the children under seven years of age will be seized by trembling and they will die in the hands of those who hold them.

"The others will do their penance in the famine. The walnuts will be worm-eaten and the grapes will rot. If they are converted, the stones and rocks will become heaps of wheat, and the potatoes will sow themselves in the fields (in the year that comes)."

There was a warning of hunger, of famine, and incredibly that year a horrid crop failure — a failure of potatoes — hit not only northern France but also the northern neighbor of Ireland. It was an epic catastrophe. An unprecedented attack of blight and failure to properly sow led to a three-quarters decrease in yield. Massive mortality ensued. Between 800,000 and a million starved, truly a *"great famine,"* and there was massive migration, a change in the very nature of northern Europe, along with outbreaks of fever and dysentery that no doubt seized the young with *"trembling."* As prophesied, the very locale of LaSalette was affected. That much took place; there was disease; there was starvation. It was the event that sent millions of Irish to America.

But as it happens, terrific as this was, as much as it was a harbinger, it had not been the end of the message. In between speaking of the grapes and piles of wheat, the Virgin had turned to each child and confided a secret. It was done separately. While she was addressing Maximin, Melanie could only see her lips move, and when the

Blessed Mother was confiding to Melanie, Maximin couldn't hear. It is these secrets I would now like to discuss; they pertained not just to a region or locality, as usual, but to the world at large. It is debatable whether they pertained almost wholly to events that followed in the 19th century, or were meant to encompass our own future. Two facts stand out: the predictions included great natural events, and while many can be interpreted as having soon taken place, some of the prophecies have not yet occurred. They pertained both to events of the time and to the future. They outlined a clear pattern that began to develop. And they were not just for Catholics. Moreover, it was an apparition that was officially accepted despite the Church's famous skepticism. Those who are not familiar with Catholicism should bear in mind that I am not speaking about the more widely known secrets of Fatima. That was a separate event, and came later. This was an experience that came on the heels of the French Revolution, which as I said had seen thousands of priests, nuns, and ministers, all walks of Christian faithful, ruthlessly slain, the symbols of Christ — the works since the first century — destroyed. A secularism was moving into the human arena — as it never had — and its tenets were about to sprout into Darwinism, Marxism, and a system of humanistic thought that was no longer in need of God.

If paganism had been the evil of too *many* gods, rationalism, when taken to an extreme, when relished as a religion unto itself, was the evil of *no* God.

There had been a notable increase in antagonists who by means new and full of deceit were striving to sap the Christian message.

Satan was many things and among them a spirit of extremes. He nurtured imbalance. He swayed people into pagan beliefs or into the void where there was no belief at all. It was Baudelaire who said the devil's greatest wile was to persuade us that he didn't exist, and this was accomplished in the 1800s in Europe through those who sought to implant the notion that reality was confined to the material. The only things *real* were those that could be seen, heard, touched, smelled. It was a philosophy that presented earth as an accident of atoms in a void of senseless universe. And because it was presented by a system of science that was producing wonderful new marvels, it had the potential of sweeping the planet for the first time, and instituting a totally non-spiritual humanity.

This was the great stirring at the time of LaSalette and it was undoubtedly what caused the warnings as mankind slid into a mindset that put itself above the "superstition" of God. Botany and anatomy were demystified. Who needed God when there was rationalism? Who needed God when there were now magnificent human inventions? Who needed God when we could now explain physiological processes? Who needed Him to heal when there was medicine?

It was the age of mathematics and chemistry and discovery of elements that let man play the role of creator.

Who needed God when heaven could be attained with a telescope?

Science was becoming a religion, and while it brought great benefits, it headed, at its extremes, into darkness. The problem wasn't so much theories like that of evolution but how they soon sought, at evil behest, to exclude God. In the case of evolution, which means "unfolding," Darwin had introduced the idea that it was natural selection — a random process based on genetic mutation — which had directed the unfolding, the development of life, instead of an unfolding that God engineered. When an animal developed wings to fly, or fur for warmth, or brains to think, it was just the product, they now said, of freak genetic occurrences that allowed these animals to outcompete other creatures and thus win a selection process that meant survival. In other words, nature, not God, directed evolution.

There was no need for a Creator. There was a new reverence for nature. It was a clever throwback to the oldest pagan beliefs, and it was remarkable. Did scientists really believe that the unique characteristics of so many animals, the humps on the back of a camel, the lengths of beaks in birds that dug for bugs, the pocket for infant kangaroos, were a matter of *chance*? There was even a fish that had an illuminative organ — a light — to see at the greatest ocean depths!

There was no problem with evolution, but a whole *lot* of problems with the idea that it had been devised, directed, and regulated by the toss of genetic dice. It was a notion that was purely physical, and with that level of physicality — of materialism — religion was in peril. Little by little such earthliness, manifesting through extremes of socialism, capitalism, secular humanism, and communism — extremes that ignored the spirit — would infiltrate institutions of learning, communication, business, and government. It would reach full stride during the twentieth century. Such was the urgency. Such was the warning at LaSalette. The current times were an incubation period. The stage was being set for a full-scale attack on the spiritual. If he couldn't do it with occultism, if he couldn't do it with a pantheon of gods, the devil, a superintelligence, was going to eradicate the very notion of the supernatural for one simple deadly reason: without the supernatural there could be no God.

It was an endgame and it was as effective as paganism. In a mood set by the concept of natural selection, belief would be extinguished, those who remained faithful would be persecuted — indeed, martyred — and the influence of evil would accelerate in all regards. There was now "humanism" in the sense that humans were seen as the ultimate form of intelligence. That was what the goddess of wisdom said, and it was what had happened during the French Revolution. It was what was still happening in France, where soon after LaSalette the government officially tried to strip the Church's power. Humanists wanted marriage extracted from religion and turned it into a strict legal matter. Churches had been turned into "temples of reason." There were bankers to fund Karl Marx and there was a German philosopher named Nietzsche who was soon to rise and proclaim the need for a new creator. Taking rationalism to the limit Nietzsche preached the evolution of a new godhead that he called "superman."

This too had been foreseen at LaSalette. Let's get back to that: the secrets. As I said, the Virgin had spoken to each child individually, and from the early days there was the feeling these secrets might pertain to more than local events, that they might involve "great events." No one could glean more than this. No matter how the children were prodded, threatened, or interrogated, they showed a remarkable ability at circumspection — to evade granting hints — despite their meager education. In fact the imparting of secrets was not even known until several days after the apparition. "Yes, there is something, but the Holy Virgin has forbidden me to tell it," Maximin had replied when asked sometime between September 21 and September 26 by the parish priest, Abbe Pierre Melin, if there had been anything else; the firmness and reserve and precision in handling the most adept and at times tricky questions never failed to impress interrogators. There was an initial inquiry by Father Melin, who interviewed Maximin a week after the apparition, then an investigation by four faculty members of a seminary in Grenoble, followed by an interrogation of the two children by a priest named Francois Lagier who questioned the children and thunderingly demanded the secret during a 15-hour session with Melanie — dragging the girl time and again over every inch of the apparition.

Still, nothing was revealed, and the same was true during investigations by secular authorities. Neither the mayor of LaSalette, who threatened the youngsters with jail, nor the Royal Prosecutor from the Grenoble district could elicit more than the children chose to be known. Two commissions of the most learned priests in the diocese examined the matter and recommended a formal juridical inquiry, which was then headed by Father Rousselot, whose investigators visited nine dioceses checking on claims of miraculous healings among pilgrims.

Strange things had occurred. A spring of healing water had erupted beside the rock on which the Virgin was said to have sat, and in October, when two lieutenants passing through LaSalette were shown a small piece of rock broken from the larger one, they split it with a hammer and when the rock fell into two pieces were stunned to see an image of Christ etched inexplicably into one of the pieces.

So it went for many months. The children were interrogated again and again and still their accounts remained consistent and theologically flawless, although they did not attend school, had not received religious instruction, and were late in receiving their first Communion. Other bishops were consulted — at least half a dozen — and after a board of 16 priests was named for a final conclusion, the LaSalette bishop, Monsignor Philbert de Bruillard, concluded the proceeding with no comment — mulling it over for the next four years.

Such was not uncommon. Other cases took longer. There was the need for great caution. Aside from the possibility of simple hallucination, self-delusion, confusion, or fabrication, there was the real possibility of demonic deception. Through the centuries the Church had logged many diabolical charades — times when Satan had come as an angel of light (*2 Corinthians* 11:14), and for that reason rejected all but the most powerful manifestations, waiting to see what the "fruits" would be (in accordance with *Matthew* 7:16). There was also a discernment by Jean Baptiste Vianney, the famous curé of Ars who would later be canonized and who in the end also came to believe what

Melanie and Maximin said. By this time hundreds had exhausted every device to trap the two children in contradictions or extract the secrets. "Threats of imprisonment and death, offers of money or other benefits, and tricks and ruses could not move the children to disclose their secrets," wrote Dr. Sandra L. Zimdars-Swartz of the University of Kansas, who has brilliantly researched the history of LaSalette. "The children's preservation of their secrets in the face of such pressures became, for the investigators, an argument for the children's integrity and thus evidence for the divine origin of the apparitions." When Abbe Pierre Chambon, superior of the Grenoble seminary, sent a report to the bishop, he emphasized "the astonishing resourcefulness" that the children showed, and others marveled that Maximin, whose inability to learn the catechism had prevented him from making his first Communion, could show what was described with "a precision, a reserve, and a firmness" entirely alien to him.

SENT TO EARTH

CHAPTER 12

"I am terrified of these prodigies"

But there were certain hints. And they indicated more than the potato failure. In 1847, a Grenoble lawyer named Armand Dumanoir had reported that the Lady had given each child "a secret which appears to consist in the announcement of a great event," and the idea that the secrets might be more than just personal messages — that they might concern the world — was also indicated by Canon Rousselot, who had been delegated by Bishop Bruillard to gather evidence and who suggested that the secrets might well involve the announcement of a future happening.

For five years the children steadfastly refused to reveal anything to anyone. After failure in 1849 and 1850 to get them to repeat what they had been told, the archbishop of Lyon, negative toward the events, wanted the secrets transmitted to the Pope, if to no one else. It was a matter of discernment. The children were asked if they would be willing, and agreed only after great initial resistance, especially on the part of Melanie, who was now in a convent. "They want my secret, they want my secret," she had been heard to fret over and again in her sleep. "I must tell my secret to the Pope or be severed from the Church."
Finally, the girl agreed if it could be done in person, or through a letter in a sealed envelope. Maximin similarly

agreed. There were hints, according to Zimdars-Swartz, that the children believed that they had been given a special sign from heaven that permitted such a disclosure. And so it was that on July 2 Maximin, now 15, was taken to a secluded room and wrote his message under the supervision of a cleric named Canon de Taxis and a local engineer, F. Benjamin Dausse, who had followed the situation closely. According to Zimdars-Swartz, Maximin recorded his secret rapidly, with no hesitation, exuberantly tossing the paper in the air when he was done, and then recopied it when the first version appeared too sloppy. "I am unburdened, I no longer have a secret, I am as others!" he was heard to exclaim. "One no longer has any need to ask me anything, one can ask the Pope and he will speak if he wants!"

Dausse then attempted to elicit the secret from Melanie. After agreeing, hesitating, and then agreeing again, the young woman, now approaching 20, finally sat down on July 3 and under the auspices of Dausse and a chaplain named Abbe Gerente, calmly recorded the secret. As was the case with Maximin, there was no hesitation or pondering. It flowed right out. Melanie's secret was significantly longer, however, spanning three handwritten pages.

The matter would have rested there, but a few hours later Melanie became agitated and asked to see Canon Rousselot, who had been designated to gather evidence of the apparition. The reason was simple: she had forgotten to write something. Rousselot agreed that Melanie could write a new version and three days later, on July 6, the girl did just that. This time, however, the session was more emotional and during it Melanie asked what the word "infallibly" meant, as well as the spelling of "soiled" and "antichrist." The secret was then taken to Bishop Bruillard, who was allowed to read it in his chambers.

The bishop emerged in an emotional state, with tears. There was something in Melanie's secret (more than Maximin's) that hit chords at deep, sorrowful, and even frightening levels. It was possessed of the kind of gravity only a supernatural missive usually has. Was it real? It seemed so, and it was then placed in an envelope and sealed for transmission to the Pope. Canon Rousselot and Abbe Gerin, curé of the Grenoble cathedral, immediately took the secrets to Rome, where they were presented to Pius IX on July 18. Of this we have few details, except that on reading Maximin's message the Pope showed little emotion. "Here is all the candor and simplicity of a child," was his only comment.

It was different with Melanie's. This of course was the longer secret, 38 paragraphs, some long, and after reading it the pontiff's face changed. Like Bruillard, he reflected inner turmoil. There were hints, unlike other messages from the Virgin, which were usually gentle, that this one contained urgency, that it laid out the situation starkly, at times even harshly, and that it railed against corruption in the clergy, as well as a general spirit of modernism, of antichrist, that challenged God. Such admonishment was understandable in a world where there was a mood of contempt for all that was sacred and a serving of self instead of God.

All eyes had turned to the earth instead of heaven.

Idolatry of the intellect — idolatry of humans — had replaced ancient idols.

It was a racheting, an intensification, of the Modern Era, and there was an assault on Christianity by men like Karl Marx, who had spent time in Paris and who cynically called religion "the opiate of the people."

Basic conceptions of human existence were now at odds with the spiritual.

Few went to Mass or read the Bible. Ties with the traditional past had been violently sundered. There was sacrilege.

"It is necessary that I reread these at more leisure," said the Pope. "There are scourges that menace France, but Germany, Italy, all Europe is culpable and merits chastisement. I have less to fear from open impiety than from indifference and from human respect."

That the issue was of great concern at the topmost Vatican levels was apparent in the remarks of Cardinal Nicolo Fornari, nuncio to Paris. "I am terrified of these prodigies," he told Rousselot. "We have everything that is needed in our religion for the conversion of sinners; and when Heaven employs such means, the evil must be very great." As for authenticity, the Pope's inclination was conveyed in the fact that he gave Rousselot a blessing for the children and presents for Bishop Bruillard, sending word that the bishop should do what he felt best. That ended up being formal approval. On September 19, 1851, exactly five years after the apparition, and having consulted the Vatican, along with dozens of others, Bishop Bruillard issued a proclamation authenticating the apparition. In Bruillard's words LaSalette was a message "that obedience and submission to heaven's warnings can spare us the new chastisements with which we are threatened, while too long resistance can lay us open to evils beyond repair." When, years later, he was asked in private about the secrets, Pope Pius is said to have responded, "You want to know the secrets of LaSalette? Ah, well, here are the secrets of LaSalette: if you do not do penance, you will all perish."

Chapter 13
"A time of darkness"

By 1853 bits of the prophecies leaked out, and by 1872 — a quarter century after the apparition — detailed versions of both secrets were published, Maximin's when it was obtained from the early copy he had made, and Melanie's at her own direction.

Maximin's was short and to the point. It focused on problems in the Church. Three-quarters of France would lose the faith, it said, and those who retained it would do so in a lukewarm way (a prediction that would be borne out with statistics compiled more than a century later in a study at the University of Michigan, which found that just 21 percent of the French were weekly churchgoers — technically less than a quarter).

That was the first point of Maximin's prophecy: The Church would enter a period of desertion. Peace would be given the world, said the message, only after men were converted. But this peace would be disturbed by a *"monster"* that would arrive *"at the end of the nineteenth century or at the latest at the commencement of the twentieth."* This seemed to dovetail with a warning that was issued by Pope Leo XIII, who on October 13, 1884, supposedly received his own vision of demons loosed from the pit. *"Up, ye children of light, and fight! For behold, the age of ages, the end, the extremity is at hand! The Church passes into darkness. The world will be in a state of consternation, perplexity, and confusion,"* said the alleged secret — alleged because the authenticity of the copy, the public version, has always been in question.

If that seemed like a stark warning, it was no more so than what was given to Melanie, who said she had been told by the Virgin that she could release her message after 1858 and who in January of 1870, after waiting for reasons her own, sent a fuller text to a priest, Abbe F. Bliard, saying it "should no longer be secret." That part and a yet lengthier version were published in 1872 and 1879 bearing the respective imprimaturs of Cardinal Xyote Riario Sforza of Naples and Bishop Salvator Luigi Zola of Lecce, Italy, the nation where Melanie was now in a convent.

It was explosive. It was detailed. It addressed both the Church and society — so searing that there were attempts to suppress it. Were words as direct as these, at times harsh, truly from the Virgin, or had Melanie, who as a nun had access to mystical literature, inserted some of what she heard from earlier seers, seers in France who wrote in a similar vein, and books of the Bible such as *Habakkuk* and *Matthew*, which had similar language? There was a great back and forth: bishops who supported it, others who sought to have it condemned. As a result the secret had a checkered history. While it bore imprimaturs and was said to have been favorably received by Leo XIII, there would be a formal Church decree against it in later years. The message said that by their irreverence and impiety, by their love of money and other pleasures, that priests had become *"cesspools of impurity."*

"Yes, the priests are asking vengeance, and vengeance is hanging over their heads," said Melanie's secret. *"Woe to the priests and to those dedicated to God who by their unfaithfulness and their wicked lives are crucifying my Son again!"*

The chiefs, the leaders of the people of God, had neglected their prayer and the devil, said the secret, had *"bedimmed their intelligence."* There had been a dumbing-down. There was blindness. It was not only the priests. It was the whole of humankind. And as a result God would allow *"the old serpent"* to cause divisions among those who reigned in every family and in every land.

Society was on the verge of the most terrible scourges, said the secret. *"Woe to the inhabitants of the earth!"* God would abandon mankind to itself. There would be hatred, jealousy, and homicides. Italy would be punished and so would the other European countries. There would be a *"general war."* There would be immorality. Carnal pleasures would spread over the earth. The righteous would suffer. There would be an antagonism to them. The spirit of dark would seek to extinguish that of light and those who followed Christ would be hunted down, made to die a cruel death. For a while one would not know who the true Pope was; the Holy Sacrifice would not be offered in churches; it would go underground — in tunnels, barns, and alcoves. Even bishops would abandon the side of truth. Demons would be loosed in 1864 and there would be such a blinding that unless blessed with special grace, many would assume *"the spirit of these angels of hell."* Several religious institutions would lose all faith, prophesied Melanie. Civil governments would have the same plan, and that would be to do away with every religious principal, making way for materialism, atheism, and vice of all kinds. God would send punishments *"which will follow one after the other for more than 35 years,"* said the prediction. France, Italy, Spain, and England would be at war. Blood would flow in the streets. *"Frenchman will fight Frenchman, Italian will fight Italian."* The general war would be appalling. For a time God would cease to remember Italy and France because the Gospel of Christ had been forgotten. After the turmoil there would be a false peace. *"People will think of nothing but amusement,"* said the secret. *"The wicked will give themselves over to all kinds of sin."* The occult would resurrect. There would be spirit mediums — something that happened in the immediate years after LaSalette with the popularization of Spiritualism. Voices would be heard. Everywhere there would be extraordinary wonders. There would be phenomena in the air. As a way to infiltrate, as a deception, evil spirits would assume the identity of those who were dead. There would rise a *"demon of magic."* The ancient rituals of Egypt and Babylon and Rome would continue their propagation through the clandestine practices of Masonry, and a false light would brighten the people. *"Evil books will be abundant on earth and the spirits of darkness will spread everywhere a universal slackening in all that concerns the service of God,"* said the missive. Convents would become *"the grazing grounds of Asmodeas and his like,"* a reference to a Persian devil who was thought to have been the spirit who had overthrown the seven bridegrooms of Sarah in *Tobit* and was overcome by the angel Raphael, who sent him to upper Egypt: the controller of gaming houses, the demon of impurity, the inventor of mindless amusements. In Solomonic legend he went by the name of Saturn! Rome would lose faith and become the seat of the antichrist, said the secret, and the devil would resort to all his evil tricks to introduce sinners into religious orders. Everyone would go his own way and everyone would seek superiority. There would be an avalanche of pride and this would lead to greed and ruthlessness. The darkness would spread everywhere; there would be a universal moral slackening.

"Woe to the Princes of the Church who think only of piling riches upon riches to protect their authority and dominate with pride," said the 1846 warning. *"The Vicar of my Son will suffer a great deal, because for a while the Church will yield to large persecution."* There would be a time of darkness. There would be attempts on the life of a pope. There would be *"a frightful crisis."*

Chapter 14

"The seasons will be altered"

It was a startling view of what was swiftly becoming the modern world and much of it, especially the first part of the secret, had immediately come true. The secret said there would be a period of turmoil — that God would abandon mankind to itself for 35 years — and indeed, by 1848, within two years, revolts had erupted everywhere. Venice. Vienna. Paris. A general economic slump and food shortages — the prophesied famine — had bred violence. Governments were swept aside or put on the defensive in nearly every major European capital. The message had said Frenchman would fight Frenchman and indeed French had fought French. It had said Italians would fight Italians and Italy was in fact in the throes of a civil conflict. Less than three decades after LaSalette, in 1870, there was another revolt in Paris that was crushed by the government with a toll of dead that equalled the great terrors of the French Revolution. There was also warfare between nations. The very year of LaSalette England had fought in India and troops from Russia entered Poland. *"France, Italy, Spain, and England will be at war,"* the message had said and soon England and France were fighting Russia. There was also war with Austria, and in 1870 France declared war on Prussia. There was turmoil in Spain, in Romania, in Serbia. Everywhere, including America, was civil war. "Fondly do we hope — fervently do we pray — that this mighty scourge of war may speedily pass away," said

73

Abraham Lincoln in an address. "Yet, if God will that it continue until all the wealth piled by the bondman's 250 years of unrequited toil shall be sunk, and until every drop of blood drawn with the lash shall be paid by another drawn with the sword, as was said three thousand years ago, so still it must be said, 'The judgments of the Lord are true and righteous altogether.'"

Things did not settle down until the 1880s, more than 35 years after the revelation. In India, in this land of Hindu gods, where lords of death, where queens of mayhem, reigned, starvation killed six million.

Militarily, philosophically, and economically, the world was in upheaval. The year after LaSalette Marx had written a major treatise on philosophy that became known as the "Communist Manifesto" and seemed inspired by sinister elements. He was a strange man whose dark side was chillingly exposed in the lyrics of macabre poems like *The Player*, which said: "The hellish vapors rise and fill the brain, till I go mad and my heart is utterly changed. See this sword? The prince of darkness sold it to me. For me he beats the time and gives the signs. Ever more boldly I play the dance of death."

A poem called *The Pale Maiden* was more blatant yet:
"This heaven I've forfeited, I know it full well. My soul, once true to God, is chosen for hell."

As forewarned at LaSalette (and by a chorus of other seers), governments began their attempt to do away with legitimate religion while forces of the occult, often tied to government, tried to create illicit new ones. There were seances, Spiritualism, and trance mediums. There was a "creature" at Loch Ness, and in the air what we would today call UFOs. Just as the secret forecast, there were wonders everywhere. A wave of strange lights began in 1878 when a man named Lee Fore Brace saw two enormous luminous "wheels" on each side of a British Indian Company steamship navigating the Persian Gulf. If they were not just figments of the imagination or bore some form of extraterrestrial explanation then, they had a spiritual component. They were *"astonishing wonders."* They were another of the prophecies that had been fulfilled.

The most startling prognostications had to do with disasters. As seldom before, the Virgin was warning that nature too would be in turmoil. She had often warned of plague, but now was expanding out. She was setting forth an entire long series of cataclysmic events that sounded much like the Mesopotamian, Roman, Bronze Age, and medieval chastisements. *"The seasons will be altered, the earth will produce nothing but bad fruit, the stars will lose their regular motion, the moon will only reflect a faint reddish glow,"* said the secret. Signs in the sky. Signs on the moon. It sounded like everything from volcanoes to asteroids. *"Water and fire will give the earth's globe convulsions,"* claimed Melanie, *"and terrible earthquakes will swallow up mountains and cities."*

The seasons would be altered.

It was a powerful statement, and it came not only at the very cusp of a new episode of global warming (a warming that Melanie could not have known about at the time, and one that would soon begin to mimic the medieval warming). And there were other events that were beginning to fit the pattern. In 1883 a huge volcano in Indonesia called Krakatau erupted with such force that it was heard 2,900 miles away and created a tidal wave that rose to a height of 120 feet and killed 36,000. Its ash faded the sun, caused weather changes around the world, and sent a glow as far away as Connecticut.

That was fire. There was also water. In 1887, 15 years after details of the secret came out, an inundation along the Yellow River in China engulfed an entire city called Cheng Chou, the population racing to shore up the walls but a gap widening to more than a thousand yards and chasing the workers away, the river in what one writer called "demonic pursuit." As the water rushed east it destroyed another city called Chungmow and over the next few days widened to thirty miles — swallowing an estimated 600 villages and towns.

The official death count was 900,000.

As A. H. Godbey, a chronicler of the time, noted, "The actual loss of life could not be computed accurately, but the lowest intelligent estimate placed it at 1.5 million, and one authority placed it at seven million."

Between 1846 and 1900 millions and possibly tens of millions died on the sunken triangle of land from Shanghai and Hanhow to Beijing.

Nor was the misery confined to Asia.

An earthquake had devastated Charleston, South Carolina; there was more famine in Ireland; and in Japan a tidal wave that hit Sanriku killed 22,000.

Clearly, if it was a pure revelation (and if negative Church judgments in 1915 and 1923, pertaining to certain versions and commentaries, did not negate its prophetic value), there was a sense of another global chastisement. And if it was like other major ones, this was just the start; more would be seen in the future; according to Melanie, much more. *"God will strike in an unprecedented way,"* the girl had quoted Mary as saying. *"Woe to the inhabitants of the earth."* The society of men, said the secret, was on the eve of *"the most terrible scourges and of gravest events."* God would exhaust His wrath upon them, and no one would be able *"to escape so many afflictions together."* These can be taken to have transpired during the revolts in Europe but it also mentioned that *"several cities would be shaken down and swallowed up by earthquakes,"* and while there were severe quakes in places like Peru and Ecuador and soon San Francisco, none had been *"swallowed."* Let's keep this in mind: earthquakes. Europe.

"Nature is asking for vengeance, because of man, and she trembles with dread at what must happen to the earth

stained with crime," said Melanie's secret. The earth, it claimed, *"will be struck by calamities of all kinds."* There would be storms. There would be fearful hail. *"There will be thunderstorms which will shake cities, earthquakes which will swallow up countries."*

As in some many previous events, there would be an astronomical element.

"All the universe will be stuck with terror," said the secret. *"The fire of heaven will fall and consume three cities."*

If that was true, it was clearly in the future; there were no asteroid hits in the 1800s. But there was the beginning of a profound change in climate. In fact, it can be argued that the year of LaSalette was precisely the year when the current warming started. By 1895 the mean temperature in the U.S. was 51.3 and it was ominously unfolding at the same speed as the Medieval Event.

At the same time, things philosophical and spiritual, things mystical, were heating up. In a vision remarkably similar to that of LaSalette, it was rumored that Pope Leo XIII had seen the devil approach the throne of God and request a century to test the people of earth, especially the Church, and this had been granted. *"Woe to the inhabitants of earth,"* the secret had announced, and so it was that occult trade unions — the freemasons who had their roots in the Middle Ages — rose to power and men dipped deeper into the belief that the ultimate power was to be found in deductive reasoning, not God. It was reasoning, it was logic, after all, that was creating all the marvelous inventions. There was the steamship. There was discovery of more chemicals. There was the telegraph. There was the linotype that led to mass media, and there was isolation of the diphtheria bacillus.

There were trolleys. There were treatises on electricity. There was the first coated photographic paper.

Soon there were the first motors powered by gasoline.

And man was becoming intoxicated with his intellect. It was emphasis on the mechanical and only the mechanical and it led to egoism. It led to faithlessness. Who needed God for illumination? When they needed light they now turned on a switch. And demons? There were no such things. With science as the new religion, it was time to purge childish notions. It was time to look at earth solely from a physical perspective. And this was extremely dangerous. It allowed the devil just what he wanted: to operate unseen. It was true: LaSalette was an intensely Catholic prophecy. It came from that part of the Christian Church. It was steeped in tradition. But it spoke to the world. It classed believers as one. And it was a battle cry. *"I call on the Apostles of the Last Days, the faithful disciples of Jesus Christ who have lived in scorn for the world and for themselves, in poverty and humility, in prayer and in mortification, in chastity and in union with God, in suffering and unknown to the world,"* the Virgin had said. *"It is time they came out and filled the world with light."* It was time to counter a trend that threatened to discard the nonmaterial. It was time to look back to the spiritual. Woe to the princes! Woe to the great thinkers who were blinded more than they could see! Suddenly, instead of seeing evil spirits as the cause of human maladies (as they had been since the time of Jesus), there were other causes; suddenly all mental, spiritual, and emotional disorders became a matter of psychology. Suddenly there was no more demonism. Despite copious evidence that spirits could cause actual physical and mental harm, cases of demonism were soon classed as "psychosis," "schizophrenia," or "multiple personality."

Philosophy was to replace mysticism and the light bulb was to replace illumination. Who needed a minister — who needed a confessor — when there was a therapist?

It was the era of Freud, and although the very female patient who inspired Freud's theory was by many reckonings a case of spiritual oppression (she was known as

"Anna O." and told Freud there was a demon inside her), he scoffed at such notions and was contemptuous of religion. As far as scientists were concerned, the realm of devils and angels was a fanciful realm. It was an opiate. It was a way for the feeble human mind to cope with a mortal world. Spiritual problems were now attributed to sexuality or childhood.

It was all in the plan of a darkness that rose with the temperature. Woe indeed! The Virgin had told Melanie that evil would come in great force beginning in 1864, and indeed that was the year of the first international workingmen's association founded by Marx, who in the poem *Oulanem* — in one of history's chilling moments — had said that "soon I shall embrace eternity to my breast, and soon I shall howl gigantic curses on mankind."

That same year Tolstoi published *War and Peace* and soon a book called *The Power of Darkness*.

There was also the swastika. Once a symbol in ancient Egypt, then Greece, Rome, China, and among Indians in the Americas, as well as the barbarians, the old sun sign was now in modern Europe. In 1875 a "magician" named Guido von List (who wore a white beard, long flowing robes, and performed sex rites to raise the "spirits") had gone to a hill overlooking Vienna, chanted his special incantations, and buried nine wine bottles in the shape of the swastika. It was a town that would soon be home to a man named Hitler.

SENT TO EARTH

CHAPTER 15

Wondrous Times

Woe, as came the fruits of rationalism; woe as came a world full of sudden mechanical wonder — celluloid film, electrical lamps, cars — but devoid of the spiritual. It was a trend that like the temperature would whipsaw into the future. The manufacture of rayon! The first telephone switchboard! Men were now creating their own material. They were designing their own reality! By 1893, Henry Ford had built the first automobile, and in 1895 came the first motion-picture camera.

Heady times. Wondrous times. Gramophones! There was the beneficial; there was insulin. And there was the insolent. Was technology the beast? Was that what Maximin had seen? Was it the discovery of radium and plutonium? Was it the artificiality of chemicals? Or was it the simple fact that instead of gifts of inspiration — gifts from God — invention became the source of human pride and the notion, always deadly, that men could become their own creator?

That was what had gotten Satan thrown out of heaven: trying to assume God's throne. And yet that's the direction in which too many were now heading. There was sensuality. It resembled the High Middle Ages. There were the first extracts of cocaine. There was murder, as LaSalette had predicted. There was Jack the Ripper in London, a town that also produced an occultist named Aleister Crowley, whose credo was, "Be strong, O man! Lust, enjoy all things of sense and rapture: fear not any God shall deny thee for this."

Do what thou wilt would be "the whole of the law," said Crowley, and for too many, for an increasing number, it was. The occult was on the march again. In their lodges Masons were spawning cults such as the Rosicrucians, movements that borrowed from Spiritualism or ancient sorcery and gave birth to the Hermetic Order of the Golden Dawn, cults that served as forerunners of modern satanism and produced characters like Crowley, a drug user and practitioner of "sexual magic"; a philosopher of the "true inner self"; a man whose own mother called him "the Beast."

He came to power right on the button in 1900. Was the spirit behind him the one Maximin was referring to when his secret prophesied that "*the monster will arrive at the end of the nineteenth century or at the latest at the commencement of the twentieth*"?

Addressing heaven at an occult ceremony, Crowley had railed against Christ Himself. "Thine hour is come," he had said with supreme dark arrogance. "As I blot thee out from the earth, so surely shall the eclipse pass; and Light, Life, Love and Liberty be once more the law of Earth. Give thou place to me, O Jesus; thine aeon is passed; the Age of Horus is arisen by the Magick of the Master, the Great Beast."

There was nothing more dangerous than that — rising against God! — and there were cults under similar inspiration across Europe. There was a move to question the virgin birth, the Resurrection of Christ, the authenticity of the Bible. It wasn't just the practitioners of black magic. It was also the scientists, the philosophers, the skeptics. The Church would be in eclipse, Melanie had said, and this too was materializing. It was coming full steam. And so was disaster. Hurricanes were astir. The climate had poured heat into the pot, and when that was released thunderstorms clustered and nucleated and began the famous rotation. Hurricanes. *Hurukan*, as Indians, as Mayans, called it. "Evil spirit." "Storm god." They were the most vicious of climatological events and in places like the Florida Keys they were lifting cattle and sending huge beams winging, rolling homes over, the ocean now coming in fulfillment of prophecy as a huge endless surge. In 1835 waves of astonishing height had hit Key West and in 1841 yellow fever preceded a hurricane that destroyed a little gambling mecca called St. Joseph in Florida. There were always hurricanes and there were always plagues and there were always local events but it was shaping up like others had, like the storms and flux in climate that had marked the beginning of every major event. Five years later a great hurricane had swamped Key West, destroying more than 500 homes and washing up a cemetery — one coffin found against a tree with its lid open, "the ghastly tenant looking out upon the scene of desolation around, as if in mingled wonder and anger that its rest had been so rudely disturbed," reported the *Florida Historical Quarterly*.

They came from the Atlantic; they came from the Caribbean; they came from the Gulf. Out on the wailing seas crews fighting to discern the horizon, to tell the gray sky from the vault-gray sea, saw uncanny electrical phenomena. "For nearly an hour we could not observe each other, or anything but merely the light," reported Captain William Seymour of a brigantine called the *Judith and Esther*, "and most astonishing, every one of our fingernails turned quite black, and remained so nearly five weeks afterwards. Whether it was from the firm grasp we had on the rigging or rails I cannot tell, but my opinion is, that the whole was caused by an electric body in the element."

Storm after storm hit, on occasion plowing north. In 1893 a hurricane reached New York City and caused a resort called Hog Island (just south of Brooklyn) to permanently vanish — the island totally washed over. Six hurricanes made landfall in the U.S. and hit St. Croix,

Guadeloupe, and El Salvador. No question: hurricanes were a product of nature (the heat caused moisture to collect), but nature was a product of God. When He so willed, said *Nahum* 1:3, His path was "in hurricane and tempest." There were clouds and wind and rain but they were the end result of dynamics that no meteorologist could lay full claim to comprehending. It was hard to tell where it all commenced but one thing stood for sure: it went beyond basic climatology. There were always dynamics that were mysterious, that seemed tied to deeper forces, that reacted not just with systems of high and low pressure or with stratospheric oscillations or with the Coriolis of the earth's rotation but with forces, with emanations, from the earth and sun that sailed in ways that couldn't be gauged or that edged into the spiritual. The very word "pneuma" as in air and "breath" meant "spirit." Christ had rebuked the wind (*Mark* 4:39) and that showed there was a spiritual element. How many places in the Bible involved weather? In *Psalms* there was the plea for God to "flash forth lightning" (144:6), there was the thunder in Moses's time (*Exodus* 19:19), there was the mention of lightning in the same breath as God's "arrows" (*2 Samuel* 22:15), there were droughts and rain and clouds. In *Revelation* it was said that thunder issued from His very throne (4:5). Thick clouds were His cover (*Psalms* 18:12). He came down in clouds. He dwelled in them. He sent them to guide Moses or to cover Mount Tabor.

Are we to believe this was all figurative? Are we to slough it off as metaphor? Are we to believe that God was once active in nature but has since relinquished that power — that weather, like natural selection, was now a random force?

There were endless accounts of God intervening through the weather. In 718 A.D. a huge storm had risen in Spain on Mount Auseva with sheets of rain that caused the Deva River to sweep over its banks and chase away an army of Moors who were about to overwhelm a little pious group in the highland and in France a storm had figured into the siege of Chartres: As the English penetrated to the very walls of the city the sky had suddenly, drastically turned overcast, "and so terrible a storm fell upon the English army that it seemed as though the end of the world had come." In 1815 during the war between America and England there had been another wonder when the British arrived near New Orleans to square off against General Andrew Jackson. As at Auseva it looked like sure defeat (the Americans were outnumbered by more than two to one), but a group of Ursuline nuns in a convent went to the Blessed Sacrament, weeping before a statue of Our Lady of Prompt Succor, and at Communion time the next day — at the very moment of the eucharist — a courier rushed in with the news that the British had been miraculously defeated, confused by a sudden fog that had sent them wandering to a mire — in full view of the waiting Americans.

So taken was Jackson with the events that he went to the convent to offer gratitude.

"By the blessing of Heaven, directing the valor of the troops under my command, one of the most brilliant victories in the annals of war was obtained," he proclaimed to his troops, describing the victory in a letter to the vicar as a "signal interposition of Heaven."

SENT TO EARTH

CHAPTER 16

A Thousand Devils

There were numerous other accounts. There was also the evil one. Could the devil raise the wind?

Perhaps the answer was in the description of him as prince of the power of the air. Many were the storms that seemed to have a sinister cast, a sense of true ill-boding, and as we know Christ had seen Satan "fall from the sky like lightning" (*Luke* 10:18). An evil feeling was common to clouds. Often it was like they were a manifestation of spiritual conflict, their thunder cannons, and that was what Christ had said: earth was a battlefield. At any given moment there were 1,800 thunderstorms on earth, which came to 16 million a year. It took warm, humid air, which was now in great abundance, and the effects could be awesome. There were blue "sprites" that shot from the tops of thunderheads and "blue giants" (which could strike twenty miles from a cloud), and chain-lightning that crawled across whole regions. Against every probability, there were people who had been struck by lightning two or even three times. Nature was an enigma and it was riled; no doubt about that. The "cannons" were sounding at the onset of the century, at the very time that temperatures were heading up, as men were straying from God. In August of 1900 a heat wave set records from the upper Mississippi Valley to the Great Lakes, Ohio Valley, and Mid-Atlantic states, and in Galveston, Texas, the humidity was close to a hundred percent.

The pump was primed for a disaster, and it was on its way to Galveston — which had tempted fate with a recent Mardi Gras that had "Beelzebub and the Devils" as the costume theme. Halfway between Cape Verde and the Antilles, a hurricane brewed. It was spotted on August 27, 1900 and picked up force as it crossed the Atlantic, made its way into the Caribbean, and then found its way into the Gulf of Mexico, where eddies known as warm core rings fed the system like fuel injectors. There was what meteorologists called "violent deepening" — a drastic drop in pressure, which meant a low-pressure system was intensifying — and suddenly it was on its way to Texas and specifically the party town of Galveston, which was less than nine feet above sea level.

It was a category-four storm, and it scutted in, blasted in, with malevolence, pushing in wall after wall of water — waves that crashed against second-story windows, furniture floating, clunking against ceilings, kids clinging to parents in terror in the attic before the homes were torn apart and they were thrown into the dark waves, the storm gusting to 180 miles an hour, killing 8,000, shrieking, whistling, sounding to one survivor "as if the room were filled with a thousand little devils."

CHAPTER 17

The Earth Rumbling

Nature was seeking vengeance. Six years after Galveston the United States was rocked by another massive disaster when a quake destroyed San Francisco. It started with a jolt at 5:13 a.m. on April 18, 1906, followed by a severe rocking motion. The earth undulated. Fires from ruptured gas lines spread in all directions. In short order more than 28,000 buildings — homes, offices, the city's grand hotels — were destroyed, sending panicked swarms onto the streets.

Babylon on the Bay was swathed in flames — fire befitting ancient Mesopotamia — and as always there were coincidences that seemed like more than coincidences. While the disaster touched both the good and bad (in accordance with the Scripture that said it rained on the just and unjust alike, *Matthew* 5:45), the most severe damage, the most blatant destruction, and the highest flames were in neighborhoods rife with swindlers, gamblers, and prostitutes. In Chinatown flames gutted a tunnel of opium dens — smoking out hidden subterranean chambers where sex slaves had been kept — and across town speakeasies and shantytowns were flattened, the ruffians who lived in them going on a rampage. Inmates from a mental hospital dashed through the streets, frantic, howling. Rodents rushed from sewers that had collapsed and gnawed on the legs of those crushed under a cupola. There was damage everywhere.

89

There was devastation at Stanford University. There was great destruction in San Jose. No one was spared. Not celebrities. Not opera stars. Not bankers who found their vaults melted and their money ash. Famous for its corruption, city hall was no more, its iron tangled, its dome fallen, its columns crushing pedestrians. More than 3,000 died and as the fire flared into evening, figures moved toward the hills of Oakland like ghosts in red twilight, in search of refuge in a world that no longer afforded it. "Death and destruction have been the fate of San Francisco," said the local newspaper. "Shaken by a temblor at 5:13 a.m. yesterday morning, the shock lasting 65 seconds and scourged by flames that raged diametrically in all directions, the city is a mass of smoldering ruins."

On January 21, 1906, there had been a magnitude-8.4 quake in Japan, and that had been followed ten days later by an 8.6 in Ecuador. Shortly after San Francisco there was a quake of equal power in the Aleutians, and just thirty minutes after that particular tremor was a yet larger one in Chile. New Guinea. Australia. Ecuador. "Normally you have one magnitude-8 earthquake every one-and-a-half to two years," I was told by Lowell S. Whiteside of the National Geophysical Data Center. "In 1906 there were about ten of them."

None was the "big one," the great seismic apocalypse that geologists feared, but they served as previews. In Sicily a quake and tidal wave killed tens of thousands, and meanwhile another part of the ancient pattern, astronomical phenomena, seemed to be coming back. On June 30, 1908, seismic stations were again set in motion when a small asteroid exploded above the Tunguska region of Siberia. Although only 60 to 200 feet in size, the chunk of rock caused an explosion that was at least 1,000 times the atomic bomb dropped on Hiroshima, a cylinder of incandescent white light that was seen falling with a fiery tail and was heard at a distance of 500 miles. Trees were blasted down over an area of 850 square miles. In a town called

Vanavara forty miles from the explosion residents were tossed into the air, their homes collapsing around them.

"The sky split apart and a great fire appeared," said one witness. "It became so hot that one couldn't stand it. There was a deafening explosion (and my friend) S. Semenov was blown over the ground across a distance of three *sazhens* (twenty feet). As the hot wind passed by, the ground and the huts trembled."

Everything round about was shrouded in smoke and fog from burning, falling trees. The forest had flashed into a column of smoke and flame and the sky took on a strange orange glow over Western Europe. As far away as England people were able to see newspapers without a lamp.

As prophesied at LaSalette, there was fire, the earth was convulsing, and more was to come. If what Melanie had said was true, a slew of events, disasters that destroyed particular cities, would presage larger disasters. These were forerunners. There would be a progression. In one part of her secret the girl had mentioned that several cities would be *"swallowed,"* and whether this related to quakes like the one in San Francisco or — more likely — was referring to a future event in which a quake would literally gulp down a major metropolitan area, there was no doubt that when all was said the secret went beyond local events.

Little by little, there would be a progression. Just as there was a progression in temperatures, so would there be an accumulation of other forces. One day the disasters, the catastrophes, would be *"widespread."* There would be *"infectious disease,"* said Mary. There would be famine. The earth would be *"desertlike."* And one day tremors would swallow not just cities but *"countries." "Woe to the inhabitants of the earth,"* the secret had said, and indeed a mind-boggling 24 million Chinese had starved as the result of a drought that was arguably the greatest known weather event. Marseille would be *"engulfed,"* said the secret, Paris would *"burn."*

CHAPTER 18

A Flaming Sword

These events served as the background for another dramatic apparition. On May 13, 1917, three children who like Melanie were shepherds spotted the Virgin on a similar hillside. "It was a lady dressed all in white, more brilliant than the sun, shedding rays of light clearer and stronger than a crystal glass filled with the most sparkling water and pierced by the burning rays of the sun," recalled the oldest seer, Lucia dos Santos.

The Virgin appeared to be only 16 years old, with a garment of the finest white and a star near the hem of her flowing robe. She held white rosary beads, her hands delicate, her expression one of wistful solemnity — not sad, not happy, but serious. She had come, she said, asking for prayers and sacrifices as an act of reparation for the world's sins. With the exception of August, she appeared to Lucia and the two others, her cousins Francisco, 9, and Jacinta Marto, 7, on the 13th of the month for the next five months, preceded by three flashes of light, accompanied at least once by a luminous globe, and leaving to the sound of thunder. It was on June 13 that the Virgin gave Jacinta a secret (as at LaSalette, separate from the others), and the following month, on July 13, to Lucia, who was 10. The last apparition was on October 13, 1917, and included a famous miracle in which 50,000 people were witness to the sun spinning and throwing off stupendous rays of crimson, causing reflections of green, red, orange, blue, and violet on the faces below; it gyrated at least three times, shuddered, and began to plunge downward in a zig-zag fashion, as if to destroy the earth.

That made news around the world, but more famous were the secrets. This was in the middle of World War One (which may have been the *"general war"* foretold at LaSalette), and there was a tremendous attempt on the part of authorities to learn what Lucia and Jacinto had been told. At one point the children were thrown into jail and convinced by the mayor, Arturo de Oliveira, a Mason, that they would be boiled in hot oil.

Still they refused to divulge what the Blessed Mother had told them in confidence. The first two parts of the secret included a vision of hell and a powerful message. *"God wishes to establish in the world devotion to my Immaculate Heart,"* said the Fatima secret. *"If what I say is done, many souls will be saved and there will be peace. The war is going to end; but if people do not cease offending God, a worse one will break out during the pontificate of Pius XI. When you see a night illumined by an unknown light, know that this is the great sign given you by God that He is about to punish the world for its crimes, by means of war, famine, and persecutions of the Church and of the Holy Father.*

"To prevent this, I shall come to ask for the consecration of Russia to my Immaculate Heart, and the Communion of reparation on the First Saturdays. If my requests are heeded, Russia will be converted and there will be peace; if not, she will spread her errors throughout the world, causing wars and persecutions of the Church. The good will be martyred; the Holy Father will have much to suffer; various nations will be annihilated. In the end, my Immaculate Heart will triumph. The Holy Father will consecrate Russia to me, and she will be converted, and a period of peace will be granted to the world."

Jacinta was shown highways and fields and roads full of people crying with hunger and nothing to eat. In a third part of the secret, they were shown a startling vision of chastisement. As Lucia later recounted, "After the two parts which I have already explained, at the left of Our Lady and a little above, we saw an angel with a flaming sword in his left hand; flashing, it gave out flames that looked as though they would set the world on fire; but they died out in contact with the splendor that Our Lady radiated towards him from her right hand: pointing to the earth with his right hand, the angel cried out in a loud voice: 'Penance, penance, penance!' And we saw in an immense light that is God: 'something similar to how people appear in a mirror when they pass in front of it' a bishop dressed in white. We had the impression that it was the Holy Father. Other bishops, priests, men and women religious going up a steep mountain, at the top of which there was a big cross of rough-hewn trunks as of a cork tree with the bark; before reaching there the Holy Father passed through a big city half in ruins and half trembling with halting step, afflicted with pain and sorrow, he prayed for the souls of the corpses he met on the way; having reached the top of the mountain, on his knees at the foot of the big cross, he was killed by a group of soldiers who fired bullets and arrows at him, and in the same way died one after another the other bishops, priests, men and women religious, and various lay people of different ranks and positions. Beneath the two arms of the cross there were two angels each with a crystal aspersorium in his hand, in which they gathered up the blood of the martyrs and with it sprinkled the souls that were making their way to God."

The two youngest, Jacinta and Francisco, were told they would die soon, which occurred when a horrible epidemic of influenza spread around the world, killing more than twenty million. That forces of nature were in upheaval, were in battle, was also indicated by a savage storm that descended the night before the sun miracle on all of Europe. "What a night!" wrote William Thomas Walsh. "It was as if the devil, somewhere in the ice and snow that could never slake the burning of his pain, had resolved to destroy with one blow all that remained of the Europe which had so long been his battleground against the Thing he hated most. Somewhere in the dark misery of Siberia, he was permitted, heaven knows why, to disturb the equilibrium of the air, setting in motion a cold and cutting blast that shrieked across the continent to the western sea. It may have passed howling over a cabin in Finland where a little lynx-eyed man who called himself Lenin had been waiting to enter St. Petersburg (he had lately sown the seeds of revolution there), and to begin, in a very few weeks, the transformation and destruction of all the world which owed what was best and noblest in it to the teachings of Christ."

The slashing rain muddied the roadside and choked gullies but the faithful continued to the site where on October 13 there was an apparition of Jesus, Mary, and Joseph, along with the burst of sun that seemed to rotate and plunge and miraculously dried the clothes of spectators. Tens of thousands bore witness, and just a month later, as prophesied, Vladimir Lenin, promulgator of Communism, returned to Petrograd, where he was to put Marx's godless notions into practice and turn Russia into an atheist country, one that absorbed and crushed — annihilated — surrounding countries like Ukraine. Soon government offices displayed corner altars with pictures of Marx, Engels, and Lenin, whose first name of "Vladimir" meant "lord" or "ruler of the earth" — which was interesting because it was precisely the language Melanie had used when in a last part of the secret she mentioned that there would be *"kings of the antichrist"* who would devise a plan to be *"the only rulers of the world."*

"A forerunner of the antichrist, with his troops gathered from several nations, will fight against the true Christ, the only Savior of the world," said the LaSalette secret. *"He will shed much blood and will want to annihilate the worship of God to make himself be looked upon as a god."*

It was what Maximin had seen as the rising beast. The spirit of antichrist was materializing. "We are going to destroy everything," Lenin once told a friend. "And on the ruins we will build our temple."

That would be followed, Melanie had warned, by *"calamities of all kinds,"* including famine and plague, *"which will be widespread,"* and indeed it was just a year after Lenin's rise that the pandemic of influenza, the greatest plague since the Black Death, started. The source was thought to be Fort Riley, Kansas, which had been hit by bone-chilling winters, sweltering summers, and blinding dust storms, where a threatening black sky had come with a stinking yellow smog from burning manure, and where, two days after the sun went black, soldiers began to take ill and spread it abroad during the war, especially to Spain. "The Spanish flu, as it came to be known, reached every continent and virtually every country on the map, going wherever ships sailed or cars or trucks or trains traveled, killing so many so quickly that some cities were forced to convert streetcars into hearses, and others buried their dead in mass graves, because they ran out of coffins," wrote Malcolm Gladwell.

Once in Europe it had mutated and swept into Portugal with virulence. Like the Black Death it moved in all directions. England infected Scandinavia; France infected Italy. In India the virus came by sea and raced inland.

SENT TO EARTH

CHAPTER 19

The Hour of Persecution

Nor was persecution long in coming. In the Soviet Union, believers would have to renounce God or die. During Lenin's takeover and the Red Terror of 1918-1920 — the years immediately following Fatima — at least two million oppositionists were killed, including a thousand bishops and priests, and millions more during the civil strife and persecutions to follow. According to one estimate twenty million perished between 1914 and 1920, and millions more during a Soviet-induced famine in 1921-1922, which was aggravated by the gyration in weather.

Millions died. Untold millions. They were hung, shot, thrown into the gulag. As prophesied too at LaSalette, priests and nuns would be hunted down, made to die a cruel death (in some instances nailed to walls crucifixion-style). Hundreds. Thousands. There were jail sentences of twenty or thirty years for simply holding Mass or services in the woods or hearing confession. Protestants, Jehovah's Witnesses, and believing Jews were eradicated. No one knows how many were slain, but this was the start of it; this was what the Blessed Mother had told Lucia. During the next twenty years nearly two million Ukrainians would be deported while another 400,000 were destroyed *in situ* — shot. With demonic vengeance, with the belief that they could form a world without God, Communists surged across the landscape like locusts, and the red dragon, also rising in China, would (as prophesied in *Revelation*) chase after the woman.

When all was said and done, the Communists would cause more martyrs than in all centuries leading up to the twentieth combined. No wonder Lucia, in quiet training for the life of a religious, handled the secret like a burden. No one wanted to know that. No one wanted to see how atheism would strip a person of caring, charity, and inner goodness. The spirit of atheism — antichrist — was a cold wind that sought to override, to chill, the power of the Holy Spirit, and there was a *railing*, a coiling of the serpent, at God's presence. The secret saw the way it would lash out at all that was good, all that was spiritual, the way it would assume characteristics of classic evil. And I do mean evil. As a child Lenin's favorite comfort was the aria from *Faust*, and in grammar school he had inexplicably torn off a cross he was wearing, spat on it, and thrown it away.

Now he was trying to do the same with all religion. It was the beast hurling blasphemies (*Revelation* 13:5), and this was at the heart of the third secret. Martyrs. There was a systematic and frighteningly widespread effort at eradicating the good. And although in less murderous fashion, the same cold spirit was filtering into the very ranks of the Church. Through cracks came the smoke of Satan. This was in the form of a sterile secular spirit that sought to strip the Church of mysticism — its charisms — replacing it with an intellectuality that put logic above spirit.

There was nothing wrong with logical thinking but there was plenty wrong with installing it in place of the supernatural, with sending in so much philosophy and robotic thinking that all that remained of a parish or hierarchy was a vacant institutional structure.

That was the result of too much rationalism. Lucia saw that. It was given to her. She saw the soot, the curling smoke, and she saw a "decisive" battle. That much she would say. It was a battle in which one side would win and the other lose.

But for years, Lucia would keep it a secret. She too evaded inquiries with remarkable deftness. She had no need for attention. Her goal was the poverty of a convent. Hers was to be a life of prayer. And it was the opposite of what was going on in the rest of the world. If it had seemed like the High Middle Ages were an uproarious time, it was less than was in progress now. This was the "Roaring Twenties," and it sounded a lot like what the Virgin had foreseen at LaSalette when she said *"people will think of nothing but amusement."* For decades men had been busy with their inventions — with proof of how masterful they were — and now it was time to kick back and drink it in. There was jazz and dance and women in frilled skimpy skirts. There was speculation. The stock market was soaring; it was the "get-rich-quick" era. It was a time of entertainment. It was a time of gangsters. It was a lawless and lavish and outlandish time. Hollywood was cranking out 2,000 films a year and sports became a national obsession.

That seemed harmless but something was happening to the family. One-sixth of marriages now broke up and there was a trend of illicit sex. On the scene was Oscar Wilde, who promoted homosexuality, and Margaret Sanger, the woman who founded Planned Parenthood and championed abortion. Sexual promiscuity was her aim and as one writer, Mabel Dodge, described her, "it was as if she had been more or less arbitrarily chosen by the powers that be to voice a new gospel of not only sex knowledge in regard to contraception, but sex knowledge about copulation and its intrinsic importance. She was the first person I ever knew who was openly an ardent propagandist for the joys of the flesh."

Her own husband complained that Sanger's movement was "not noble but an excuse for a saturnalia of sex."

A saturnalia was a pagan sex festival and so we see how society was coming full circle, and how, in a more sophisticated, often unknowing way, it was performing the rites of witchcraft with saturnalia and a blood sacrifice with abortion, a sacrifice of the innocents. Paganism, a form of demonic worship, was infesting not only philosophy and politics but personal morality. Sanger was a Rosicrucian — one of the cults spawned by masonry — and the motto of her newspaper, *Woman Rebel*, was "No Gods, No masters."

A massive sex rite! If Spiritualism was the demon of magic, this was the demon of lust. The sexual revolution was on its way, along with its fruit of abortion. For centuries, since medieval times, witches had promoted precisely what Sanger was promoting: free, extramarital sex and the sacrifice of babies. The occult spirit engendered by Spiritualism, nurtured by secret cults, and so lucidly foreseen at LaSalette, was now integrating itself in society's mainstream under the guise of liberation.

Sanger also advocated the control of population, including the weeding out of the crippled, the mentally defective, and those of "inferior" race.

"The propagation of the degenerate, the imbecile, the feeble-minded, should be prevented," wrote this strange woman, railing against "chaotic breeding" from our "stupidly cruel sentimentality."

This, to emphasize, was the most dangerous of trends: humans as controllers of life, as creators, the age-old treachery. Were humans really expendable? Was it in the domain of science to engineer life? Would it one day lead back to the murder of Rome? Was that what life was all about: survival of the "fittest"? And did that spell the end of mercy? Was man naught but an advanced rendition of the mammal?

It was the era of the Scopes Monkey Trial and men indeed began to look on themselves as a species, something to study, something expendable.

And no one was questioning science. No; that was a sacrilege. Its accomplishments were astonishing. There was ammonia, cellophane. There was the x-ray, the airplane.

There was the first telegraphic transmission of pictures. Who could question that kind of ingenuity? Who could stand against *that* magic? It was a new religion and when it went too far, dragging men to nothing but a material view of life, of the world, it was what Lucia was to call a "diabolical disorientation."

It was paganism but in some ways it was worse than paganism because this was no longer ancient Egypt. This was an era with access to the Gospels. It took a conscious decision to deny the truth, but that's what was in progress. If before there had been worship at the altar of goddesses and amulets and sphinxes, now there was the reverence of objects that whirred, that functioned on the magic of electricity, that fizzed as new potions.

CHAPTER 20

The Dark Horseman

The Twenties were roaring but so was nature. The progression that had begun with LaSalette was like a great grinding gear and it was rotating faster. In 1920 an earthquake had claimed 200,000 victims in the Kansu province of China, and Japan was hit by a typhoon that destroyed tens of thousands of homes. The storm was followed a few short years later by a magnitude-8.2 quake that ravaged Tokyo, sparking a fire that dwarfed the one in San Francisco.

As yet it wasn't a major global upheaval and these were not the greatest events in history (nothing to compare with the drastic climate changes during the Great Mesopotamian Event), but events were beginning to point in that direction. In London an extraordinary tide caused the Thames to bust through its banks and in the United States tornadoes hit record proportion — one traveling from Missouri to Indiana and spending three horrifying hours on the ground, killing 669. In Florida a lighthouse swayed so violently during a hurricane at Jupiter that mortar squeezed from it like toothpaste.

Then in 1926 came the Great Miami Hurricane. At category-four it was the potency of what had destroyed Galveston, and the debris was tremendous. Yachts were dumped in front of hotels, Miami Beach was washed over, and the building where the famous Miami Follies Girls frolicked was left looking in the words of one eyewitness like "the Rheims cathedral after the German bombardment."

Not a single palm could be found in whole stretches of South Florida, pines also gone, casinos razed, bars ruined. Waves thrashed the bottom floors of apartment towers and if it wasn't the action of water it was the whip of wind. Large doors were blasted open as the hurricane entered thousands of homes, crashing lights and exploding plaster. The eye moved directly over Miami and the force around it scattered furniture, clothes, and anything else it could lift for miles. Patrician neighborhoods, the hoi poloi, were devastated beyond knowing. So immense was the destruction that the very viability of Miami as a city, as a safe place to live, was called into question. "Six days ago this City of 200,000 people was one of the most prosperous, beautiful, and delightful communities in this country," said a citizens committee in appealing for help from the rest of the country. "Today, as a result of a disastrous tropical hurricane, which devastated our coast last Saturday, it lies prostrate."

A few years later, at Lake Okeechobee, nearly 2,000 died in another storm that sent water surging over dikes, where it carried one house for half a mile.

That too was a category-four. From 1910 to 1929 there were five storms at that level. Each increment up the scale — each new category — meant five to ten times the damage. The storms were hovering, down-blasting, and destroying huge swaths from Louisiana to Texas. Warm air was speeding upward, the barometer was dropping, and even Galveston had been hit again.

There was also drought. While Florida was awash, the Midwest was desperate for water. It was the Dust Bowl, and through the Thirties, as America reckoned with both drought and economic collapse, banks, churches, and schools were boarded up and the very character of the country changed. In the Soviet Union, drought was also causing a crisis, a famine greatly aggravated by the forced collectivization of farms. The fruit of Communism, the fruit of godlessness, was a famine that cost at least five times as many lives as the Irish Famine. "*The good will be martyred, the Holy Father will have much to suffer; various nations will be annihilated,*" it had said at Fatima, and if what happened during the 1920s, if the execution of landowners and freethinkers and priests wasn't enough, there was now the horror caused when Stalin, seeking to quash Ukrainian nationalism and terrorize private farmers, hauled all that republic's wheat to Russia and created a severe, almost incomprehensible famine. In 1933 alone at least 4.6 million and perhaps as many as ten million Ukrainians perished. It was the dark horseman of the Apocalypse. "Practically every village has a mass grave from the artificial famine of 1933," Dr. James Mace, director of the Commission on the Ukraine Famine, told me. "There was tremendous demographic damage — epic figures."

According to another scholar, Lubomyr Hajda of Harvard, the number of dead from this period alone was comparable to the number killed during the Nazi Holocaust. Said Hajda: "In terms of absolute data the Ukrainian numbers are probably higher than any other mass atrocity we're familiar with. It's not proportionately as high as what happened to the Jews — whose entire European population was nearly exterminated — and we don't have a good reckoning from China, but the Ukrainian experience has certainly been one of the most horrific of this century."

Their crops stolen by the Muscovites and their herds slaughtered for Russian consumption, Ukrainians were forced to eat nettles, tree bark, leaves, milkweed, worms, rodents, and crows. Entire villages were devoid of life — the cats and dogs devoured when the crows and rats were gone, followed by numerous incidents of cannibalism. In cities where children were abandoned by parents who couldn't provide so much as a morsel of black bread, trucks came each night and picked up corpses that littered every major thoroughfare. There was a black market in human meat. "We arrived at a nameless village," recalled one survivor. "There was not a soul to be seen. Our purpose was to weed beets. It was spring and the beets were still growing. I asked the leader why there was such a stench coming from a neighboring village. The name of the village was Katerynivka. There were some peasants gathering wild garlic to make dinner, he answered. Later on, I grew thirsty and they wouldn't give us water, so I went toward the village without permission. There I saw a truly horrible picture. Everywhere bodies were sitting and lying and they were decomposing." Added another witness, "People died of hunger in their houses, the fields, in the yards, streets, railroad stations, on the roofs of train cars. Bodies were collected everywhere and taken to a large hole where they were covered with lime. One spring day I heard the cries of a child. Going up to the yard where the cries were coming from, I saw a young mother sitting on a bank of earth against the house. There was an infant on her breast which was frantically trying to suck its mother's breasts, which were as dry as empty bags. It seemed at first that she was asleep, but when I touched her shoulder, she fell like a blade of grass. She was dead."

So enfamished was the populace that mothers butchered their deceased children and children consumed their parents.

"I believe the famine deaths to have been about seven million — five million in the Ukraine, one million in the Kuban and North Caucasus, and one million in the Don and Lower Volga," said Ukrainian scholar Robert Conquest.

CHAPTER 21

A Horror in Paradise

Back in the U.S., the horror of Lake Okeechobee and the Great Miami Hurricane were exceeded on September 2, 1935, when a monster, category-*five*, hit the Florida Keys like a superstorm out of the Middle Ages.

Known as the Labor Day Storm, it started as a tropical depression near the Bahamas and wasn't a hurricane until it approached Nassau and underwent violent deepening — its pressure plummeting to a mind-boggling 892 millibars (a record compared with 935 in the Miami hurricane). Where storms like Galveston had blown at 130 miles an hour, the Labor Day Hurricane had sustained winds of 150 to 200 and gusts that detonated at 250.

Hysteria reigned. At Alligator Reef wind shattered the thick glass on the beacon at a lighthouse (carrying the lens ten miles) and titanic swells rushed ashore.

Once more Hurukan came in the dark of night, the fiercest winds blasting across Islamorada, a small island that was 65 miles southwest of Miami and saw water rip rails from thirty-foot bridges, the surge overtopping the entire island.

Hundreds drowned, flushed out of ravaged homes, unable to keep a grip on roofs, poles, and trees, the air whipping so savagely that corpses lost distinguishable facial characteristics. It was what one chronicler called a storm with "the most awesome storm effects imaginable."

"I was a manager of structural engineering for Pan Am and many mechanics were in that storm because Pan Am was contracted to do cleanup and body recovery," recalled Erle Peterson, now manager of recovery for the Dade County Division of Emergency Management. "There were a lot of stories of what they had to do down there and the big similarity was the business of bodies simply not having any skin on them. They were sandblasted. They were found in the trees and in the water and all over the place. I've talked to dozens of people who had to pick up after the 1935 hurricane and the procedure was if you went to work you punched in and then you put both your arms up to the shoulders in a barrel of mercurochrome and every hour or so you came back and dunked your arms."

It was an explosion of wind and it lifted sand with such force that it generated an electrical charge — looked like fireflies. That was accompanied by terrific lightning that scorched the horizon. There was no overstating this storm: barometric pressure, the most important gauge of a hurricane's force, dropped a full degree over the span of just six miles — a plunge exceeded only in tornadoes. At Alligator Reef a huge cruise ship was carried four miles inland and at Islamorada a train sent to rescue veterans working in a relief program was swept from the tracks, the waiting veterans grasping onto the rails and blowing like laundry on a clothesline.

"I was almost nine at the time," recalled Floyd Russell, whose large family ran a plantation. "During the storm most of the family stayed in their homes on the ocean, but my father and his immediate family and his brother and his family went to a little one-room packing house where they used to package and ship key limes up in the middle of the island, which was a little higher. But it didn't matter a whole lot where you were. I remember the water was coming in under the door and my uncle reaching down and tasting it and saying, 'It's salt water.' That meant that it wasn't rainwater, that the ocean was coming in, and shortly after the building started going to pieces and the adults grabbed all the children and went out into the storm and the water was probably eight or ten feet over much of the island.

"It was pitch black, the middle of the night, and you couldn't see anything. There was no way you could know what was happening. I was just a child but you can imagine what parents went through, trying to decide which child to hold onto. It had to be the worst experience. You couldn't hold onto any child or anything. It was just impossible. It was the will of the Good Lord that I survived. As best that I can remember I was separated from my father and apparently tried to hold onto a piece of a house or something. But during the storm I had a head wound, a big gash in my head, and perhaps I was unconscious and maybe that's one of the reasons I survived: I wasn't struggling so hard but I remember I was old enough to pray and I was just praying that I might get through it and it was just the Good Lord who got me through it. There wasn't anything a nine-year-old boy could do to survive something like that. You were just out and you were at the mercy of the wind and the waves. It's a miracle that anyone survived in this area. My uncle was severely injured. Something big hit him in the hip and knocked a hole in the meaty part. Another cousin was pinned up in a tree. There were 15 of us in that building and 11 died, including my mother, two sisters, and two brothers. Only my father, my uncle, my cousin Bernard, and I survived."

A few years older at 17, Bernard remained conscious. It was a horrifying ordeal.

The main part of the storm had let loose around 8:35 p.m., and wave after wave pounded the island, which like many of the keys had an elevation of just four to 12 feet above sea level.

It was all the more horrid because of the dark.

"You couldn't see your hand in front of your face, you couldn't see anything," said Bernard. "You didn't know what was going on around you. You didn't have time even to scream. When we started going out of the building my dad said, 'Everyone grab a hold and hold onto someone when we go out and then when you get out hang on,' but when you got out of the house the wind and waves just separated you. There was no way you could hang on together. I was with my sister and her little boy, who I was holding onto, and we went out but the wind spun me around and I never saw either of them again.

"The Good Lord was looking out for me because I was washed around in a pile of trash and coconut trees and lime trees and it was just a big boiling pot, along with all the houses and stuff floating like a tidal wave went over the island. Whatever you could grab hold of you did, but you still didn't know what you were doing because you couldn't see. You grabbed hold of anything you could. It might be a piece of a house. It might be a telephone pole. It might be a bed. You couldn't tell. And you couldn't hang on with the force against you. There was no way you could control it. The initial wave went across in a hurry. A piece of debris hit me in the back and pushed me down to the ground and I took a couple gulps and thought it was all over. Somehow I got back to the top but swimming didn't help you. It was like a boiling pot, houses, trees, boats — everything all in one pile and everyone trying not to be washed off the island. A lot of people, that's what happened: they grabbed on to something and it took them across the island and it put them out in the bay and of course that was the end of that."

This went on for at least an hour, thrashing, going under, struggling back to the top. But even when the water settled, there was the entanglement of debris and the wind, which was still at terrific force.

Bernard came to rest on a mound of wreckage. Miraculously, his father also survived. "After I got down I heard a voice. It was my dad. I didn't know it was him at the time. I kept telling him to yell, to yell, to yell and I would yell back, and I finally crawled on the ground not knowing where I was going or what I would run into because I couldn't see until I told him to keep yelling and I got over to where he was and we just sat there and waited it out until daylight."

The winds had raged until five a.m. and the sight in the light of morning was beyond anguish. There were 53 Russells before the storm and only 15 after.

"You knew that everything was gone and your whole family was gone with it," Bernard recounted. "My dad survived but my mother and three sisters and little nephew passed, along with my grandmother and all my aunts and uncles. I had a first cousin who had a little baby and she was swept from the island to somewhere near a place called Flamingo on the mainland, near the Everglades, which was near Cape Sable — thirty miles away. When they found her she still had the baby, died there with the little child, but she apparently had been alive when she got on the other side on the beach on the bay side, because they could tell where she dragged herself up in the sand."

SENT TO EARTH

CHAPTER 22

The Great Sign

Not since records were kept had there been a storm like that, and it came with record temperatures. Slowly but surely, and sometimes not so slowly, the climate was smoldering. At the Armagh Observatory temperatures reached another spike in 1938.

That year, peering out her lonely window at a convent in Spain, where she had become a nun, Lucia dos Santos was fascinated by a display of the northern lights. "God manifested that sign, which astronomers chose to call an aurora borealis," she later wrote. "I don't know for certain, but I think if they investigated the matter, they would discover that, in the form in which it appeared, it could not possibly have been an aurora borealis. Be that as it may, God made use of this to make me understand His justice was about to strike the guilty nations."

It all flashed back to the secret. *"When you see a night illumined by an unknown light..."*

War, famine, and persecutions would follow.

It was the most brilliant display of the "northern lights" in at least fifty years. "Aurora Borealis Startles Europe; People Flee in Fear, Call Firemen," said *The New York Times* on January 26, 1938. "Britons Thought Windsor Castle Ablaze," said a subhead. "Scots See Ill Omen — Snow-Clad Alps Glow."

In London awestruck residents had watched two magnificent arches of light rising in the east and west, "from which radiated pulsating beams like searchlights in dark red, greenish blue, and purple."

Astronomers said it was from sunspot activity, and indeed the sun was beginning to act up, to burst with the same kind of energy as during the Middle Ages. From an airplane it looked like a "shining curtain of fire," said reports. The phenomenon disrupted wire services, telephone systems, and all transatlantic radio communication was down. Tonguelike rays rippled up. There were coronas. The lights were seen from Italy, Austria, and Morocco to New York and Canada.

Effects were reported by the Associated Press in Grenoble — the city closest to LaSalette.

It was the *"great sign"* which Mary said would precede war, and indeed on February 4, 1938, a week after the aurora, Hitler promoted himself to military chief in Germany and a month after marched into Austria. It was the takeover of a nation and in many ways the beginning of World War Two. Soon Hitler was meeting with Mussolini in Italy, where anti-Jewish legislation was passed, and there were pogroms in Germany.

War. Hatred. The ancient god of war, Woden — revered by the Huns and barbarians and Vikings — had returned. Fatima was right. There would be more persecution. Eerie was the fact that in 1889 an artist named Franz von Struck had painted Woden rampaging on horseback across a landscape and while this was decades before the rise of Nazis, the god was portrayed with a clipped mustache and forelock combed over the left brow that so resembled Hitler (who, it turns out, was born that year) that many thought it was an undiscovered portrait of him!

It was no coincidence that Hitler was fascinated by gods like Woden, researching the pagan deity, and no coincidence that Woden was also known as Odin, an old Norse storm god. There was also resurrection of the swastika. As

The Great Sign

I said this symbol had been used in ancient Egypt and during the following centuries found itself in nearly every part of the world, with the exception of Australia. Although often used as a sun sign — an emblem in solar cults — it was also associated with the worship of another storm deity, the infamous idol condemned in the Bible, Baal (to whom children were sacrificed, and who like the Minoan idol was part bull and part human). Thought to carry the power of nature, the swastika had been imprinted on coins in ancient Greece, carved on Near Eastern pottery, and used as a symbol of spiritual magic by the Hopis, the Navahos, and the Aztecs. It had also been found in Israeli ruins and although it was often intended as a good-luck charm, it had deep roots in occultism, which pervaded the Third Reich and was witnessed with Hitler's well-known fascination with magic.

The Nazis were steeped in mysticism — derived in part from the ancient cult of the templars, with inspiration from Crowley — and so we had the SS, hiss of the snake.

Death was in the air. It was about to cut down Europe. That was the fruit of evil. No wonder, then, that Adolph meant "noble wolf," and that throughout his life it was said that he was in touch with something preternatural, hearing voices, conversing with the wind. Many believed he was possessed, and he often complained of something that visited as a shadow at night. Perhaps it was this "shadow" that inspired him to eradicate the Jews, to attack Christians as well, to do it in the name of Woden. This he had initiated upon rise to power, reaching a milestone in 1938, the same year as the aurora borealis, when there was a bloody pogrom.

By 1941 eradication of Jews was in full progress and there was a *holokaustein* or "burnt offering." Another aspect of witchcraft had arrived — and at a ghastly scale. Millions were shot, gassed, starved, and another 44 million died in the war itself, which made it the greatest human disaster up to that point. Among the first targets were Christians, and Himmler publicly advocated execution of the Pope. Small bombs were dropped on the Vatican (this in retribution for giving sanctuary to 15,000 Jews), while Gypsies, Jehovah's Witnesses, and homosexuals were also persecuted. In Poland one third of the nation's clergy — 2,700 priests — were eliminated. Woden was in a fury. And a sacrifice this was, the greatest calamity in Western civilization, comparable to what was progressing in China, where Christianity — where all religion — would be attacked, and where the rise of Mao with men like Hitler and Stalin raised the question of whether these were indeed what Melanie had referred to when in her secret she claimed there would be *"kings of the antichrist"* — that men were coming who would *"have one and the same plan,"* that plan to extinguish religion, a plan that was underway on many fronts, in politics and philosophy and science, with everyone from Marx to Hitler — who in fulfillment of another warning from LaSalette, which had mentioned that fire would destroy the French capital, had tried to incinerate the major cities of Europe and in a famous question had insistently demanded of his chief lieutenant, "Is Paris burning?"

At the height of the war, with Nazis everywhere, with the world in the type of turmoil the Blessed Mother had so exactly foretold, Lucia was asked by the Fatima bishop to sit down and, for the first time, write the full prophecy. The bishop was concerned that Lucia, suffering from an acute infection, might soon die. The order had come in October of 1943 and though she tried three times, Lucia encountered a strange, frustrating, block. The impediment "was not due to natural causes," said Lucia. Finally, however, in January of 1944, she was able to write it down. As at LaSalette, the secret was placed in an envelope, sealed with wax, and given to the bishop, Dom Jose Correira da Silva, who took it to his chancery in Leira.

CHAPTER 23

"Tsunami!"

We know now that the war Fatima had prophesied, and perhaps LaSalette, too, was ready to end. On May 13, 1944 — anniversary of the first apparition — what became known as the "victory of Garigliano" liberated Rome, and on the anniversary of the last apparition, October 13, 1945, Allied bombers pounded Nuremberg, turning the Nazi headquarters into rubble. At Hiroshima the mushroom cloud, if it was like mushroom clouds at test sites, caused reflections and striations that resembled the northern lights. Thus, the great sign had not only predicted when the war would start, but the way it would end. Among the few survivors at Hiroshima were eight Jesuits who were reciting the Rosary each day at Our Lady's Assumption Church, just eight blocks from the explosion, and were the only ones to escape the effects of radiation, which even science had to admit, was a wonder.

The war god was now quiet, but the chastisement was rolling, was slogging on — in its own dangerous way, was quietly gathering momentum — and as war had alternated with natural events in the prophecy of *Matthew* 24, so was it now nature's turn. On April 1, 1946, a quake of magnitude-7.8 hit the Aleutians, causing a tidal wave that slashed against Unimak Island before sweeping 2,400 miles across the Pacific to Hawaii. Though a mere ripple in the middle of the ocean, the wave (which was not really a wave so much as an entire parcel of ocean) caused a strange withdrawal of water before it arrived at Hilo Bay, but then there was the relentless rise as water piled at the shore to heights of fifty feet, drowning at least 173, many teachers and students at a school in Laupahoehoe. "On April 1, which was a Monday, we had one more week before spring vacation and I lived with three other teachers, all from the mainland," recalled one teacher, the only one who survived from her cottage. "The first we knew about anything was when a boy came and knocked on the door and said, 'Come and see the tidal wave.' We were very curious, so we went out to a promontory to see this tidal wave that had sucked out a little bit and came in a little bit and we thought that was it."

It was a curious sight. They could see the bottom of the bay. Fish flapped on the suddenly waterless inlet and the locals were out in force to gather them. At first it didn't seem like anything to fret about. When the water came it was like a tide, no breakers, no surf. But it kept coming. It was the way of tsunamis. It crept past the high-tide mark and almost up to the teachers, hanging there, lapping at their feet for a few seconds, then returning back toward the horizon.

Another built up, but it still wasn't what the teacher had expected, although each was getting a little bigger and in between the bay was withdrawing farther. "We were in our pajamas and bathrobes and were thinking that school was going to start — all the school kids were there — so we went back to the cottage to change our clothes," she said. It was then the big one hit. "The ocean drew out once more, fast this time, with a vast, deep sigh," she was to later write. "The deep pool just off the rocks, where we had gone swimming, drained suddenly dry. A tremendous wall of water was gathering out to the left of the lighthouse. For the first time I felt fear, an almost paralyzing fear."

The teacher and another named Fay ran inside, where they joined two other teachers, one named Helen, and slammed the door — trying to decide if they should remain there or make a dash for the hillside.

Already it was too late.

"There was a roar like all the winds in the world," she wrote in an article. "I looked back to see brown water fighting at the windows, heard the crash of shattering glass as the windows burst in, and the sharp cracking of parting timbers. The four of us clung to the sides of the doorway as the cottage began to tilt and move. 'It's going to tear the cottage down,' Helen said. She spoke calmly, and there was more wonder than fear in her voice. No one screamed; we just braced our feet against what suddenly became nothing, and then the four of us were thrown into the water. Helen, struggling to keep her head above water, sank right in front of me."

The cottage was swept away and the teacher with it. She and Fay managed to cling to the roof, which spun like a merry-go-round and headed at what seemed like great speed toward the open ocean. "Two of us climbed on the roof and then it sucked out again and we got caught on the rocks," she told me. "There's no beach there, just rocks. It sucked out very swiftly and I remember the principal's car was parked in the garage next to it and was just tossed like a tootsie-toy. It sucked us way out and we got clunked down on a rock."

When she got back to shore another hit. This time all she could see was a mass of white bubbles. And all she could feel were lungs about to burst. "We climbed off the roof but didn't get very far and a huge wave came in and that's when I went under," she explained. "Somehow I came up from that. There was a lot of rubbish and the third time I came up I was right by a lighthouse there, right at the top, and I was surprised that I could move anything, that everything wasn't broken. It seemed like I was underwater forever. Finally I was clinging to a door."

At Hilo, a city on the east side of the big island, residents were likewise under assault. There were yells of "Tsunami!" and a wall of dirty water and palm trees 35-

feet tall suddenly submerged. "Seawater came up to my knees," recounted Mieko Browne, who was also carried away in her house. "I decided to change clothes, in case we had to swim. When I opened the closet, the back wall was gone! All I could see past my hanging clothes were waves and dead fish. It looked like a strange painting. Through the windows we could see people floating by, holding onto whatever they could. A boy was clinging to a piece of lumber. The waves carried us far out into Hilo Bay and back again three times."

One boy was afloat for 27 hours and as he fought the hunger and dampness, especially the hunger, he spotted a trail of debris bobbing by. The wreckage was from a house and included a photograph. Grabbing for it, he was amazed to see that it was a photograph of a family he knew — a portrait of close friends. And on it was a piece of fruit.

CHAPTER 24

Something Underneath

There were always God's little touches, His reminders that He was with us in even the most tumultuous of events, but He was getting hard to see. There were more waves. There were tornadoes. The sky was darkening. More than two hundred had died when a twister drilled into Tupelo, Mississippi, and on April 9, 1947, 181 succumbed as one blasted through Oklahoma.

They were strange things, clouds. People saw things in them. There were formations of mist that resembled devils and curls of cumulus, wisps of clouds, that looked like angels. Scientists said this was in the mind of the beholder and maybe that was so but if nothing else it was a symbol of spiritual tension.

Year by year, evidence of an up-cycle in hurricanes arrived. There would be quiet years but overall warm seas, favorable stratospheric air flow, a strong Atlantic current, and rainfall patterns in Africa caused a profusion and in 1938 a category-three had whipped through New England, followed by another of the same force in 1944, which meant winds of 111 to 130 miles an hour. "From 1944 to 1950 Florida saw *tremendous* damage," I was informed by Roger A. Pielke Jr. of the National Center for Atmospheric Research. "Multi-billion damages every year for that seven-year period."

Indeed, 23 hurricanes hit America's mainland during the 1940s and while they would simmer down during the

1950s, there were still years that saw as many as 11 develop in the slowly stewing Atlantic. A category-four named Hazel made it as far north as Toronto — causing severe flooding — and this was accompanied by a flurry of earthquakes. From 1933 to 1944 four hundred miles of the Anatolian fault in Turkey ruptured and this was portentous because it was where quakes had destroyed ancient Troy.

Were the tremors of the Bronze Age returning?

And as in the Bronze Age, there were massive floods in China. In 1931, 3.7 million had died along the Yellow River and a short eight years later 200,000 were counted dead as floods savaged the Hubei and Shandong provinces. In 1954 the Yangtze engulfed an area the size of Texas. A year later monsoons caused eight rivers to flood southwest of Calcutta, inundating 10,000 hamlets. For days survivors clung to trees that were also the refuge of cobras.

While there was still no single event or series of events that affected the entire globe — no volcano, asteroid, or weather event that quickly turned the ecology upside-down — the temperature continued its upward trend and events were building. A new decade, a decade that would define cultural life for the rest of the century, a decade that was remarkable in wondrous and horrible ways — a decade that was the beginning of a very deep spiritual descent — was marked at its very outset by a seismic uproar. On May 22, 1960, a huge stretch of fault ruptured in the ocean off Chile (in an area where one continental plate was grinding under another), and at magnitude-9.5 it was not only 250 *times* more in total energy release than the San Francisco quake, but the most powerful movement of earth ever recorded, occurring about a hundred miles offshore along a strike length of 600 miles and so forceful that it released more than a fourth as much energy as *all* other earthquakes up to that point in the century combined.

Not since the advent of quantitative measurement had scientists gawked at one like this, and it devastated the coastal towns of Chile. A huge portion of the crack had slipped and the shore of Chile had dropped like a plank. The trough of a tsunami, the withdrawal, arrived ten minutes after the quake and was followed by thunderous breakers that swept along 300 miles of coast and sucked boats into a terrifying vortex. Some said the wave was eighty feet. Some said that near Valdivia it may have reached 165. It also radiated westward and that night — moving at the speed of a jet — was attacking Hawaii. There — again at vulnerable Hilo — the entire oceanfront, homes, stores, hotels, was bulldozed. "We had recorded the earthquake and we knew that if a tsunami occurred it would take it fifteen hours to travel from Chile to Hawaii," recalled Don Richter, a retired geologist for the United States Geological Survey (USGS). "The first arrival was about midnight. The first thing we noticed was that there was a withdrawal of water from the bay. It withdrew so far you couldn't see it anymore. And then there was a gentle rise over a twenty minute period and it came up three or four feet on the bridge piers. Then there was a tremendous withdrawal of water and even with the lights on we couldn't see water at all. We could hear a noise out in the bay and shortly after we could see a white line, which was the wave breaking. We realized we were in trouble. We had to get out of there. So we ran up onto the road ten or fifteen feet just about the time the wave hit, and we could see it go through town. Lights went out on the poles and finally it hit the generating station and everything was dark."

So powerful was the wave that it bent parking meters and pushed sediment into corked bottles of wine. Bulldozers tumbled; cars were wrapped around palms. A shock wave circled the globe three times.

As forecast at LaSalette, the earth was beginning to "tremble." It was something the Protestants also said. There were men like Billy Graham warning that the bottom was falling out of morality and that God would react. Deep in the earth, forces were shifting in darkness. A "bizarre" quake had been recorded under the Atlantic — 370 miles below the floor of the ocean — as huge masses moved like blobs of warm plastic. No one knew what was going on down there but it was suspected there were cyclonic subterranean movements that mimicked cyclones above, churning, burbling, rotating. When it got to the surface, when it broke through the mantle as lava, it sent the stench of hell itself. In the craters of Kilauea near Hilo forces converged as they did also along the "ring of fire," a great seam that stretched from Chile up through California to Alaska and down through Japan. Off Hawaii lava flowed in blazing streams toward the sea, where it fell into the water with great rises of steam and a scene that was primeval. The spirits were agitated. They sent more sulfur. They hurled more waves. "We had terrible tsunamis from 1938 until 1965," I was told by a professor named Gus Furumoto, and indeed of the ten largest quakes during the twentieth century, seven occurred in that period. As I wandered among the craters, as I drove past the burnt caldera, I could feel the spirits. There were altars to a volcano goddess, and there had also been occult rituals up with the Kwakiutl in Alaska, where on Good Friday, 1964, the second strongest quake on record, a magnitude-9.2, struck and caused great damage in Anchorage, Valdez, and Seward — along with a seismic wave that hit from Alaska to California and caused strange effects as far as Texas.

"I was 13 and a half and it's still very vivid," said Tom Gilson of Valdez. "There were trees going back and forth, there were telephone poles flopping, and the wires were busting, so we had live electric wires flopping around. They were dancing and the telephone poles were dancing and the trees were dancing. The first thing that came to mind was that it was the end of the world. It was pretty hard to koop on your feet. I remember going to my knees several times. We had about five minutes of shaking. I saw the fronts of a couple of block brick buildings fall down. There was a rushing sound and the rumbling. A lot of people described it as like a freight train coming. A rushing, roaring noise. We had a gradual slope to the bay and we had all this groundwater coming up and I remember after the shaking stopped we were concerned about a tidal wave coming, so the tendency was to get away from the water. I was about a block and a half away and we moved up another half a block and then I started farther away and heading home, which was another five blocks east of the water, and all of the groundwater was coming up through these huge fissures and you could see the water coming down and dropping into these holes. Probably about midnight all the big fuel tanks ruptured and all of a sudden the water came in and picked up the fuel, and so the fuel was floating on top and somehow there was a fire near the water and so all of this fuel reached the fire and lit and went clear across the waterfront back to where the fuel tanks were and there was this thunderous explosion. One of the tanks blew and just lit up the sky like it was daylight."

At the town of Seward a construction worker and local fisherman named Doug McRae made an even narrower escape. As he was driving he spotted two elderly people who had climbed up on the boom of a crane and were shouting for him to head back because a tidal wave was coming. "And then we could hear it," he said. "It was like a jet trying to land on your house. A tremendous roar. We backed up as fast as that car would go, maybe two or three hundred yards to the house, hollered to my family to come, and they came just in time. Luckily there was a 500-gallon oil barrel alongside the house with steps going up it, and we ran up that, jumped on the oil barrel onto the roof of the garage, where we could really hear the wave then. It was just deafening, the crashing and banging. Then we saw the wave hit a couple houses across the street from us and they just disintegrated. We realized the wave was much bigger than this flat-topped garage that we were standing on, so we were able to jump off the garage up onto the house, which had a peaked roof, and really didn't even set down when the wave hit. Luckily it was the only one of about a dozen houses that survived. Both ends were ripped off and we took off like a surfboard between the trees."

Waves from the quake swamped parts of Vancouver Island, Crescent City, and Santa Catalina Island just off Los Angeles. At Depoe Bay in Oregon, tragedy struck when four youngsters sleeping on a beach were swept to sea, leaving their parents childless. There was also a wave in the Gulf of Mexico, one that lashed at Texas.

Although it was unconnected with the wave in the Pacific, many wondered if the Gulf disturbance had been caused by shocks penetrating the earth. Witnesses described it as "spooky" and "weird." "The water was rolling and bubbling up throughout the Houston ship channel," noted one witness, "as if something was underneath it."

Chapter 25

"There were tornadoes all over the place"

Wave after wave. Was *this* the subterranean beast rising? *"Woe to the inhabitants of earth,"* Melanie claimed she had been told, and however controversial parts of the prophecy, there was no denying its prescience. She claimed there would be a spirit of rebellion and by the Sixties it was exploding everywhere.

I remember it well. I took part in it. It was a cultural revolution and while many of the revolts were justified — the demand to eliminate racism, to halt war, and to stop the mistreatment of women — it had quickly veered into extremism. Much of it started with music, which spoke directly to the soul and preached wanderlust. At first it seemed innocent. Elvis. The Beatles. Then the beat got faster, stronger. The hair longer. What started as movements of social justice turned into an orgy of self-indulgence and there was the feeling that society — that the traditions of our parents, including religion — were about to be rejected.

It became corny to believe. And there was no more evil. There were only "hang-ups." What had once been sought in prayer was now sought through the *pharmakeia* of drugs, and everyone was okay. Everyone could do their own "thing." Long condemned by the Bible, sex outside of marriage — fornication — became the rite of passage.

There was the playboy philosophy. There was gay "liberation." It was the old Crowley credo: Do what thou wilt would be the whole of the law, and indeed his face was to be found on the cover of a famous music album called *Sergeant Pepper's*, which, like so many my age, I played until I wore it out.

It was the "Age of Aquarius." There was astrology, as in Babylon. There was "pyramid power." There were displays of public nudity that would have done Minoans proud. There was also the peace symbol, which for centuries had been known as the "witch's foot" or the "cross of Nero" because it originated from the upside-down cross that Romans used to crucify Peter.

More than anything, there was chaos. Rape was surging as it had in medieval times, and there was ESP. There were UFOs. There was one massive ongoing psychedelic experiment. The portals of the soul had been thrown open and it came to a crescendo in San Francisco where a riot broke out (and a man was murdered) as the Rolling Stones — no strangers to the occult — played a song called *Sympathy for the Devil*.

Violence was the order of the day and so was lust; even institutions like marriage were now in question. Tune in and drop out, said a Harvard guru. There were riots. Sit-ins. There was an orgy of lawlessness. There were the Hell's Angels. Streets seethed with the spirit of revolution, which the Bible called the spirit of witchcraft (*1 Samuel* 15:23), and while there were righteous causes, darkness crept in. It seemed like there were now only two choices: belief in the occult or belief in nothing. In 1966 the Church of Satan was formed and the cover of *Time* asked, "IS GOD DEAD?" Three years later the first satanic bible was printed.

That year, the high point of the Sixties, the year of "Satyricon" and "Oh! Calcutta!" and "Aquarius" — the year of Manson and Woodstock — saw nature aim at the very underbelly of America, striking like so many events that came as *yet* in warning at an out-of-the way place, at a place that would serve as a victim soul — an example.

This was in the way of the only category-five, the most powerful and frightening hurricane, to ever hit the mainland United States. It was Hurricane Camille (the name derived from *camillus,* a legendary warrior maiden), and though at first it looked like it would strike the land of voodoo, New Orleans, head on, it veered just east and ravaged the coast of Mississippi. More than 5,000 homes were destroyed by winds that gusted to 207 miles an hour. Forests were blown leafless and large cargo ships tossed on land. In Harrison County, the damage was compared to what would be inflicted by a one-megaton bomb.

"I think I was a little nervous because it was an eerie feeling, and also everybody here just lived and breathed Nash Roberts, who was the weather anchor for WDSU-TV in New Orleans at the time, and he said at about noon that day, 'Everybody, hear me: Get out of there now,'" recalled a survivor named Robert J. Sawyer, who lived in Gulfport, a teen, and believed it was a miracle he survived. "We had never left our homes in other storms but we did this time. We went downtown. As far as I know we were the only family to stay there during the hurricane and it was at my dad's real estate office. We were in the main part, which was up front on the street. We went there because it was brick, about two blocks from the beach. I remember a news guy walked by and asked if we were going to stay and we said yes and we asked if he wanted to stay but he said, no, he had to use a phone. We told him he was welcome to use ours because it was still working at the time but he said that he still had to get the sound effects of the wind outside and we never saw him again. That was probably about six o'clock. The intensity really started around nine or ten p.m. There was a clothes store across the street and I remember an explosion and mannequins flying through the air and when there was lightning I could see the mannequins, a quick glimpse while the lightning popped and lit up the area.

"There were tornadoes all over the place and at about one or two a.m. it was really creaming us. The pressure was so bad that our ears were popping, hurting so much we were literally in *tears*. I'd been lying on the floor in the conference room looking out the big window there and I saw a big green steel mail box on the corner of the street *floating* through the air down the street. My dad came in and said, 'Get away from there and let's close the door!' Just after he closed the door the window blew out and the conference table, which was probably ten feet long, was sucked out.

"We rushed back to a suite of other offices and you could hear things flying down the street. At one point the walls were breathing in and out. It was paneling and you could *feel* it when the pressure of the storm was greatest. We were very, very scared, just frightened terribly. I had my grandmother, my brothers, my sister, my mother and father, so there were probably ten of us. My mother just kept reading from the Bible and I know it was only God Who kept us alive. There was no other way to survive that one, not where the eye was. One man who lived close to us was named Sam and I remember hearing on the police scanner that Sam had called in — it was around nine or ten — and he and his wife, who had stayed in their home, were going to leave. They thought their house was hurricane-proof, but they called and said they were going to try to get out of there, that it was terrible, but they never made it. Later, when officials found their bodies, the only way they could recognize him was the ring on his finger.

"We had eight of our neighbors killed. There were millions of pieces of board and nails and everything just flying at you, and you became ground beef. It was horrible. It was just total, *total* devastation everywhere. We lived five rows from the beach and after it was over we were the *second* row from the beach. Everything was so destroyed. A guy who lived two doors from the beach sent off his parents and stayed in his home to try to protect everything but he started to see the walls caving in with water, gushing in, so he went upstairs to the second floor and water started coming up there, so he went into the attic and water came in there and he had no way to get out. Water was coming straight in and what he did was take his fist and break through the ceiling and crawl out and when he came to, he was downtown a mile and a half away.

"There were also three young ladies who were hitch-hiking through town, hippies. They died — all three of them — and nobody ever found out who they even were."

CHAPTER 26

"Fire will fall"

That was the way the Sixties ended. The next year hail as large as 17 inches in circumference was recorded in Kansas (nearly the size of a skull) and the most terrifying tornadic outbreak in U.S. history hit from Alabama to Ohio, where there was a funnel so fierce that scientists wondered if it went beyond the ultimate F-5 category.

"When I first saw the tornado I didn't know what it was because it didn't look like the regular tornadoes that I had seen on TV," recalled a woman who was at ground zero in Xenia, Ohio. "It was huge and seemed to be the same size from top to bottom. I went into the bedroom to get a better view of it. By this time it was much closer and I saw two small funnel clouds come out of the large cloud and go back into it. It was so close by this time that I saw the debris in it. I ran to the living room and turned a large piece of furniture over and grabbed my daughter out of her bed where she was taking an afternoon nap. The roar was awful. My little dog was going crazy and of course my daughter was screaming. I was just praying."

The outbreak spawned 148 tornadoes and at one point there were 15 on the ground at the same time. More than three hundred people were killed. In all, 13 states were affected. Xenia, which the Indians had called "the place of the devil wind," was all but totaled. But it was no better — and in fact worse — in other countries. Asia was under constant bombardment and by calamities the likes of which America has never seen — had never come *close* to seeing. On Friday the 13th in November 1970 a cyclone (the name for a hurricane in the Indian Ocean) struck Bangladesh with a 50-foot wall of water, flooding so far inland that it drowned between 300,000 and 500,000. It was hard to get an actual count in Third World countries, but it was at least thirty times what happened in Galveston. So strong were the winds that people who fled were rolled along the ground before the ocean washed over them. Corpses clogged bends in the rivers, too numerous to dispose. Beginning around 1970 the episodes of catastrophic winds around the world doubled and in Texas the skies were nothing short of diabolical. "I distinctly remember seeing four different levels of clouds going four different directions at different speeds and of different colors," recalled a truck driver who witnessed an F-5 tornado at Wichita Falls. "As I was standing there the wind was alternating every which way, and I looked south and saw a cloud form and shoot west. I thought, 'Wow! That was fast!' In a few moments another one formed and shot to my right, so I looked southwest, and *whammy*. These clouds were forming and flying straight towards this big black cloud on the ground. The little clouds that were shooting towards it were being whipped upwards into the tornado and power lines were sparking and stuff was flying everywhere."

More dead. More hail. The pressure was imploding homes, detonating them, all but carrying away whole trailer parks. That year there was also a large twister near Hartford, Connecticut, where you wouldn't expect it.

And the earth itself was having conniptions. On July 28, 1976, a magnitude-7.8 quake struck Tangshan, China, displaying phenomena that was unnerving. The night before a thick mist had developed and on the day of the quake a dense black fog enveloped this area in the northeastern part of the country. Well water began to rise and fall, muddying or even turning odd colors, and residents saw luminosities. Rays of light with rainbow colors flashed across the sky, perhaps the result of fractoluminescence, silicates that were grinding against each other, emitting a charge. Some saw what looked like rolling fireballs. And in coastal areas there were reports of luminous belts in the water. Miners working night shifts said they heard what seemed like a howling wind. Others described a rumbling. Gases spewed out of wells and survivors reported bizarre animal behavior. Mules refused to enter sheds, chickens clucked about in agitation, and a goldfish in Xiangnan scooted wildly in the water and less than two hours before the quake jumped out of its tank and kept jumping despite the best efforts of its owner.

At 3 a.m. (which, of course, was the bewitching hour) a fireball was seen rolling from the northwest, followed by ear-splitting blasts from the same direction.

"At around the same time people in the city of Tangshan saw flashes of radiational rays which were followed by tumultuous roars," wrote a team of scholars. "At 3:42 on the 28th, following climatic blinding flashes and an ear-splitting bang, the earth began shaking violently."

It was one of the greatest seismic disasters in world history. At least 240,000 — a quarter million — were killed, and in one 11-square-kilometer area 95 percent of the residential units incurred serious damage. Most victims were crushed in their sleep, the ground twisting from east to south and then from west to north. The whole process took just two or three seconds, but in that time an industrial city of more than one million people was reduced to rubble.

It was like armies were clamoring from the netherworld. There were always disasters, but one day these would look like precursors, or at least examples of what could happen. And there were more wonders in the air, as had occurred before the onset of bubonic fever. It had started with UFO reports in 1947 and by the 1970s the phenomena were exploding, with accounts of lights that levitated, that appeared and disappeared, that bore "aliens" who looked like old Anatolian idols or voodoo statues and came with the smell of sulfur. *"The demons of the air together with the anti-christ will perform great wonders on earth and in the atmosphere,"* it had been alleged at LaSalette, and there were so many in the twentieth century that a secret study called "Project Blue Book" was conducted by the U.S. Air Force.

A large number of demons would be unloosed from hell, it had been said at LaSalette, especially *"the demon of magic,"* and it was seen in all the occultism, the seances that had led to psychic phenomena and to the New Age. This was the Seventies and while it wasn't as blatant as the Sixties, the straying from God was becoming *institutionalized*. Agnosticism — spiritual apathy — was the cultural chic, and drugs — once the realm of hippies — were now for lawyers, teachers, and bankers. There was *pharmakeia* as never before and the sacrifice of innocents as the Supreme Court, in the most dangerous decision ever reached by an American judicial body, decided that a woman had a "right" to abortion. The fetus was no longer an individual existence but an appendage, part of a woman's body — an inconvenient piece of pulsing tissue — and more than 1.3 million would be carried out each year in the U.S., vastly more victims than the most ruthless of Roman emperors could claim. Few women were aware of it, but the taking of an infant's life had long been considered a sacrament of witchcraft, an offering to demonic idols such as Baal, Molech, and Asmodeas — who had been specifically referenced at LaSalette. A sacrament! Nearly fifty million worldwide! The Supreme Court had opened a floodgate!

And that very year at another convent, this time Akita, Japan, a nun named Sister Sasagawa received a startling message from the Blessed Mother on October 13 (once more a Fatima anniversary): *"As I told you,"* said Mary, *"if men do not repent and better themselves, the Father will inflict a terrible punishment on all of humanity. It will be a punishment greater than the Deluge, such as one will never have been seen before. Fire will fall from the sky and will wipe out a great part of humanity, the good as well as the bad, sparing neither priests nor faithful. The survivors will find themselves so desolate that they will envy the dead. The only weapons that remain for you will be the Rosary and the sign left by my Son."*

This was stunning because it connected directly with what would later be revealed as the content of the third secret: falling fire just as Lucia had seen an angel with flames coming from that sword — *"flames that look as if they could set the world on fire."* If it wasn't bad enough that evil was pervading society, the work of the devil was also infiltrating even into the Church, said the message from Akita (which bore initial Church sanction), and cardinals would oppose cardinals, bishops turn against bishops, the priests who venerated Mary scorned and opposed — churches and altars sacked, the Church full of those who accepted compromise, the demon pressing many priests and consecrated to leave the service of the Lord. *"If sins increase in number and gravity, there will no longer be pardon for them,"* warned Mary in language that approached the toughness of LaSalette. *"Pray very much the prayers of the Rosary. I alone am able still to save you from the calamities which approach. Those who place their confidence in me will be saved."*

She needed sacrifices and acts of reparation and the locution came in association with a weeping statue — a statue that shed tears as many statues began to shed tears around the world. Abortion! That was obviously the greatest danger, the one to which so many were blind, but there were others. There were many ways that humans were usurping God at the same time they were losing their own dignity. A cut-throat attitude in business had done the same, had degraded our humanness. Gone was what Christ had said: that one could not serve both God and mammon (*Matthew* 6:24), that it was easier for a camel to go through the eye of a needle than a rich man to enter heaven (*Matthew* 19:24), that to have the love of God was to disdain the world (*1 John* 2:15). It became the American way to gauge success by how cleverly, how selfishly, one could horde money. It was the "Me Generation" and sleekness was now paramount, as in the 1300s. In a way that only the devil could accomplish, the words "love" and "lust" had become interchangeable. Some of the best and brightest were starting to practice what the Bible forbade, and no matter how good they otherwise were, this was an area of terrific moral blindness. Any illicit sex — any sex outside of marriage — was a hazard: a danger at an emotional, spiritual, and soon physical level. That wasn't a fundamentalist opinion. It was a simple factual statement. In the Garden God had made it plain that life was not a place for dalliance — that utopia was not be found on earth — but that it was a place where there was testing, purification, and the mystery of suffering. Who understood suffering? Who understood the deeper mysteries of God? No one would be able to see clearly until they were on the other side but it had always been clear, it had been clear in Babylon, it had been clear in Egypt, it had been clear on Thera, that a lustful lifestyle was the way of destruction.

Yet this was no longer seen by a society that was heading ever deeper, that was driving head-first, into worldliness. It was God we were to have our eyes on, heaven, not this passing physical place. But now, more than ever, there was a move to make earth into paradise, to evade the suffering, the trials. This was one of the devil's greatest wiles, and it was working: worldliness was once again hip, fashionable as it had been in medieval Europe. That was the name of the game. Materialism. You did what you could to get *all* that you could and whoever died with the most toys won. That was the new bumper sticker. There was an aloofness, a chill, and it was reflected in art, which had grown cold, abstract, and confused. There was deception and it was at the topmost rungs of government. There was racism. There was obscenity. There was a level of lewd-ness that had not even been reached in Roman times, that was worse than the graffiti at Pompeii, that was seen in hard-core pornography, movies that went by titles like *The Devil in Miss Jones*. The seeds of lust were becoming trees and the party had moved from Woodstock to the discos. There were actresses and singers who dressed like Cleopatra, like Nebuchadnezzar. It was one huge reincarnation of Mesopotamia. There were even Pharisees — intellectuals who had taken the French Revolution and instilled it at every level of education at the same time they got rid of school prayer. And at the same time that the devil tried to get rid of the Pope, as had been foreseen in the third secret. In 1981 a remaining prediction, the prophecy that a *"bishop clothed in white"* would fall *"under a burst of gunfire,"* was realized when John Paul II (as Pope "bishop of Rome") was shot at St. Peter's Square on the Fatima anniversary of May 13.

SENT TO EARTH

CHAPTER 27

The Warnings

The predictions of martyrdom, war, influenza, and the attempt on a pope had brought Fatima to the cusp of fulfillment and now a month after the shooting another apparition burst on the scene, an apparition that bore the same potential as Fatima.

This was Medjugorje in what is now Bosnia-Hercegovina and like the last apparition at Fatima it was preceded by a storm so fierce it scared seasoned farmers. Lightning hit near where the young people had established their first discotheque and the following afternoon two teenaged girls tending to animals on a stony hillside as at Fatima and LaSalette reported a figure in a rotating light, a woman who beckoned them.

Soon the two girls and four other youngsters began receiving daily apparitions, falling together on their knees with perfect simultaneity when the Virgin arrived with three flashes of light. The Blessed Mother came as "Queen of Peace" and despite the opposition of local Communist officials (who as at Fatima detained the seers), the young visionaries, four girls and two boys, aged 10 to 16, persisted in visiting the place of apparitions, where they were given a flurry of messages, including secrets.

"Peace, peace, peace," the Virgin said. *"You must seek peace. There must be peace on earth. You must be reconciled with God and with one another. Children, darkness reigns over the whole world. A great struggle is about to unfold. Light and darkness are fighting each other. The peace of the world is in danger. You must warn the bishop and the Pope with respect to the urgency and the great importance of the message for all of mankind."*

There was darkness because man was disobedient — was progressing as if God did not exist — and the result, warned Mary, would be severe. With some of the strongest language in the history of apparitions she told the youngsters that she had *"come to call the world to conversion for the last time."* She called the present hour *"the hour of Satan,"* as I indicated in the first chapter, and urged direct prayer to Jesus, prayer from the heart. *"You cannot imagine what is going to happen, nor what the Eternal Father will send to earth."* The time was crucial. A denouement approached. Satan had been given a period of time to test God's people, to test the Church, and now that period was reaching its high point. In a report to the Vatican on December 2, 1983, the parish priest at Medjugorje, Tomislav Vlasic, reported that the Virgin had told one of the seers, 18-year-old Mirjana Dragicevic, *"Excuse me for this, but you must realize that Satan exists. One day he appeared before the throne of God and asked permission to submit the Church to a period of trial. God gave him permission to try the Church for one century. This century is under the power of the devil, but when the secrets confided to you come to pass, his power will be destroyed. Even now he is beginning to lose his power and has become aggressive. He is destroying marriages, creating division among priests, and is responsible for obsessions and murder. You must protect yourselves against these things through fasting and prayer, especially community prayer. Carry blessed objects with you. Put them in your house, and restore the use of holy water."*

That message had come after an instance in 1982 when Satan had appeared to Mirjana in a bright flash of light and told her to renounce the Virgin. In that way, he promised, she could be happy in love and life. It was the easy road, but it was also the road to chastisement.

"*The devil tries to impose his power on you,*" said Mary, "*but you must remain strong and persevere in your faith. You have to pray and fast. The devil is trying to conquer you. Do not permit him. Keep faith, fast, and pray.*" It was crucial, said Mary, to read the Bible and invoke the Holy Spirit. It was the Spirit Who brought peace. It was the Spirit Who brought discernment. It was the Spirit Who brought knowledge of God's will. Life was a test and it was only the paraclete Who could guide. In what sounded like a last-ditch effort, the Virgin was calling God's children to carry His light "*to all the people who are in darkness.*" There was no more time to waste. There had been warnings since LaSalette, since the Miraculous Medal. Pray, pray, pray, she begged. Everyone was needed to help the world. "*I want you to comprehend that God has chosen each one of you in order to use you in a great plan for the salvation of mankind,*" she said. "*You are not able to comprehend how great your role is in God's design.*" The goal was "*conversion of the whole world.*" It was the last call before major events. It was a plea for the opening of hearts. "*Be strong in God. I am calling you to love your neighbor. Without love we will achieve nothing. Make a decision for love. Prepare your hearts for these days when the Lord particularly desires to purify you from all the sins of your past. I ask you to abandon yourselves completely to God. Put your lives in God's hands. Let your only instrument be love. By love turn everything into good which Satan desires to possess and destroy.*"

Destruction had always been Satan's plan and as an emissary of Christ the Virgin was coming against that, was trying to counter it as she had tried to halt the famine at LaSalette. If the devil had too much of a grip, the Lord would have to break that power with chastisement, she warned. He would have to purify. He would have to reorient society as He had reoriented it so many times in the past — too many times. He would have to send events to purge the contamination of Satan, who was working hard and because his time was drawing to a close, was becoming all the more aggressive (exerting control as seldom, if ever). The trend set in motion after LaSalette was ready to heighten — to greatly heighten, perhaps to peak — and some of the events, perhaps the climatic events, were given to the youngsters in secrets: confidential predictions that they and only they knew, as many as ten per seer, secrets that would begin to unfold in their lifetimes. All they would say, no matter how hard one pressed (and I myself had spoken to nearly all of them about it), was that events would be sent to the world as "warnings." That's how the secrets would begin: with warnings. According to Mirjana, there would be three "admonitions" and then or as part of the third warning there would be a "great sign" — precisely the term that had been used at Fatima even though the seers knew virtually nothing of Lucia. A forerunner was said to have occurred on October 28, 1981, when a large fire was spotted near Medjugorje, a fire that burned brightly on the hill where Mary had been spotted and lasted for fifteen minutes. At the time the hill was under the guard of Communist police who were attempting to halt the apparitions. On investigating they had found no signs of fire.

It was like the bush that "was not consumed" in the time of Moses (*Exodus* 3:2), some form of herald, and this, we were told, would mark the end of the warnings. That was the first set of secrets, and from what Mirjana said they sounded like regional events that would be reported through the media to the rest of the world. The regional nature of what sounded, at least in her secrets, as disasters was obvious when Mirjana remarked that her secrets were "for mankind generally, for the world, Medjugorje, some other areas, and the sign." They would not say where the "some other areas" would be. When another visionary, Marija Pavlovic, was asked if her secrets involved the West, she only flushed and dropped the subject as if it impinged on the confidentiality of what she had been told. In his letter to the Pope, Father Vlasic was only able to report that "there will be three warnings to the world. The warnings will be in the form of events on earth." There was no timetable. The kids were astonishingly reserved, adroit in evading the cleverest of questions, queries that would soon pour in as thousands and then millions began to travel to this remote outpost. What would the great sign be? Would it be like the aurora? Would it be seen only in Medjugorje? There were already major phenomena there, phenomena strikingly like the great sun miracle. On August 2, 1981, the sun seemed like it was falling to earth as at Fatima and on countless occasions pilgrims saw it move and whirl with splendiferous colors. I witnessed this myself, the sun appearing as if a disc moved in front of it, a host-like form that softened the rays and allowed me to stare for minutes on end, to watch in disbelief as it shed gorgeous shades of red and yellow and crimson, as a huge pinkish cast surrounded it, as rays shaped like a cross suddenly beamed to the ground. Looking up at the moon one evening in May of 1990, I was startled to see a bearded face, a face that resembled a statue I saw the next day of the prophet Elijah. Although I didn't know of LaSalette at the time, Elijah was mentioned in the secrets. Others saw angels or doves and in 1981 hundreds had seen the word *MIR* — "peace" — in fiery letters above a mountain.

SENT TO EARTH

CHAPTER 28

"They have no idea what awaits them"

Now another sign was anticipated, one that would be more distinct than the aurora, preceded by warnings. It was where things grew intense. When Mirjana was asked about the events in the first secrets, she said they would "give the world something to think about." In an interview with her spiritual director, Mirjana, referring to the Madonna, said, "She not only asks, but *pleads* with everyone to convert, to pray, to fast. They have no idea what awaits them, and that is why, as their mother, she is in deep anguish for them. She stresses again that everyone should pray much, fast, do penance. It is not enough to simply pray; it is not enough to just quickly say some prayers so that one can say they prayed and did their duty. What she wants from us is to pray from the depth of our souls, to converse with God.

"There never was an age such as this one," continued the seer, "never before was God honored and respected less than now, never before have so few prayed to Him. Everything seems more important than God. This is the reason why the Blessed Mother cries so much. The number of unbelievers is becoming greater and greater. To such people, as they endeavor for a better life, God Himself is superfluous and dispensable. This is why I feel deeply sorry for them and for the world. They have no idea what awaits them. If they could only take a tiny peak at the secrets, they would convert in time. I now know things that are not particularly pleasant. I believe that if everyone knew about these same things, each one of these people would be shocked to their senses and would view our world in a completely different light."

She said her secrets contained certain "horrors." The last ones were "*really* unpleasant." During a vision on October 25, 1985, Mirjana, whose daily apparitions ceased in 1982 (but then proceeded on occasion), was shown the first secret like pictures projected on slides and said that it shook her badly. "That was, of course, due to *seeing* the first secret," she said. "If the people saw the first secret, as it was shown to me yesterday, all of them would most certainly be shaken enough to take a new and different look at themselves and everything around them."

"The manifestation of that secret, will it be a momentary thing or will it be something that will last for an extended period?" she was asked by Father Petar Ljubicic the day after the vision.

"It will last for a little while," replied Mirjana in the interview.

"Will its effects be lasting and permanent or will its effects be momentary and passing?"

"How can I explain that without encroaching on the secret?" said Mirjana. "Let me just say it won't be good at all. It won't be pleasant."

"Will the interval between the first and second secrets be lengthy?"

"That varies according to the secrets," answered Mirjana. "What I mean is that, for example, the time between the first and second secrets is of a certain period, between the second and third is of different length. For example, *and I stress*, the first secret may take place today and the second one already tomorrow."

"Are they of a notable, distinct character," asked the priest, "or more of a spiritual nature?"

"Distinct. Distinct. It will be visible. It is necessary in order to shake up the world a little. It will make the world pause and think."

"Something like a catastrophe?"

"No. It will not be anything as huge as that," said Mirjana. "That will come later. These first two secrets are not all that much severe and harsh. What I mean is, yes, they are severe, but not as much as the remaining ones. [The first] will be something that will give the world something to think about seriously, allow it to see [Mary] was, indeed, here, to see and realize that there is a God, that He exists."

"And after that, will there be anyone who will say, 'This is some sort of a natural phenomenon,' or something along those lines?" asked the priest, who Mirjana had chosen as her confidante.

"Perhaps some staunch unbelievers might say something like that after the first and second [secrets]," replied Mirjana.

They would be events, she said, that "everyone everywhere will immediately hear about."

It would be "something that people will hear about very far."

The apparitions, said Mirjana, were a preparation. "Just as any mother, [Mary] cares for her children. She wants us to come and meet God the Father well-prepared. She doesn't want us to weep and wail when it's too late. God said that He forgives at any time — providing the soul repents sincerely. All she asks for, the one thing she waits for, is for all of us to repent so that we may be forgiven. What follows are the secrets which are *really* unpleasant. I would be happy if everyone would finally understand that. I cannot tell them [much more], but once they begin to be fulfilled, then it will be too late."

That was a constant refrain: repent while there is still time, and it was what John the Baptist — whose feast day it was when the first apparition took place — had likewise warned.

"It will make the world pause and think," Mirjana repeated, referring again to the first secret. "If they could only take a tiny peek at these secrets, if they could see, they would convert in time. Still *Gospa* [the Blessed Lady] gave us God's ten secrets. They may still convert, certainly God always forgives all those who genuinely convert."

Convert. Pray. Repent. There was no lessening the serious nature of the message. Something was coming. A *number* of things were coming. Obviously, it wasn't the end of the world, not from the sounds of the first secrets, at any rate — but there was an unmistakable gravity. Mirjana called knowledge of what was to transpire enormously stressful and said that it caused her depression. Although one was not to obsess on it, one was to understand the serious tone of Mary, who had shown Mirjana some kind of desolation, *"the upheaval of a region of the world"*; who had warned that when the events began *"people will tear their hair, brothers will plead with brothers"*; and who said that by the time the sign appeared it would be *"too late"* (according to another seer named Vicka Ivankovic). Although there were those who tried to sugarcoat this and although the seers themselves discouraged any further fretting (after all, Mary often came with joy), there was no denying the underlying gravity of the message. The world had become what Mirjana described as "very evil." The hour of mercy was dwindling into the hour of justice. It had not arrived as quickly as some expected (and as quickly as certain lesser-known seers had predicted), but it was coming faster than the average person knew. Though it didn't seem like the first secrets were global cataclysms, neither were they minor. They would be distinct, Mirjana had said, visible. They would make the world "pause and think." When asked by her spiritual director if people would flock to the place where the first secret occurs, Mirjana had replied, "Well, father, surely no one wishes to watch disasters, distress, and misfortune. I don't think that this kind of thing attracts people at all. Why would people go to see something of that sort? Who would, for example, go to Italy to see a dam collapse? Who has that kind of a desire? I don't think that anyone does, and that is how it will be with this secret."

In mentioning a place like Italy Mirjana seemed to be hinting again that the first secret was regional. It would occur at a particular place or places. It would be unusual. Perhaps it had to do with water. A rush of water. She wouldn't tell Ljubicic where it would occur. That was "forbidden." She said only that it would be "something that people will hear about very far."
If people could see it, if they could glimpse the first several secrets, Mirjana told the priest, they would reform; they would rid their avarice.

Three secrets. Three warnings. It wasn't clear if the third was the concurrence of a disaster with the great sign or if the sign itself was counted as another warning, and it wasn't known how long it would take for the first three secrets to conclude. As they began to unfold, said Mirjana, the devil's grip would loosen. It would be the end of his extended reign. It was hard to tell if the first secrets would be impressive due to their severity, or because Mirjana said they would be announced shortly before they took place, proving that Medjugorje was supernatural. Depending on the seer, these secrets were followed by ones that sounded like they had to do with the future of Medjugorje, the Church (which was under precisely the assault warned about at Akita), or developments that were personal. It was the seventh through tenth secrets that got back to what sounded like disastrous events. When asked by another priest about her last secret, Mirjana shied away. "But

I can tell you that the eighth secret [actually, Mirjana said at another point that it was the seventh] is worse than the other seven," she allowed. "I prayed for a long time that it might be less severe. Every day, when the Madonna came, I pestered her, asking that it be mitigated. Then she said that everyone should pray that it might be lessened. So, in Sarajevo, I got many people to join me in prayer. Later, the Madonna told me that she'd been able to have the secret lessened. But then she told me the ninth and it was even worse. The tenth secret is totally bad and cannot be lessened whatsoever. I cannot say anything about it, because even a word would disclose the secret before it's time to do so."

It was unclear if the seers shared the final secrets as they shared at least part of the third secret (all having been told about the sign), but there was no doubt others had been told of "chastisements" and in the case of Vicka it was the seventh that had been lessened. Although at times it sounded like the events were inevitable, with prayer and penance, emphasized Vicka, such punishments could be "substantially" decreased. It was unclear to what extent the same was true of the final messages. "The ninth and tenth secrets are serious," the letter to the Vatican had advised. "They concern chastisements for the sins of the world. Punishment is inevitable, for we cannot expect the whole world to be converted. The punishment can be diminished by prayer and penance, but it cannot be eliminated. After the first admonition, the others will follow in a rather short time."

Should people be afraid, Vicka was asked?

"Not if they are prepared," she firmly responded. "If we are afraid of these kinds of things, we don't have confidence in God. Fear of this kind does not come from God. It can only come from Satan who wants to disturb us, so that we close ourselves to God and are not able to pray. With God, you can only have confidence — and strength to go through any troubles."

Many pretended to see Jesus or Mary, said the Virgin, *"but are in fact lying."*

Regarding catastrophic predictions, she had said, *"that comes from false prophets. They say: 'Such a day, on such a date, there will be catastrophe.' I have always said that misfortune will come if the world does not convert itself. Everything depends on your conversion."*

SENT TO EARTH

Chapter 29

Edge of Catastrophe

With prayer there was no room for fear but it was hard to lighten the warning. God, said Mirjana, was "at the end of His patience." Desolation. The pulling of hair. Cursing their lives without God. When each seer was given his or her tenth secret, the daily apparitions for that visionary ended, and so far Mirjana, a seer named Ivanka Ivankovic, and the youngest, Jacov Colo, had gotten all ten. Speculation was rampant that the secrets would begin when the last seer stopped having daily apparitions. According to the visionaries, the extended power of Satan, his "century," did not solely pertain to the twentieth century, indicating that it would carry into the new century for a while. In the meantime, smaller warnings, the build-up, continued. The year Medjugroje started, Mount St. Helens erupted like a reminder of Thera and the next year the Pacific developed a record El Niño, one that caused drought, forest fires, floods, erosion, great ocean fog, unusual bird migration, desert rain, and tropical storms. Although temperatures had briefly leveled during the 1970s, they had since resumed their upswing, and hot air was whisking moisture from one region and dumping it on another. So great was the shift in air circulation that it slowed the rotation of the earth by 800 microseconds.

There had never been an El Niño like this, not in the recent annals, not since ancient storms.

And at the same time there were more prophecies — this time from Africa.

At Kibeho, Rwanda, seven youngsters claimed that they too were seeing the Virgin, along with Jesus, and had been informed of impending disasters. It seemed apocalyptical. Sexual promiscuity, said Mary, would bring about ruin. They were shown entire villages deserted. They were shown war, a "river of blood," decapitated bodies. During 1981 and 1982 natives in the outbacks and for that matter neighboring countries murmured that something horrible, something far more frightening even than a savage tyrant, was about to occur. The world, it was said, was about to end. Strange sights could be seen in Rwanda's skies, the sun spinning and pulsing or splitting into two separate suns. In Bantu and Watusi lore, signs in the sky were beyond question an indication of major upheaval, even doom. It was a time of recall. The Virgin urged those at Kibeho to forsake attachment to worldly things and follow the narrow road. She told a seer named Agnes Kamagju that the people must renounce fornication and *"make of their bodies an instrument destined to the glory of God and not an object of pleasure at the service of men"* — as so many prostitutes along the Kinshasa Highway were.

The world wasn't just indifferent, said Mary, but had turned against God. As a result, there would be events. The seers were shown terrifying glimpses of the future: a tree in flames, decapitated corpses. The world, said the Virgin of Kibeho, was on *"the edge of catastrophe."* This message was being repeated as apparitions, some real, some questionable, all serious, cropped up or soon would in country after country. Italy, Venezuela, Ireland, Nigeria, Argentina, Ecuador, Canada, the U.S., Ukraine, Slovakia, Mexico, Spain, Switzerland, and even Iraq — where a girl would claim to see the Virgin at Mozul, a city that encompassed the very ruins of Nineveh! In Nicaragua in an apparition that was granted rare Church sanction a man who was soon to become a priest said he was warned that an atomic war was close at hand, a warning repeated in Argentina.

It was the claim of Sister Lucia that such a war was scheduled to occur in 1985, but that a consecration of the world and implicitly Russia by John Paul II in 1984, in obedience to the Fatima request, had prevented or at least forestalled it. The light from the Blessed Mother had drowned out the angel's sword. It was a time of great tension between the U.S. and Soviet Union as Ronald Reagan squared off against Soviet leaders who, it was darkly rumored, thought a nuclear war might be winnable. That was averted, but the crises, the close brushes with chastisement, were far from over. On April 26, 1986, explosions at a nuclear reactor in the southern Soviet republic of Ukraine sent wafts of plutonium and other radioactive material into the air, killing 237 outright, making 15,000 ill, and exposing 12,000 children to high, potentially carcinogenic doses. This was especially chilling for those who looked at the Book of Revelation and saw in it a star that fell from the sky and turned a third of the waters sour with "wormwood" (*Revelation* 8:11). In Ukraine was a bitter herb called "chernobyl" (from which came the name of the plant) and in English it translated into "wormwood." There was also a description of "something like a huge mountain all in flames" that was "cast into the sea" (*Revelation* 8:8). This was all in the section of *Revelation* that compared most closely to Lucia's vision of the angel and on the first anniversary of the disaster, Mary was reported at a small chapel in Ukraine that had been closed by the Communists. She came dressed in black and warned of more fire. *"How many warnings must mankind be given before it repents?"* she asked one seer. *"I see a large field of flames and upon it are many nations. There is not even the time to dig graves. There is no water. The heavens and the air are on fire. Who wants to receive the grace of God should pray constantly and take upon himself voluntary penance. Be merciful. Remember that the Rosary will preserve mankind from sin and perdition. My children, all of you present are dear to me and please me. I do not make distinctions as to the color of your skin or your religious faith. Love is longsuffering. It was because of the envy of Satan that death entered into the world, and everyone who is now serving him will receive death. The wicked of the world are gorging themselves on depravity and impurity. The people are falling into the hands of Satan."*

For a short time, said Mary, Satan would rule; godlessness would extend from one end of the earth to another. He was preparing a massive deception. Lightning was shown in this vision, and clouds rolled. Half of the ocean was dark and stormy and lightning was cutting through the horizon. An awful noise rumbled over the ocean. It did not sound like the danger was over. Not by a longshot. Angels of chastisement were clearly on the scene and these admonitions from the Virgin were admonitions from Christ and were to be heeded not just by those who were Catholic or carried a special devotion but by all God's endangered people. It was time to put aside religious bias. It was time to stop the animosities that had begun in the 1500s. Christians were Christians and God's people were His people and all were of concern to a Lord Who had shed His blood, Who had warned of natural upheaval right there in *Matthew* 24, and Who through His messengers — especially His mother — was warning again.

And storms there were. From 1985 to 1988 the increase in temperatures took another jump and it was heating all over and getting strange, with huge unexplained fish kills as there had been fish kills before bubonic fever had hit and a miasma, a foul wind, blowing. In 1987 freak winds blasted down 18 million trees in England, the worst gale since the 1700s, the wind howling through the night, toppling trees that had been there for centuries, back to the famous kings, to the roundtable. Whole communities were barricaded with debris. There was no getting out of the house. Wave heights were swelling by a third in the Atlantic. Reports came of rogue waves that reached heights of up to 85 feet while in the south a truly massive hurricane called Gilbert spread itself over half of the Caribbean and at 888 millibars, below even the Labor Day Storm, set a record for lowest barometric pressure, its *radius* stretching from the Yucatan in Mexico to Louisiana. There were also quakes. Mexico City had been slammed, and the total number of global tremors rose steadily upward. And then there was the threat from the sky. In 1989 an asteroid, a cosmic boulder larger than an aircraft carrier, much bigger than the one in Tunguska, missed earth by six hours. Shaken, the American Institute of Aeronautics and Astronautics recommended studies of how many other close calls or "near-earth objects" there might be and soon there were estimates of 2,000 objects larger than a kilometer that crossed the earth's orbit, a size that was not only much greater than what had struck Tunguska, Siberia, but one that, coming at speeds much faster than a bullet, could toss up enough dust to blot out sunshine and kill one of every six people on earth.

The odds any given year were low — one in up to 500,000 — but there were no reliable estimates and astronomers suggested various periodicities, ranging from every 500 to 1,500 years for smaller but significant strikes. "We've gotten to a position now where we can understand roughly where these periodicities have come from, and they're to do with the circulation of this cosmic material called the Taurids," I was told by Dr. Victor Clube of Oxford. Every few centuries, said a report from NASA, "the earth is struck by a near-earth object large enough to cause thousands of deaths, or hundreds of thousands of deaths if it were to strike an urban area." During our lifetime, said the report, there was "a small but non-zero chance that the earth will be struck by an object large enough to destroy food crops on a global scale and possibly end civilization as we know it."

The prospects of that were tiny, but there were far higher odds that a smaller yet severely damaging object could hit — an object over a couple hundred yards in size

— and even one that was only the width of Tunguska would be the equivalent of more than 650 Hiroshimas. "Extrapolation from smaller yields suggests that the local zones of damage from the impact of a 1-kilometer object could envelop whole states or countries, with fatalities of tens of millions in a densely populated region," NASA had concluded.

There was also concern for solar storms. Every so often the sun flared, sent huge licks of flame, especially around sunspots, and the energy came in the form of great magnetic pulses. That caused upper atmospheric effects that influenced cloud formation and possibly systems like El Niño.

Was this why the sun was spinning? Was that what God was trying to show us? Was something changing on the sun, something that affected our weather, something, for all we knew, that affected the depths of the earth? Solar activity had been rising through the past hundred years (the magnetic flux had more than doubled), and in 1989 there was such a pulse that it knocked out electricity at the Hyrdo-Quebec power system in Canada, leaving six million people without power, while in Siberia the flow of energy corroded a gas line and caused a powerful explosion.

It was called a solar maximum and it had been responsible for the warming in the Middle Ages. Now it was coming in peaks once more. It was a long-term up-cycle and according to an astrophysicist at Harvard named Sallie L. Baliunas the cycle likely had a century or more to go. "When the sun's total output of energy changes, ultraviolet radiation changes by quite a bit, and that can change the stratospheric ozone layer and then profoundly affect the circulation of the earth's climate," Dr. Baliunas told me.

It was what was called an "amplifying mechanism" and while the slight change in luminosity might not seem enough to cause wholesale changes in climate, there was a complex set of reactions between the upper and lower atmospheres, both of which were affected by changes in heat, cosmic rays, and ultraviolet radiation. The more magnetism from the sun the more it deflected cosmic rays — rays that were related to cloud formation. Electromagnetic wind dissipated high clouds by changing the charge of wafting particles and this in turn allowed more solar radiation to reach the earth. Meanwhile ultraviolet radiation affected layers of ozone, strengthening winds and displacing the jet stream.

It was a complex list of interactions but it reduced to this: even slight changes in the sun had a huge affect on climate and the changes — the intensity of sunspot cycles — were increasing. The sun was at a high magnetic level. It wasn't quite as high as the tenth and eleventh centuries, which had set the stage for the Medieval Event, but it was getting there. This was not to discount the aspect of pollution. When men pumped millions of pounds of carbon dioxide and other gases into the atmosphere, it distorted the air. No doubt about that. Pollution trapped heat close to the earth. But there were other forces that were more mysterious. The solar surge was recurring. If low sunspot activity had accompanied the Little Ice Age, now there was the opposite; now the same sun that formed mystical signs at Fatima and Medjugorje and Kibeho was altering the climate.

SENT TO EARTH

CHAPTER 30

An Hour of Fire

And as the sun heated, there were more warnings. On October 17, 1989, San Francisco was hit by what became known as the Loma-Prieta quake, and although it was a relatively small quake (magnitude-7.1), it caused $7 billion in damage in a city that had all but totally reverted back to the lifestyle that had gotten it in trouble in 1906. We remember the quake as the one in which an interstate in Oakland collapsed, and Candlestick Park was shaken during the World Series. Just two days before, there had been a major pro-abortion rally at City Hall — and now workers ran from the swaying building in terror. It came right after a Supreme Court decision granted states the right to decide abortion issues, and a number of governors immediately signed a declaration backing a woman's right to "choose." This was the year that kicked off the remarkable run of natural disasters in the U.S., and there was agitation elsewhere as well. In 1989 12,290 quakes were registered around the world (nearly double the 7,747 seven years earlier), and 40,000 died during a quake in Iraq — old Mesopotamia.

Tremors were beginning to cluster where they had in the Bronze Age, the sun was entering a particularly stormy period, and it was the onset of the 1990s, a decade that would not just see another temperature spike, but records obliterated.

This lead to an hour of fire. On October 20, 1991, dry winds and a scorching sun caused another major disaster in the Bay Area when a fire erupted in the foothills near Oakland. It was the greatest conflagration of brush in the history of northern California, the wind blowing so hard that helicopters had to disperse their payloads before reaching it. Vortices of flame (what firemen called "little whirlwind devils") danced and skittered across streets and for a while, for a terrifying several hours, it looked like the inferno would incinerate the historic Claremont Hotel and burn all the way to the bay — taking the campus of Berkeley with it. A thousand students were evacuated. Frantic ash-covered residents poured out of the hills. There was a pall of dark smoke. Ash and embers whipped by the wind were carried across the bay and over San Francisco. Soot blew through open windows 15 miles away. Ashes rained down on Candlestick Park — this time during a football game. Eucalyptus trees had a vapor around them and when the fire reached them the aerosol exploded. It took two days to control. Before it was over the hills overlooking Berkeley, America's New Age center, were a blackened hell, with 3,000 homes destroyed and $1.6 billion in damage. "Things were burning very, very quickly," recalled Don Parker, assistant fire chief in Oakland. "We have very narrow streets, with heavy vegetation. As the fire was burning it was starting to build a wall of heat in front of it, like a welder's torch, and the buildings were *exploding*. The wall of heat was traveling before the flames. A friend of mine said he saw it move a hundred yards in fifteen seconds. Another friend of mine had a sister and he called to check on her and she said, 'I can't talk right now. My home's starting to catch on fire.' She never got out of that home. We found her remains days later. As it progressed it went to townhouses made of wood siding and wood shingle roofs and these homes, about 400 of them, burned to the point where there was hardly any ash. It was like a [self-cleaning] electric oven. Four hundred town homes burned in a matter of 16 minutes.

Through the early part of the fire it was estimated we were losing a home every four seconds. There were some high-voltage lines coming down to a power station and the fire caused carbon-arcing, which created these great big flashes and explosions."

SENT TO EARTH

CHAPTER 31

"Behold, I will destroy them with the earth"

Few were putting the pieces together but the chastisement that had started the year of LaSalette was now moving at high throttle. Up to now there had been peaks and lulls but now portents filled the news. Fires. Blazing, threatening fire. Mudslides. Rivers of muck were coursing down the roads in Malibu just north of Los Angeles. Volcanoes. In the Philippines Mount Pinatubo erupted for the first time since the Middle Ages, tossing up enough ash to affect global weather patterns. There were typhoons (hurricanes in the Pacific). There were earthquakes. There was also war. Ethnic groups were clashing in former Yugoslavia around the very vicinity of Medjugorje (though miraculously not touching the village itself) and in Africa famine — hunger and plague, as foreseen in Kibeho — had returned. The disasters were forming exactly as they had at the beginning of past convergences and however much scientists wanted to deny it, the public knew it wasn't normal, that no matter how they rationalized it, how they said it was just a matter of monitoring, or the luck of cycles, that what was in progress escaped normal bounds. In their hearts they had to know. It was the beginning of the period in which at least seven of America's top ten disasters occurred. Air was colliding and extruding and in 1992 came a big one: a strong category-four called Andrew in Florida.

There was only one word to describe the reaction of experts: horror. They didn't know a storm could do what Andrew did (even those who had flown in hurricanes for years were astonished), and what made it doubly frightening was that it missed Miami by just twenty miles. Ground-zero was an area known for its Santeria (a combination of voodoo and Catholicism). It wasn't a category-five — it wasn't as powerful as Gilbert, Camille, or Labor Day — but at 922 millibars it was plenty potent and it had sustained winds of more than 140 miles an hour — razing neighborhoods in such a way that even though the National Hurricane Center was only a few miles from the strongest winds, officials were aghast when they viewed the damage (including destruction in many cases of their own homes).

This wasn't a hurricane; it was a bomb. In a typical fully developed hurricane heat was released at a rate equivalent to a 10-megaton nuclear bomb exploding every twenty minutes (it takes more than sixty Hiroshimas to make a megaton) and Andrew was not a typical hurricane. It was intensity personified. Survivors told of hiding in bathtubs — cowering under mattresses — while the rest of their homes, the kitchens, the living rooms, the bedrooms, were smashed, sucked up, and blown apart. Men strained to keep the storm out by desperately holding on to doorknobs and dogs hiding with families in closets cried like they had been hit by a car. So forceful was the storm that ocean coral was damaged. Vents in the eyewall shot air down at tornadic intensity — a storm within a storm — and bits of roof, metal, and wood speared tires. Power lines slashed across one building with such force that it was embedded in the cement, and I was told of one man who watched a large steel tool box wing through the cinder-blocks at the front of his house and exit out the back wall. Another witnessed a tool shed rotating above his yard. The wind wasn't blowing; it was exploding. So damaged was Homestead Air

Force Base that afterward the government simply *abandoned* it. Officials told me the hurricane was more like a thirty-mile-wide tornado. A new breed. A storm they had not seen before. It was a small hurricane — covering a fraction the area of Gilbert — but whatever it touched was obliterated. Mirjana had hinted at something like a dam collapsing and whether or not natural disasters were in those first secrets, that's what these walls of water, the surges of ocean, were beginning to resemble. She said the warnings would be regional and that's what was starting to happen: regional events heard from afar. Foretastes. A turning point. The steeper part of a curve. At first the media was slow to grasp Andrew's extent, because its damage was so widespread that it couldn't all be grasped from a helicopter. If this was a precursor, what was in the secrets? There had been the horrific sound of wind and the sight of strange blue lights as there had been blue lights in other hurricanes and as inexplicable lights also accompanied quakes as if forces yet unknown were conspiring to cause havoc. It was this storm that helped convince the National Hurricane Center to construct a building with fortress walls and one chamber that could withstand an F-5 tornado.

For they expected the big one. Meteorologists knew the big one — the really big one, greater than Andrew — was out there somewhere in the heat of the ocean. A hurricane forecaster named William Gray told me there would be an increase in frequency for 15 to 20 years as the speed of ocean currents shifted according to salinity and there were also favorable conditions set by global temperature, rainfall in Africa (where storms like Andrew were spawned), and gyrations in the upper atmosphere.

That was the short cycle. There was also a long-term cycle, periods of intensification that lasted for a thousand years, and the question was whether this too, this greater cycle, last seen around 1000 A.D., was returning.

There were indications something was up, and officials were screaming about it, shouting at developers who were building close to the water. There had been a lull from the 1970s to the early 1990s but it was ending and now there would be turbulence for at least the next couple decades as there had been back during the Great Miami Hurricane and perhaps as during ancient onslaughts. Nature moved in cycles; there were seasons of the year; there were long-term cycles. God worked through them. He enhanced aspects of them. He could swing them into especially dramatic mode. And it was time to prepare for it. Florida was what Gray described as a "sitting duck, a recipe for disaster." Its population had grown to 15 times what it was during the previous up-cycle. Where there had been 200,000 residents in the Miami-Fort Lauderdale megalopolis in 1926, there were now more than three million. They had narrowly missed Andrew and that's what Andrew was: just a warning. A shot over the bow. Monster hurricanes were brewing, and if it followed other trends, there would be quiet years followed by ones that were explosive. There would be Gilberts and larger than Gilbert. They may not have articulated storms the size of the ones that seemed to have occurred during the Bronze Age, but meteorologists sensed it. They saw what happened in Andrew and no matter how long they had worked in the field, no matter how many storms they had flown into, no matter how many radar images, the hurricane had left them scared.

"The weekend before Andrew actually came it was a tropical wave out there in the Atlantic and we were all watching it from a meteorological standpoint and it wasn't any threat at that time," recalled Jim Lushine, warning coordinator at the National Weather Service. "We lived in Dade County near the Metro Zoo and that weekend there was a birthday party for a friend of ours up in Broward County. We got to the party and before we left that night my friend said, 'Let's flip a coin and see which county is going to be hit, Broward or Dade.' I flipped the coin and I lost. By Sunday everyone knew it was coming somewhere in southern Florida. I was called back in to work the midnight shift and had to work from 8 p.m. Sunday night until the next morning or whenever the storm was over. My wife and daughter, who was just graduating from high school, were in the house and they had some friends over, people who lived closer to the water and had come over to our house as refuge. So there was my wife, daughter, and seven other people and a dog at the time of the hurricane. When I'd left, I'd done what I could, put the shutters up and prepared everything, but I didn't realize even at that point how devastating the hurricane was going to be. I knew it was a major hurricane, a category-four hurricane, but having never actually lived through one, I wasn't absolutely sure. In theory, as a meteorologist, I knew what hurricanes could do, but in actuality I wasn't clear as to what would happen to my house.

"My wife sensed I was nervous when I left. I got to work and was watching the hurricane and writing statements letting the media know what the situation was — where the hurricane was and how strong the winds were — and every once in a while I'd call my wife to see how things were. She'd say, 'Nothing much is happening here. It's really not blowing much.' I could see it on the radar and satellite but didn't know the exact effects. It was close to a category-five. I was watching the anemometer and it got to be 165-mile-an-hour gusts on the roof of the Hurricane Center, which was 13 stories high but out of the maximum wind that's in the donut-shaped area around an eyewall. The eyewall passed just south of our building.

"Then the anemometer broke, so the wind had to have been above 165 and that wasn't even in the maximum area. There was a huge thud and everyone got real quiet at the Hurricane Center and the whole building had shaken. The radar had blown off along with the anemometer, which weighed a couple tons, a big white dome that rolled down the Dixie Highway.

"I had one more phone conversation with my wife around 4 a.m. The phones were still working but the winds were really going and then the phones went down and that was the last I heard from her until I got home later the next morning, which was about ten a.m., after the winds had died down, drove down the South Dixie Highway, and saw the beginnings of this destruction. As I got farther south it got worse and worse and I started getting more nervous about my home and didn't know exactly what I was going to find when I got there. When I did get home the family was out in the yard and all the people were there and the house itself didn't look all that bad but when I got closer I could see that the entire roof had been ripped off and everything inside ruined. The storm had trashed the entire inside of the house. There was nothing salvageable except a few pictures from our albums. Everything else — all our clothes, the furniture — was ruined. During the height of the storm my wife was in the bedroom, which had shutters on it, but a tree came down and punched a hole in the roof in the bedroom. So at four or five in the morning she had run out of the bedroom with my daughter and they went into the dining room and got underneath the table and were there for a while but then the china cabinet collapsed onto the table, so they ran from under the dining room table and went down with the others into the bathroom and bedroom closet, which I had told them were the best refuge if the worst was realized. There were five in the closet and another four in the bathtub, along with the dog. They held on to the door during those tremendous forces all night long and managed to keep the door closed. Those were the only rooms in the house — the closet and the bathroom — where the roof stayed on. The rest was totally wiped out. When they opened the door the house looked like a bomb had gone off. It was just trashed. I have no doubt that it was gusting at close to 200 miles per hour and the best proof I could see was a billboard on South Dixie Highway not too far from my house. Its I-beams, which were about a foot thick, had actually *bent* from the force. In the morning my wife had gone out to a phone that was working two blocks down the street and when she got down there she was lost. She couldn't figure out how to get back. Everything was gone, even the trees. It was totally amazing. Unbelievable. There was nothing."

"I've told people I would never write this because it wouldn't be believed, but I'm going to anyhow," said another whose home, save for his library, was trashed, Howard Kleinberg, former editor of *The Miami News*. "Only one book was ruined by Andrew. It was in the front bedroom and it had been flung to the floor from a desk top to be soaked when the roof came apart over it. It was the Holy Scriptures. And to make it more unbelievable, it was open to that part of *Genesis* dealing with Noah and the Great Flood: 'And God said unto Noah, the end of all flesh is come before me; for the earth is filled with violence through them; and behold, I will destroy them with the earth.'"

CHAPTER 32

Valkyries on a Rampage

It was getting intense and, hard as it was to believe, Andrew was followed by a "storm of the century" in Hawaii. The Pacific too was rising. The great storms were growing fiercer. Because the pressure of the Pacific was generally below that of the Atlantic, the lowest storm readings were now dipping below even that of Gilbert and some set records. There had been a typhoon named Tip with gale-force winds that extended for a radius of 680 miles!

That was not just daunting but terrifying; at 876 it was 16 millibars below the Labor Day Storm.

Something was transpiring in the oceans and it was resembling what had happened between 2500 B.C. and the medieval warming. That was when hurricanes had hurled gigantic storm surges, the evidence found in cores indicating that at one time category-five hurricanes — storms a magnitude greater than Andrew — had hit Florida, Louisiana, Mississippi, and as far north as Virginia Beach, possibly to New England, with catastrophic regularity.

In other words there had been a time when the strongest hurricanes known to man — considered in recent centuries to be a threat only in the western Pacific or down in the Caribbean — had meandered up the Atlantic. Meantime areas like the Caribbean were threatened by storms *bigger* than anything modern meteorology had witnessed. And the threat was not just from cyclones. In Peru was evidence of major El Niños during the run of Mesopo-

177

tamian disasters and these looked like they were on their way back as parts of the Pacific heated to 86 degrees and El Niños now came so often it was beginning to look like one huge *ongoing* El Niño. As the planet heated, molecules of water expanded and, added to glacial melt, caused a rise in sea level that in some years increased storm surge. This terrified residents of islands such as Tuvalo, Kiribati, and the Marshalls. Ancient graveyards were washing out and palms, undermined by an expanding tide, were toppling. Great was the fear that sea levels would increase by as much as 37 inches by 2100, which (if it kept up; it varied) meant something close to doom for islands several feet above sea level. "These aren't storms, they're surges," remarked a newsman in the Marshalls. "It's nice weather, and all of a sudden water is pouring into your living room."

The landscape was changing — washing away — and the sun's rays were stronger than ever. By 1992 average global temperature was half a degree warmer than during the rise in 1933 and a full degree warmer than the initial peak around the time of LaSalette, by some reckonings even higher.

The pot was boiling over. In Australia a storm had caused a 42-foot surge, and on Reunion Island a cyclone set a record with 18 *feet* of rainfall.

The ancient storms, the hurricanes thought by some to have caused ancient Aztecs to flee shorelines, that had once ravaged Peru, were coming back. On September 11, 1992, Hurricane Iniki swept across the island of Kau'ai in Hawaii. It was just 18 days after Hurricane Andrew; 10,000 homes were damaged. "All morning the air had been dead calm and the sky overcast," one resident reported. "The high humidity and the absence of breeze made it seem particularly oppressive. As the countdown continued into late morning it appeared that all our neighbors were outside checking each other's preparations. The sky was getting darker, and it was no longer still. The first gusts from the east had begun. Apparently, our uninvited guest was arriving early. Very quickly the wind increased to gale force, and we retreated inside the house. The phones and electricity were already dead. It was definitely showtime. Our children dutifully picked out their 'emergency toys' and took their places in the hall. Suddenly, a violent gust slammed into the house and I saw shingles fly into a guava grove in our backyard. They were off of our house and decision time was near, stay or leave. A few minutes later another gust rocked the whole structure on its pier beams. It was time to run, the house was already coming apart. We took our emergency stores and got in the car to make a run for safety. I suspected that the nearby country club would be empty. I also knew that it had thick concrete walls and was likely to withstand everything. We were completely soaked, but we made it. The clubhouse is an impressive structure featuring a lobby full of windows that ordinarily afford a spectacular view. These windows are made of hurricane-proof glass, and this would be a relatively safe place to see what was going on outside. At about three p.m. the doors at the main entrance blew in with a crash. The hurricane was inside now. It sounded like a wind tunnel. Trees were coming down everywhere, large metal conduits weighing a ton were blowing around the golf course like paper cups, and every power pole in sight was on the ground. The noise was unbelievable, shattering glass, twisting metal, flying debris impacting, and of course the piercing howl of the wind. At times the gusts would reach frenzied crescendos where it felt like the whole building would explode. On the east wing of the building there was a large banquet room set up for a wedding reception. The suction in the room was so great that the doors which open out were immovable. All twenty or so large hurricane windows were bowing dangerously inward. The low pressure in that room was lethal. Finally, during a peak gust, the entire room imploded. Every window, wall, and door, inside and out, disintegrated at once."

It was the Roaring Nineties. Tornadoes were raging too. They had gone from an average 800 a year to over 1,100 and by the end of the decade would reach 1,225.

I heard incredible stories. In Kansas a woman named Brook Williamson was picked up by a funnel that fluctuated between an F-4 and F-5 — the worst wind our planet has to offer. She was with her mother, brother, a friend, and an eight-month-old daughter. "We just got finished eating and just kind of flipped the TV on and all of a sudden we heard there was a tornado, take cover," said Brook. "And so we looked out the door and it was such an enormous storm that it looked like it was right in our backyard headed for our house. It was half-a-mile wide. We got in the car and tried to get to a neighbor's, a house that had a basement. We're in the car and we could tell it was getting too close. The cows on one side of a pasture were freaking and running to the other side of the pasture and it started hailing. We knew we were not supposed to be in a car, so we jumped out and got into a little depression in the ground. We were all saying the *Lord's Prayer* and everything was real calm and then not two seconds after that you could hear the tornado. It was bursting our eardrums. And the next thing you know it gets pitch dark. Rain was violently falling to the point where it hit the earth and then washed up in our faces. The temperature changed and it got real cold. You could hear it and smell all the electrical stuff in the air and hear trees just being broken and then you're getting hit with boards and bricks. I could hear my car shaking back and forth and then the car was just *gone*. And the tornado got a lot more violent. I picked up my head and that was my big mistake. It picked me up and my mom yelled at me, 'Lay down!' but I said, 'I can't!' I was picked up and thrown down and picked up and thrown down. It carried me for about a quarter of a mile, probably five or seven seconds, and I screamed, 'God take me! Take me and get it over with!' You couldn't hear anything because of the roar, but for some reason, I could hear my daughter screaming, and I just focused in on her screaming and heard her the whole time while all this was happening. I was whipped everywhere. There were cows flying around. We were right next to a field of cattle and it was picking them up and throwing them all over the place. I heard a cow just shrieking, horrible. I never heard a cow sound like that before. I did somersaults and I was dragged and flung violently. I went through barbed wire and when it finally dropped me I grabbed hold of a big board or something that was stuck in the ground and held on to that and the tornado didn't pick me up anymore and then I could hear my friend yelling my name. It was black. All the debris and all the stuff just made it pitch black. You couldn't see anything. I jumped up and started running toward her voice and we met and she held me up and carried me back to the ditch where everybody was," continued Brook, whose lung collapsed and who fractured her collarbone, shoulder blade, right arm, and two vertebrae. "We were all just covered with mud. We were in the ditch for two hours before anyone could get to us, and I was in and out of consciousness."

That was Andover. In the East, it was nor'easters. In 1992 a gale threw so much water at the City of New York that scuba divers were sent to aid trapped motorists. Whitecaps broke over roads and flooded a runway at LaGuardia. Sections of Wall Street were submerged, the wind howling "like Valkyries on a rampage," said *The New York Times* — which was ironic because Valkyries were the mythical maidens of Woden.

More storms were coming and officials knew it. At the emergency center in Manhattan the director told me that all it would take would be a category-three hurricane making landfall midway up the New Jersey coast to send the worst of its winds into New York Harbor, where they'd pile a thirty-foot surge and put Lower Manhattan under water. There was no way to evacuate. The bridges would swing like chandeliers. Waves would break over wharves in Brooklyn. They would lap at the feet of the

World Trade Center. Residents would flee tenements in Far Rockaway in panic. So concerned were officials that they had located their center in a building with a third-story entrance.

CHAPTER 33

Threats Close and Distant

Woe. There were even scientists at NOAA who believed storms came as "judgments," and they were quickening. In 1993 the largest system ever to strike the U. S. sprawled from the Gulf of Mexico to New England, closing every major East Coast airport and affecting at least half of the country's population.

In California storms spawned by El Niño led to disaster declarations in all but one of the 58 counties.

Mud oozed down slopes and poured into palatial beachfronts, exiting over stilted back decks to the frothing infuriated ocean. The signs were there. They were knocking on our very doors. Scientists said it was because warm air had diverted the jet stream, but there was more to it than that, and the very term "El Niño" meant "Christ Child."

It sounded like God was saying something. Floods raged. At Monterey they had to rescue pets with surf boards. Every time I went to California something was going on and the same was true across the nation. From 1991 to 1996 the number of severe storms jumped from 6,500 to 9,200 and reports of large hail *tripled*. In Texas it came crashing through windows. It was like what had fallen during the Roman events, the hail as big as "pullet's eggs" — or larger, as big as rock melons, the storms coming in a way they had not come before and surprising, even stunning, weathermen.

In Scotland wind knocked out the national power grid *twice* in twelve hours, sparking fears at a nuclear facility of another Chernobyl.

In Africa a single bolt of lightning killed all 11 members of a soccer team from the Congo.

In Hong Kong were what weathermen now called "black rainfall alerts."

In the Philippines there were supertyphoons.

And in the U.S., in a fantastic display of force, the Mississippi flooded to such an extent that 17 million acres, an area four times the size of Israel, were under water.

Weathermen called that a 500-year flood and there was also a "500-year" flood in Georgia the year after.

Inundation. "Storms of the century." No wonder there was an explosion of seers who saw huge waves, who saw great storms as Melanie had said there would be storms, *"thunderstorms which will shake cities,"* which was what it was doing in San Francisco, which saw its greatest display of lightning ever.

There were extremes of all kinds. The climate was switching. In Israel the Dead Sea dropped as it had in the days of Gomorrah while in places that were normally dry — in deserts, in the Atacama (normally the driest place on earth) — it was raining!

Rain. And ice. In 1998 an unprecedented weeklong storm toppled huge transmission towers in Quebec, 27,000 utility poles, and immobilized a *fifth* of Canada's work force. It was a taste of apocalypse as a 600-mile swath of Quebec, New Brunswick, and Ontario was coated with up to four inches of ice. Residents went without light, heat, and running water for days and even weeks. At one point the three million residents of Montreal were tethered to civilization by a single power line. So desperate were people that they began to chop up their porches for firewood. "It was a hundred-year storm no matter how you look at," said David Phillips, a senior climatologist at Environment Canada. "It could be a storm of the millennium for all we know. It was the most destructive, disruptive storm in Canadian history. We've looked in our weather files to see something like this, but nothing exists there. Maybe in the X-Files, but not in the weather files."

And there was plague. In Zimbabwe 47 percent of women tested in prenatal clinics were positive for HIV and by the end of the Nineties 24.5 million Africans were infected, turning villages into ghost towns — towns foreseen at Kibeho as the result of promiscuity. There was also the fear of ebola, a virus that likewise rose from the jungle and consumed every part of the body, causing skin to bubble and hemorrhage in every portal of the body, including the eyes.

In Zaire a nun had thrashed with such horrible convulsions that her blood was on the furniture and walls.

And in the sky, a series of warnings. In 1992, 1993, and 1994, there had been more close buzzes by asteroids. And 1994 was also the year a spectacular comet called Shoemaker-Levy Comet hit Jupiter in 21 fragments — several large enough, had they hit earth, to end civilization. The first struck on July 12, feast day of Our Lady of Mount Carmel, which was how Mary had come (swathed in brown) at the last Fatima appearance. Two years later another asteroid, JA 1996, came as close to earth as the moon and a year after *that* was the Hale-Bopp Comet — a 30-mile-wide object that hung in the night sky as Halley's had once hung in the sky over Jerusalem and gave everybody a jolt because astronomers did not know it was coming (nor that it even existed).

Hale-Bopp was spotted twenty months before its closest pass and it was one of millions of others, countless chunks of debris that came from so far out that astronomers had no way of seeing them. The same was true of asteroids, which were often burned-out comets. They too were stealth. But they were closer. There were asteroids between earth and the sun, or just beyond our orbit, and where in 1989 astronomers had known of 90 asteroids with orbits that intersected the earth's, by 1992 the figure had grown to 128, and by 1995 to 250. At one observatory asteroids were being discovered at a rate of five a month, and by the end of the decade NASA had logged 1,076 near-earth objects that were either earth-crossers or came close to intersecting our orbit, of which 405 were a kilometer or larger, a size that, if it hit, would cause a global cataclysm.

Some said we were centuries away from having to worry about a strike, while others warned that a cycle of asteroid hits would result by 2300 from the Taurid belt, and still others — a group of scientists known in government circles as "the X-Files Committee" — warned that the earth was already overdue for a rendezvous large enough to extinguish ten percent of the population.

Such an asteroid struck earth every 100,000 years, they argued, and by their measure it had been that long or longer since the last.

CHAPTER 34

The Warning in L.A.

Was this what Christ meant when he mentioned "signs in the stars" and "in the sky fearful omens"? Was this how the "powers in the heavens" would be shaken (*Luke* 21:11-25)?

Did it apply to our own time?

The prophecy of Jesus had come in the same breath as a warning about "great earthquakes," and while the big one had not yet struck, the precursors of these too, it seemed, had come. At 4:31 a.m. on January 17, 1994, a magnitude-6.7 sent a shock to Los Angeles that collapsed freeways, busted pipelines, and caused fires. The quake's epicenter was in the northern suburb of Northridge and that was interesting because Northridge was where at least 80 percent of the nation's pornographic videos were made.

It was what *The New York Times* called the "porn center of the world" and if that wasn't enough to make people think, the production centers were not just close but within a five-mile radius of the epicenter. Destruction in California's video-Sodom had been close to apocalyptic. A survey of Northridge and other Valley studios showed that with no exception every such company (and there were nearly 70) "suffered some major damage." It was one of the most site-specific quakes since the tremors that shook Pompeii in 62 A.D. and it wasn't just the X-rated industry but also the headquarters for Warner Brothers, Universal, and ABC Entertainment that suffered. Was there something basic wrong? Had the decisions of mankind in the Nineties triggered this flurry?

As the President surveyed damage there was an aftershock.

A light fixture swayed precariously over his head.

And it was not just aimed at Northridge. No, that was the epicenter but the scene was Los Angeles, where, as in the Bay Area, there were many good Christians but where Sodom was revived and where there was an ongoing saturnalia. Along the "Walk of Fame" were shops dealing with porn, magic, tattoos, skull posters, psychics, strippers, incense, obscene t-shirts, and skimpy degrading lingerie. Anything was now okay. It was Hollywood. There were orgies that would have drawn the nod of approval from Caligula. And producers made anything — no matter the harm to kids — as long as there was a payday. Occult. Violence. Adultery.

Too often that was Hollywood's electricity; that was its drawing power. And power there was. Lots of it. Money power. Satan could grant that. He could grant all the kingdoms of the world (*Matthew* 4:9). And he was. Those who were doing his bidding, who were allowing him to maintain the hold he'd held since the French Revolution, were basking in unprecedented wealth. All he asked was that America forget its Christian roots and export the evil of lust as Russia had once exported the evil of atheism. At Fatima Jacinta had been told that fashion led many to hell and now the world was the domain of feathered costumes, piercing body jewelry, and colored hair that cast straight back to Babylon. Ankhs. Snakes. The "stars" made no bones about it. They wanted Mesopotamia back. And on the streets, there were shops with signs that said "Royal Flesh," "Naughty Devils," or "Necromance" (which meant communication with the dead). Once harbored in seance rooms, demons had been set free to the extent that they climbed out of televisions and videos and from the internet as self-righteous actors acted as if what they were doing was moral. They had been blinded to their own transgressions, their perversion of the young, their own profound contamination. Demonic images were paid greater respect than those of Jesus or Mary. The time-honored representation of a demon (and what seers saw in their visions of hell) were now shown in horror movies or as aliens. This was to let them touch the populace, to familiarize us, to bring the power of evil into every functioning living room. The demons of the air would appear, said the secret of LaSalette, *"and men will become more and more perverted."* They had been described at Fatima as bearing *"terrifying and repellent likeness to frightful and unknown animals,"* and now they were all around us and our children. They had been summoned, called. And they had only too gladly responded. They had risen and were now everywhere with their blasphemy. There was a movie mocking the Virgin, another that made the Archangel Michael look like a swinging bachelor, and a horrid portrayal of Jesus in *The Last Temptation of Christ*, a movie that would not have been permitted at the height of medieval decadence.

If at LaSalette a great famine had come because men were using Christ's name in vain, how much worse was in store for a society where His name was now a curse in every movie, on every station, in conversation? If farmers using His name had helped provoke the famine in 1846, how much greater an event would now come when the name of Jesus was not just a swear word in private but in front of millions and tens of millions and hundreds of millions? What awaited a society that had children who gave a finger salute to the devil and a rock star who was said to be a formal priest in the Church of Satan?

CHAPTER 35

The Ocean Afire

The answer was disaster. In three years the United States had thus incurred its three costliest events (Hurricane Andrew, the L.A. quake, and the Mississippi flood). And it was heating up. Oh, was it heating up. At least seven of the top ten warmest years on record were logged in the 1990s and NOAA was warning that the "rapidly changing" climate now presented a situation that had grown "critical."

The signs, once a curiosity, had grown drastic. In the Arctic, ancestral Eskimo ice cellars were melting. In the Urals, tree-growth was exploding. In Central Park, they were ice-skating in December in t-shirts. If there had been peaks around the time of LaSalette and then at the time of the Labor Day Storm, now the graphline was Mount Everest. In 1997 the record for all-time warmest year was set, lasting only until 1998, which became the warmest 12-month period since invention of the thermometer.

A trend that had begun in the 1840s and moved with a certain degree of gradualness (except for the spikes in decades like the 1930s) now threatened to go off the charts. Things were heating like no one expected and science was unable to come to terms with it. They'd hoped 1997 was a fluke, but then came 1998 and a graphline at NASA literally *did* shoot off the right corner.

Whatever the cause, whether the sun, pollution, a combination, or an entirely unknown dynamic, something very major was happening and it bore unknown consequences. In 1998 each of the first nine months set all-time heat records and Dallas saw temperatures hit 100 every day for more than a month. In what climatologists said was a 1,000-year event, the thermometer stayed above 80 for 12 consecutive nights in Tampa. Average global surface temperature was now hovering above 62 and increasing by a third of a degree a decade.

It had never been this hot in the lifetime of any living person and according to climatologists not since 1300. In Antarctica massive ice shelves were breaking up — creating one berg that was larger than the state of Delaware — and now scientists feared a true global cataclysm if what was called the Western Antarctic Ice Sheet collapsed, causing a sudden 15-foot rise in the oceans. Huge regions of the Amazon were on fire (an expanse the size of England) and in Mexico fires had reached rare cloud forests. There were flames in Russia. There were fires in Montana. There were blazes in Florida, where auspicious red clouds hung over Miami.

In Indonesia, children wore masks to school and tigers fled burning forests and millions of acres of land, land that had never burned before, were turned to ash.

I can't enumerate them all. But some have to be mentioned, some clearly showed the increment, the way God in His mercy kept trying to get His point across, harder now, with ever-larger figures. Brazil, Uruguay, Paraguay. In Bangladesh twenty million were affected by floods. In New Guinea a tidal wave caused massive casualties. It rolled ashore with a sound like a jet taking off and swept away thousands of sleeping natives, a scene right out of a horror movie. Survivors reported sparks flying from the water and thought the ocean was on fire as bioluminescent microorganisms were churned up by the current. In Hong Kong more than a million chickens were killed when they were found to carry a form of flu that was fatal to humans. A bullet was dodged. The bug was stopped before it spread. But there was much sweating at the Centers for Disease Control. This was what they most feared: a global influenza epidemic like the one that had killed Francisco and Jacinta in the early part of the twentieth century.

There were signs of a coming pandemic. Soon after Hong Kong word came of a new virus in Singapore that spread from pigs.

Now the alarms were ringing.

"A flu virus no one has ever been exposed to, one that can move swiftly, causing illness and death, social chaos and political disaster around the globe, could be incubating right now in a remote part of China," said a report on *USA Today's* front page. "The prospect of pandemic influenza has scientists stacking up the public health equivalent of sandbags in anticipation…"

In the Atlantic, there were 65 tropical storms between 1995 and 1999 and 41 hurricanes, at one point four storms making their way across the ocean at the same time.

In 1999 five category-four hurricanes formed in a single season for the first time.

In Latin America — in Nicaragua, in Venezuela — it was already doomsday. In 1998 a massive storm stalled over Central America and dumped so much rain that people floated from one country to another. A whole crater lake collapsed and sent a wall of mud pounding down a mountain.

"*At the first blow of His thundering sword, the mountains and all Nature will tremble*," it had been said at LaSalette, and while 8,000 died in Central America, another 20,000 or more died as mountains collapsed in Venezuela in what the bishop publicly declared a "chastisement."

"Suddenly mountainous landslides became avalanches and streams of water became raging torrents," reported a shaken relief worker. "The huge wall of water, mud, and trees roared through the streets of Caracas like a freight train, sweeping away everything and everyone in its path. Thousands upon thousands of small red block homes were imploded by the force of the mud and with entire families inside were either swept down the ravines of the hills or violently sucked into underground water channels. People watched as their neighbors were ripped from their beds and drawn into the brown wall screaming helplessly, half of whom were children."

CHAPTER 36

A Haunted Countryside

This was in the future? This was just the warm-up? These were precursors?

In one terrific sweep, in one agonizing meander, the storm over Central America had ruined seventy percent of crops, ravaged a system of bridges that had taken fifty years to build, and set back the entire infrastructure of this region for decades — the terrain affected to such an extent that officials had to use satellites to remap rivers.

For months starving sallow-skinned children haunted the countryside while a volcano began to rumble and glow 22 miles from the collapsed lake.

In America officials recorded a tornado in Oklahoma City with the greatest recorded winds. It occurred on May 3, 1999, during an outbreak in the Oklahoma City area and registered at *318 miles an hour.*

"We had a good thirty-minute warning that it was coming," recalled Barbara Redman, a receptionist at First Baptist Church in Moore, a suburb. "When I heard it I was probably a mile from it and it was just a constant roar. I've heard stories from people who say they could feel themselves being sucked out of their homes, they could see themselves going around and around and around in front of a bathroom mirror, spinning around. It was like a monster coming. A *monster*. We at the church were like a command center and I can tell you a lot of stories of people who were thrown out of their homes. I remember one story of a man who put his two daughters in a bathtub and he himself was thrown out probably 150 yards from his house and when he got back into his house the girls were not in the bathtub but just hanging onto the toilet. The bathtub was gone. We had one school that was totally, totally destroyed. Then one of our high schools was very, very badly damaged and in the parking lot at this school cars — you cannot believe how the cars were. I saw a van that was about two feet tall. Totally squashed. Many, many, many cars destroyed and right in the middle was a dead horse. There was part of an airplane that came from many miles and we had people here in the church whose family pictures were found a hundred miles away. It was incredible the amount of stuff that was in the air, absolutely incredible. Homes were just totally destroyed. They set their big floodlights to shine up on the cross on top of our church and all they could do was just tell people to come to the cross. People began coming in and they were in shock. One of our members had a mobile home that was found just totally wrapped around a tree — I'm not sure how far away — and we had railroad cars moved and trees without a solitary leaf and no bark. Stripped absolutely clean. Devastation as far as you could see."

The righteous would suffer greatly, it said in Melanie's secret. There would be a *"continuous series of evolutions for three days,"* she also prophesied — she quoted Mary as prophesying — and the earth would *"open up its fiery bowels."*

This was now said too by modern seers. One I visited in Caracas had warned specifically of natural events, had said another epidemic was in the making, and that there would be earthquakes because the core of the earth was "not in balance." There was also the seer at Akita, Japan, and this concerned me: that the great rise in events would begin in Asia.

Was the land of Akita now about to experience what Venezuela, what Rwanda, what Nicaragua had? Was the sun rising here or ready to set? It was on the "ring of fire," the belt of hot volcanism and colliding plates — *fiery bowels* — and one had a sense that this region, if not in the secrets of Medjugorje, had a major disaster in its future, a disaster that would gather global notice, a disaster that might be part of the secrets, or at least a major precursor, announcing the onset of yet greater events elsewhere. Across Japan and also Taiwan, quakes rumbled on a daily basis. Taipei rocked. The buildings in Tokyo — where there was a "felt" quake on average once a week — swayed. There was no doubt that a big one would come and this was of urgent concern because at more than 27 million people Tokyo was now the most populated metropolitan area in the world.

Quake after quake. For the moment, small. But officials were threatened. I saw that when I toured their emergency center, sat where the mayor would sit, where the chiefs of industry would gather when the inevitable big one arrives. There were three major continental plates rubbing and grinding and subducting, tho most dangerous seismic zone in the world, just massive potential for ruin, and so the countdown in Tokyo was on. It was a matter of time. Officials knew this. They had huge cisterns of water stored at strategic places underground and expected a magnitude-7.5, which sounded optimistic. Sixty miles away in Tokai they expected an 8.5. There, a quake was "imminent," according to Keiji Doi, a senior scientific officer at the Japan Meteorological Agency's seismology division. Too much time had elapsed since the last and now the birds were coming to roost and it was this sense that was felt by the seers, by the prophets, and by the signs, including strange crows that had invaded Tokyo, birds described by *The Los Angeles Times* as "huge, jet-black creatures with intimidating beaks, killer claws, and a caw that sounds like a sea gull on steroids." They were eating everything, said the report, the rotten and still-living. They were stalking humans. They measured up to two feet and attacked those who made eye contact with them. They were blamed for starting a fire, "a blaze sparked when the birds picked up incense from a graveyard and dropped it on a nearby forest."

They were like a personification of evil and were all over: around the world the presence of crows, in England, in Ireland, in America, was at what seemed like an all-time high but I want to stay a minute on Asia. It was serious there. There were crows and quakes and on September 12, 2000, Japan had its worst rainstorm in a century. This was true across the region: storm after quake after flood after all forms of strange natural happenings. God had held back but now the time was short. You didn't need to be a seismologist to know it. In fact seismologists knew little. They were like the rest. They were feeling in the dark. Nature had evaded discovery. They knew a billion little pieces of the puzzle but no one knew how to put them together. An 8.5 in Tokai: at that level all the homes would collapse. *Imminent. In the near future.* Those were the words Doi used when I sat down with him and an array of top geophysical officials in Tokyo. There were also major volcanoes and they too were restless. There were evacuations every other week and a threat of tsunamis so severe that one town had erected a vault-like wall around itself — with gates that would be urgently slammed shut by a brigade upon a tsunami warning. As it was a quake-generated wave that reached up to a hundred feet had scoured the island of Hokkaido.

To walk beneath the endless glass skyscrapers in Tokyo was to see future panic, a density of population that would bear up poorly against a magnitude-7.5, not to mention an 8 or higher, and it was hard to believe that a place on such a hotspot was not going to see something at least that high.

Here there would be chastisement. Here there was great need of prayer. Here there was atheism and indifference. When finally I found a church to go to, a crippled old priest did the Mass and I was the only one in the pews. That kind of secularism had sent Tokyo's suicide rate soaring and opened the way to an unpleasant future. The events would come and when they did there might also be a typhoon. Recently a "supertyphoon" had narrowly missed causing what one risk analyst estimated would have been $100 billion in damage to Tokyo.

Would Japan continue to be so lucky? Would typhoons — typhoons that had strengthened, typhoons that were roaring now with winds of 185 miles an hour — continue to miss? "In all the traditional hurricane-forming belts — Fiji, the Caribbean, the Bay of Bengal, the Philippines, the Sea of Japan, the China Sea — and even outside the tropics we're finding very severe weather developing," Russell D. Thompson, an authority from the University of Reading in England, told me. "Certainly within the Philippines and Bay of Bengal there's been an increased frequency and intensity of storms."

The Pacific was at least as roiled as the Atlantic and the Philippines — the poor lowly Philippines, where there were *also* apparitions — was smack in the middle of it.

Waiting, knowing it would come due, hardly above sea level. God chastised those He loved. The Philippines were proof of that! It was getting pummeled; in one storm there had been 46 inches of rain! Throughout the region, throughout the troubled island states that hung there in the middle of the vast Pacific, conditions were ripening for an event that would garner world attention, that would announce or join in the coming run of events that would form global chastisement. The fires? In Indonesia they returned in 2000, flaring at the same time that quakes rattled the capital of Jakarta. One of the tremors was deep under the Sunda Straits, and that was eye-opening because it was the general area of the huge Krakatau volcano and also the suspected location of a volcano that may have upset the climate during the 550 A.D. event.

There was bound to be another epic cataclysm here, in the Philippines, or in Japan. There was bound to be a run of events. The signs were obvious across the breadth of Asia, especially in China, which had no moral compass, was showing the kind of antagonism to Christianity once reserved for the Soviets, and was engaged in the most atrocious persecution and degradation of human life since the Nazis. There was a policy that forced Chinese women who were carrying their second or third child to undergo abortion, and those who bucked it were jailed, brainwashed, and refused food until they went along with it. Many were in the third trimester, when the baby was six months or more in the womb, and the manner in which it was conducted turned the stomach. Shots were administered that caused babies to slowly die from heart failure over the course of several gruesome days, or formaldehyde was injected into the soft spot of the skull, or the head was crushed with forceps. A half a million died in the third trimester in such a fashion each year. "Chokers" were also used — white twisty things like garbage-bag ties that were yanked around the baby's neck at birth, causing a painful strangulation over the course of five minutes. Babies were drowned in buckets of water — often in front of the mother, if she had been uncooperative — or suffocated by stuffing towels into the young mouths and plugs in the noses. Most despicably, some fetuses were ground up in China and used in a broth as a health food.

Were we supposed to ignore this? Were there still Pollyannas who considered this "pro-choice"? Were we supposed to leave it unspoken so as not to *upset* ourselves?

CHAPTER 37

Signs in Asia

It was that kind of thinking that was taking the world to the brink. No way was God going to stand for that. It was why it was flooding in China. It was why that strange country, still steeped in Communism, still the "red dragon," had disaster after disaster. It was why floods came with such force that a million soldiers frantically sandbagging on the Yangtze along with four million peasants with shovels and picks and even using their hands couldn't stop it. Rain. Days and days of rain. It was either a drought or raining to the point of ruin, with 68 inches falling in 1998 in Qinzhou in eight weeks. Despite the effort of sandbaggers, five million homes were destroyed, 12 million damaged, sixty million acres of farmland were under water (more than three times the amount of land flooded by the Mississippi), and with agriculture, commerce, transportation, and water supplies disrupted, *an estimated 240 million Chinese were affected.*

Such numbers had not been seen in the West but were on the way; what happened in Asia would happen elsewhere. It was on the way. It would come soon. Mirjana had said the secrets were necessary to "shake up" people, to "make the world pause and think," and that too was coming for Asia, that would join the famine and drought and flood: great tremors, a shaking of the earth that would cause fatalities on a scale larger than even historic disasters. In 1556 830,000 had died in Shaanxi but there was one coming that would be bigger, from faults like those that near Beijing resulted from the accumulated force of India pressing into Asia and more importantly from the spiritual depravity. Like all good atheists Communist Chinese thought life was cheap; they were brutal. In one case officials had injected a woman with saline to abort her fourth child and when the baby managed to survive, they ordered the father to kill the child outside the hospital. He refused but was so scared he left the baby in an office building, where it was found by doctors shortly after and reunited with its mother at the hospital. When the woman and child were sent home, five officials were waiting for them in their living room and during an ensuing argument grabbed the baby, dragged it out of the house, and drowned it in a paddy field in front of the parents. That was the ugliness. Everything they had done in the Soviet system had also been done here and still *was* being done. To be a Christian was to be among the hunted. The faithful were forced to attend underground Masses, and at one, a large celebration in a remote field near a place called Dong Lu, four bishops, 110 priests, and 30,000 underground Chinese — all risking imprisonment — were reciting opening prayers when they saw the sun spin. "Rays of various colors emanated from the sun," said a report by the Cardinal Kung Foundation. "With the passing of the minutes, the sun changed colors, first to yellow, then to red and blue, followed by other colors. Subsequently people saw different apparitions in the core of the sun: a holy cross, the Holy Family, Holy Mary, and the Holy Eucharist. At times the sun would approach the crowd and then retreat. People were heard crying out, 'Holy Mother, have pity on us, your children.'"

This was another sign. Soon there was bound to be an epic disturbance here. There was a seismic pulse throbbing across the breadth of southern Asia and it was ensuring that in short order something above the normal seismic event would occur. There was going to be major destruction. It was going to come in waves, first the report of hundreds dead, then thousands, then many more. Perhaps hundreds of thousands.

For now, tremors. Every week, sometimes every day, a quake in Taiwan. A build up. Small quakes into larger. It was a myth that they relieved pressure; just as often they were forerunners. From 1993 to 1997 the number of small tremors had jumped from 5,500 to 15,000 in Taiwan — tripling just as hailstorms had tripled and leading up to a quake that had killed 1,700 in 1999.

Small quakes had led to a larger one. Elementary. And Taiwan wasn't alone. The same was happening in Turkey and now we were really returning to what had occurred in the Bronze Age. That's where the ground was rumbling and it flashed back to the ancients in their sandals and the flaming falling courtyards and the busted pottery tainted with soot.

It was returning. There were quake storms, a series of ongoing tremors. On August 17, 1999, at least 17,000 were killed as a quake erupted on the North Anatolian Fault, the crack responsible for Bronze Age destruction.

Quakes shook India, Turkmen-istan, and Pakistan, killed thousands in Iran and Afghanistan, trembled under Greece, hitting all the old territories. They were clustering, and in a most curious manner, they were accompanied by typhoons. On July 5, 2000, a storm swiped at the Batanes Islands in the Philippines at the same time — on the exact same day — that a quake shook those islands.

The typhoon then made its way to Japan and socked the eastern part of *that* country — and just hours after an earthquake with a preliminary magnitude of 4.7 rocked Kozushima.

Mongolia. India. Quakes were ready to let go of pent-up energy near the Himalayas where high magnitude-eights could occur. There were many places that were prone and had been quiet too long. There was too much evil. "The devas who are worshipped as gods or goddesses by pagans are actually devils because, in hundreds of cases of exorcisms, I have come across these devas or devils under various names confessing against their wills that they are coming from the depths of hell," wrote a priest named Robert Lewis in a letter from his post near Ajmer, and indeed, there was an eruption of demonism. It was out in the open. In Mochi Para, Loot Para, Jaruadih, and Rasikpur were tales of an "invisible" assailant called the *Murkatwa* that was haunting the night and causing such fear that people in remote areas like Godda and Sahebganj were fleeing to West Bengal.

There was possession. People thrashed on the ground. They went into convulsions. It was said that powders (or *prasaads*) dedicated to Kali — a violent, snarling goddess — were slipped into the food of the unsuspecting.

The same was true in Africa. During the summer of 2000, schools were closed over a wide area near Nairobi in Kenya after dozens of students claimed to have been assaulted by voodoo "ghosts." It was as weird as it was remarkable. First a secondary school in the central province 120 miles from Nairobi was closed, then a high school about 30 miles from Nairobi. The students claimed that stones came from nowhere, that they were slapped and punched by unseen hands. That they felt as if they were being strangled. Dozens made this claim, and it spread like an epidemic. Was it just hysteria, a prank, drugs? Or as students claimed were there practitioners of voodoo in the school system? I know only that there were too many strange things going on in Africa for it all to be a product of the imagination. "On July 3, students from Wang-uru Girls Secondary School, Kirinyaga (113 miles northwest of Nairobi) stormed the office of the Central Provincial director of education protesting the invasion of their school by ghosts," reported the Panafrican News Agency. "The students said they were terrified by the alleged demons, which they claimed appeared in the form of cats and black snakes. They further claimed the creatures, which run around their dormitories, had been introduced by their head-teacher. Angry parents had stormed the school and took away their children for fear they might be attacked by demons."

There were other cases, as if, truly, hell was unbound. Spirits were said to have invaded a primary school in Kitui and a girls' school in Macakos, where they supposedly entered St. Theresa Dormitory and had sexual contact with students like a classic incubus. Exorcists were called in. A legislator warned people to protect themselves. The hauntings were followed by some of the worst road and rail accidents in Kenya's history, a major fire in Nairobi, a blackout that affected the entire nation, and the murder of a priest. Whatever was behind it, there was widespread witchcraft in too many African countries, there was still rampant sexual promiscuity, and the combination of evils had lead to suffering and was about to lead to much more. If it wasn't enough that AIDS was on its way to claiming 25 million lives (and if the other diseases that arose from here like voodoo itself — like the potion of a witch doctor — weren't scourges enough), now the Dark Continent was about to go through a series of floods, droughts, and famines. The name of the game was extremes, and the same was true for the Mideast, with temperatures in some countries breaking 130 degrees.

As the Middle East heated like the Sahara, its old climate was creeping north to southern Europe, where rain had become sporadic, rivers were drying, and fires raged. Italy, Spain, and Greece were starting to feel like Israel and it was the same in the south of France while just north in Switzerland, Germany, and Austria, in England and Ireland, in Poland, the problem was the opposite: too *much* rain.

The collision of pressure systems had bumped into a high mode and dragged in air like a vacuum. There were storms in Austria and Germany, and Holland was seeing frightening floods at the same time that it was leading the way with free sex, abortion, and euthanasia. Europe was getting the equivalent of hurricanes, gales of 95 miles an hour, and they were reaching as far as Italy, where the Colosseum — the ancient arena where so many Christians had been martyred — was being readied for its first spectacles, a series of plays, in 1,500 years.

CHAPTER 38

A Change in Landscape

This was startling because the LaSalette secret had referred to *"pagan Rome."* It had also mentioned the *"king of kings of darkness,"* the beast with his subjects, at the same time that the world was swiftly heading for a new order that would serve as a platform for such a "king." It was happening with the unification of countries at the United Nations right on America soil, soil that had been stained with the blood of abortion and now had been cursed as had the soil that absorbed the blood of Abel (*Genesis* 4:10) — crying for justice, which was coming. America had let evil happen and now waited for disasters of its own, knew a number of them were in the wings, and more than anything sensed the coming of mega-hurricanes.

Somewhere out there in the Atlantic, Caribbean, or Gulf was a storm as no one had seen.

Great hurricanes were coming.

Their way would be paved by a change in our surroundings. It would warm, and then possibly chill, as it had in the time of the Vikings. In any major chastisement there was a change in the very nature of physical surroundings. And this too was starting. In Monterey crabs were moving north; on the East Coast fewer robins were heading south for the winter. And like the Middle Ages, ice was vanishing. There was a fundamental change in the very nature of northern territories. Glaciers were melting so swiftly it was now expected that within fifty years there would be no more ice in America's Glacier National Park. Arctic ice had shrunk by 14 percent; there was such a melt that Greenland was in need of remapping. In parts of Alaska temperatures reached eight and even ten degrees above normal during the winter and Checkerspot butterflies, once indigenous to Mexico, were spotted as far north as Canada. There was now a third of a degree rise in average global surface temperatures every decade, and that rate was projected to double. No one had any idea what such an increase would mean. But it was dangerous. It was very dangerous. If a degree or two could melt glaciers, if ice shelves in the Antarctic were already threatened, if there was already very erratic weather, what would doubling it all bring? And could it go higher? And faster? Could it reverse into a severe spell of cold?

No one knew. There were too many variables. But scientists were aware of one thing, and that was the fact that during the past 100,000 years there had been at least 22 events that they described as climatic "jolts": times when (in geologic time) change came nearly instantly. "It seems when we look to the past, those transitions happened very, very quickly," I was told by Dr. Peter B. deMonocal of Columbia University. "Really, really large transitions seem to have occurred in the tropics and elsewhere too. There was a time when the Sahara Desert was covered with lakes and completely vegetated. During that time there were crocodiles in an area that today receives no rainfall at all. The end of that happened about 5,500 years ago and the transition happened on the order of a hundred years."

In just a century a territory the size of the United States had changed from one vegetal state to another that was completely different. "We used to think climate changed gradually, like slowly turning up a dial on an oven, but it's more like a light switch," said Dr. Jeffrey P. Severinghaus of the Scripps Institution of Oceanography, who found that there had been times in the past when temperatures in the Arctic had increased *nine to 18 degrees* in less than three decades.

At the high end that averaged to six degrees a decade and as one scientist from the University of Maryland phrased it, a change of five degrees in a decade "would be a calamity."

There was no reason (as yet) to panic over that. The figures cited were for the Arctic (where variations are often extreme), and usually for periods that, unlike our own, were coming out of an ice age. They were not for climates like ours, not that anyone knew. But still: just a *third* of such a jump would be of major concern, a "runaway" climate. And whether or not the temperatures remained on the increase (there was a chance that the climate jolt could kick earth into a sudden cooling trend), the graphline was bound to form a zig-zag. Gone were the smooth gradual curves. The climate was swerving, and for now was in an up pattern, as during the onset of the Medieval Event, which ended, of course, with a drop in climate.

Was the switch about to be thrown again? Was the oven on high or just warming up — still heating? The official estimate was that temperatures could increase by as much as six degrees this century! Whether that was accurate or not, there was this to consider: with less ice in the world there would now be less reflection of heat back into space. That might further push the rise. And all the wildfires, the flames from Oakland to the Amazon, the Indonesian peat burns, were pumping all the more carbon dioxide into the air, which added to global warming. There was thus an exponential effect. It was also true with the oceans: the warmer they were, the more carbon they released. A vicious circle. The same release of carbon occurred when permafrost thawed.

So there was the chance that temperatures would bolt further, but how far up? Virtually all major governments agreed that the trend was sharply up but not one could be certain of the future. No one could see more than a few years down the road. There could be a sudden plunge. There could be a rocketing. Right now it looked like sweltering years ahead. God was loosing the forces of nature. He was allowing commotion in the natural order. There was one overriding factor in climate, one force that bore on all others, and that was the Holy Spirit. He controlled the forces under Him. He controlled sunlight and magnetism and gravity; He was in ultimate control of the wind. And He was shaking things up. He wanted change. We could only plead His mercy. The current heating could reverse. Eventually, it would; what went up would come down. But for now there was great heating and that augured yet more dramatic change in landscape. Already New England was becoming more like New Jersey and New Jersey more like Maryland. With each degree of warming it was said the landscape shifted 100 miles north. While overall the warmth would pump more moisture into the air, there would be pockets — sometimes huge pockets — of drought. It was starting. There had been great dryness throughout the United States. In 1999 the longest drought on the East Coast of the U.S. in decades was followed by drought in 2000 that set off wildfires in California, Colorado, Washington, New Mexico, Montana, and Arizona. This hearkened to ancient droughts that used to stretch from Minnesota to Mexico, from the Great Plains to California. At one point Texas sought declaration of three-fourths of its counties as disaster areas. It was that dry. It was that hot. It took soldiers to fight the flames. Curious was how several of the fires directly threatened federal nuclear facilities in New Mexico, Idaho, and the state of Washington — at one point causing the evacuation of Los Alamos, where the first atomic bomb was constructed. It had been a century since the Mid-Atlantic was as dry, and then came more rain than anyone wanted. There was no overriding trend except the trend of extremes and a general unraveling. *That* was the trend. And much more was on the way. There would be huge monsoons. There would be cyclones that took two or three times the toll of the one in 1970. There could be a surge that killed more than a few hundred thousand. We were approaching disasters that could cost the lives of millions. Without prayer winds would hurtle trees in India and Bangladesh and blast thatched homes out of existence.

SENT TO EARTH

CHAPTER 39

The Storm Next Time

Great storms were coming in whatever direction the thermometer swerved but especially if more heat was pumped into the system.

No one knew the full story but besides the cycle lasting two to four decades and involving temperature, ocean currents, and stratospheric winds, there was also the distinct chance that the ancient cycle of hurricanes a magnitude higher than even the highest current category was kicking in. Was the Middle Ages, so similar to what was now going on, going to repeat itself in this regard also? Were we going to see the kinds of storms that had been witnessed in the medieval warming, and before that in the Bronze Age? If so it meant hurricanes the likes of which we can only imagine, and it wasn't just a product of climate. The forces were more mysterious than that. They operated in a way that transcended science. And it was a true use of the word awesome. There were indications that in the past storms had hit with surges twice what was seen during Andrew, up to forty feet, inundating a vicinity near Naples, Florida. "From the historical record there's evidence of some extreme hurricanes that hit this state from A.D. 800 to 1400 in the last global warming period," I was told by Erle Peterson of the Dade County emergency office. "There's a classic work where they found a Calusa Indian village on Marco Island in Collier County that was buried underneath a 20-foot sand dune. The thing that was unusual is that everything was intact like a Pompeii event. The sand was put there, as near as they can tell, all at one time. And the only thing that could put a twenty-foot sand dune there all at one time is a storm surge."

Although some claimed the sand was a remnant of ancient Indian burial mounds, Peterson argued that burial mounds contained skulls (which were detached from the body) and broken pottery (which had been ritually shattered when no longer used), where these heaps were not layered and contained unbroken pottery and whole skeletons.

It was as if something huge and unexpected had come upon them. And Peterson believed that "something" had been a hyper-hurricane with sustained winds of 250 to 260 miles an hour.

Were these the type of storms that Gilbert, that Andrew, had hinted at? Were they coming back?

Over the past twenty years at least ten percent more moisture had been pumped into the atmosphere, and that was like octane. This was what fueled superstorms. Big storms fed off moisture. Moisture and turmoil. It wasn't just heat. A sudden flux that caused an atmospheric "wave" in the tropics was enough to trigger it, and it didn't even matter if it was a busy hurricane season or a quiet one: The big ones — the Gilberts, the Andrews — had come in calm times, and so there was a constant risk that could only be discerned through prayer. For now what we could know was that there had been a substantial increase in precipitation and it was concentrating in the large events (*half* of the increase in rainfall was in the top ten percent of intense storms), which meant high-end storms were heading higher. There was going to be greater than Andrew. It was going to be greater than the Labor Day Hurricane. While it wasn't a prerequisite, the more hurricanes the better chance there was of one ballooning into an event that would be apocalyptical, and some years, as in 1995, they were lining up like planes at an airport. Would they continue? Would they combine? Would they join moisture? Would a storm the size of Hugo, which had devastated the Carolina coast, or Typhoon Tip, which had a reach of a thousand kilometers, develop a level of intensity known previously only to smaller hurricanes like Camille, Labor Day, or Andrew?

A bullet had been dodged when Hurricane Floyd, a massive system, looked for a while like it might reach category-five status and hit the east coast of Florida in 1999, which would have been the first time in recent centuries. There had been panic. The President had cut short a trip. It was a storm larger than the state of Texas. Officials ordered the largest evacuation in American history. That had been a close call, but the warnings were ending and soon there were going to be direct hits. As always, it was conditional (there was still time to convert, there was still time to pray), but the tremendous fortune we had seen with recent hurricanes was ready to give way and storms that were both larger and more powerful than Floyd were stored in all the energy flowing in huge ocean gyres. There were going to be hurricanes that combined force and there were going to be hurricanes that came one after another, that wandered where they had never gone, that stalled over areas like the one had in Nicaragua, that hit the same places more than once, or that battered different parts of the U.S. at the same time.

Some of them would be larger than any we had seen and at least one would be the most powerful on record. That was my take on it. It was in the milieu that would compose or usher in chastisement. And it was coming. The question was when, where.
While there was an increasing chance of a big storm heading north, all the way to New York or Cape Cod (where Dr. Liu was starting to see indications of major storms in ancient times), and while Pacific hurricanes were begin-

ning to circle close to California (as had a monster named Linda), the key threat, the nail biting, remained on coastal land from Virginia to Texas.

Houston was three times likelier to get the big one than New York and Florida half-again likelier than Texas.

In the middle of that stretch, on the way to Texas, at the most vulnerable part of the coast, was New Orleans, and this was a truly special case; this was enough to raise goose bumps. We have to stop here a moment. This is worthy of special consideration. For New Orleans had a long history of violent hurricanes, had been escaping them for an inordinate length of time, was thus overdue (a word we will see used over and over), and was not only low to the water but below sea level.

Emergency managers in New Orleans and neighboring Jefferson Parish told me that all it would take would be a direct hit by category-three or four to put the entire city under water! There were parts of New Orleans that were below sea level by 12 feet, which meant that a hurricane with a 17-foot surge (far below what may have occurred in the Middle Ages) would put the entire City of New Orleans under more than twenty feet of surge!

The whole area was like a bowl surrounded by levees that in normal times protected against river flooding but in a hurricane would trap water that came from the Gulf or sloshed from Lake Pontchartrain. On Bourbon Street there would be water to the second story. Those who didn't evacuate would head for their attics with axes (in case they had to chop their way to the roof), while others would get trapped on the sole interstate (which emergency planners said was totally inadequate).

There were 900,000 in the metro area. It would take a minimum of 48 hours to evacuate them. At that point forecasters still would not know within a hundred miles where the storm was going to hit. In the best of circumstances officials believed that at least 100,000 would be stranded. There were that many without personal transportation, and many who would choose to brave the storm — not knowing the kind of storms that once had hit, that had caused mayhem as recently as the 19th century. Hundreds of thousands coming from the lower parishes would likewise find themselves trapped. All in all Walter Maestri of emergency management in Jefferson estimated that a direct hit by a major hurricane — something that happened in this area before it had grown so populous — would cause between 25,000 and 75,000 dead.

SENT TO EARTH

CHAPTER 40

Kings of the World

The return rate for a category three in New Orleans was 31 years, a category four 65 years, and a categoty five 170 years. There had been significant hits in the 1800s and Camille had missed New Orleans by a mere thirty miles.

Clearly, something would come here soon. If it was a five, said Maestri, if it made landfall somewhere between New Orleans and Baton Rouge, it would be "the most catastrophic hurricane in the history of the United States." At first residents would watch in fascination as tides built, but that would quickly turn to horror. It would be one big bathtub. The water would rise to the ankles, the hips, the knees, would quickly climb up porch steps as it poured into the heart of the city.

At the Gulf swells would crest and spray blindingly. Refineries and chemical plants would be blown out of existence. Hotels would be leveled. The surge would sweep across bayous, blast open restaurants. On the coast residents would scurry for trees that snapped, and were swept into seas that looked like rapids. Water that has piled into the northwestern corner of Pontchartrain would slosh toward the city like a tilted saucer. It would dwarf Galveston. It would be like the last of voodoo, every curse, had been answered, had been exiled — as if God were finally cleansing this poor area of the evil that had infiltrated, that was now so pervasive. Would the people of New Orleans wake up? Would they pray? Would they get rid of the pornography and strip joints or keep tempting fate as Galveston had tempted it?

Every year there was the Mardis Gras, and while this had started as "Fat Tuesday" before the fasting of Lent, there was no longer fasting, just this extravaganza with huge devilish faces on floats surrounded by the pomp of barely clad dancers who would have felt right at home in the gardens of a Roman emperor or on a barge on the Nile or in a Venusian temple — the streets overflowing with revelers wearing bizarre dark masks.

It may once have been good fun but now it spoke to the demonic. It was like the Mardis Gras in Galveston that had been called "day of the devils" and would lead to similar consequences.

There were voodoo shops and graveyard tours and psychics on the sidewalk in front of the cathedral.

Now, there would also be events. I heard it everywhere I went. No matter the state or country or town, people sensed it. Things were coming. Close. Closer. It was an intuition and it was not meant to bring fear but prayer. She had been shown *"many horrors,"* Mirjana had said. *"Really distressing"* things. Like a dam that collapsed somewhere. Like a dam: It was why there was such a call to prayer. And to fasting! At Medjugorje Mary had said that we could prevent wars, we could suspend natural laws, but it had to be done soon. The United States was headed down a path of destruction. It would melt like the snow in spring. Its remarkable ascent, its run of luck, would be breached by a series of disasters. That was coming, events that would cause the whole world to tune in, that would be heard from afar, by everyone, everywhere, that would be what Mirjana said was a wakeup. People were greedy and as the official exorcist from Rome, Father Gabriele Amorth, warned, there was a veritable flood of demonism, infestation, and obsession. "Unfortunately, in the past fifteen years, we have witnessed an increase, almost an explosion, of these types of associations," wrote the priest about all the occult organizations. "The first factor that influences the increase of evil influences is Western consumerism. The majority of people have lost their faith due to materialistic and hedonistic lifestyle." He had exorcised people who were diabolically afflicted because of drugs, abortion, magic, false visions, and money, he said, and it was all the worse because mainstream churches no longer addressed it. The devil wasn't mentioned from the pulpit. They were too concerned with "scaring" people, offending them, sounding old-fashioned. It didn't fit with the atmosphere of "feelgoodism," and so the example of Christ and His disciples warning of devils and casting them out had been all but lost. There was silence. Utter fearful silence. Which let it fester all the more. The majority of people had lost their faith due to lust and materialism, said the exorcist, and while church attendance was higher in the United States than in many nations — far higher than parts of northern Europe (which in Scandinavia was as low as four percent), and higher than most of Latin America. The majority felt that abortion was murder but in what can only be termed extreme indifference, the majority also felt that it was up to the woman to choose!

Murder of this kind was okay as long as they couldn't see it. When films depicted Christ in a derogatory way, or when a museum exhibited a "portrait" of the Madonna with elephant dung thrown at it (as happened in New York), there was no real clamor against it.

Most simply tuned it out, switched to another website or channel. Unless it affected the stock market, few took notice. And we would pay for this. Oh, would we pay for this! Christ had said He would spit out the lukewarm (*Revelation* 3:16) and this kind of apathy had preceded other chastisements. Society hadn't advanced; it was mimicking societies that were now 4,500 years old; it had taken huge steps into the past.

Such was the darkness and it was dangerous because Christ had warned that bad trees, bad wood, would be tossed into the fire. He had warned of hell. I wasn't making this up. It was Christ Who was tough. It was Jesus Who warned because Jesus loved. He had come to bring people to a place of eternal happiness, and if that meant chastising, here on earth, so be it; it was better than letting more of His children fall into the clutches of His eternal enemy, and so, yes, storms approached, great winds, winds that no meteorologist would be able to anticipate. There were more than a million infants being exterminated in the U.S. each year and 46 million around the world (just short of the total casualties for World War Two), and it was hard to see how God was going to put up with that, a practice abhorred even by the Romans. A world war every year! And done by doctors, by those who were supposed to save, but who now looked at the practice of medicine as one looked at a car dealership. Profit. Money. It was the idol. It was paid the greatest reverence. The worst known disasters, the famines that had swept Africa — the drought and hunger that killed millions of Chinese — couldn't compare with the number killed by abortion, and so, if God now sent events that swept away entire areas, if it looked like He was being "cruel," one had to weigh that against how many were being "terminated" (sacrificed to Asmodeas) in that area.

God was trying to purge. It was His mercy. It's what He used when we didn't take the hint as there had now been *so* many hints. Incredible as it seemed, the United States, founded on God, in the spirit of Christianity — invoking His name constantly — had now degenerated into a nation so ruthless that babies were yanked from the womb in late-term procedures that forced open their skull and sucked the brains out as the little legs frantically wiggled. There was a market in fetal parts! Actual corporations had been set up to "harvest" limbs and organs and brain tissue, with medical researchers now able to specify how much of the pelvic bone they wanted or how freshly cut they needed a leg.

No ancient society had been any colder than that. Fetal parts were being shipped via overnight delivery! It was done under the guise of donations (so as to avoid illegality) and quiet, too, equally discrete, was the research into cloning. Dangerous experiments were ongoing. We were changing the makeup of plants, tinkering with the very genetic code, manipulating human eggs, combining human and animal cells to create spare human parts (trying to grow a human ear on the back of a mouse), designing ways of incubating human eggs in rats, cloning sheep and an array of other animals, and heading of course to the greatest feat science could conceive: the cloning of an actual human.

That would be ascendancy; man could transcend mortality. Who needed God? Who needed religion? Who needed the Spirit? That had all been for primitives who didn't understand nucleic acids — who didn't know DNA — but now we could forge to a new future where man and only man ruled the kingdoms of the world.

SENT TO EARTH

CHAPTER 41

A Remarkable Horror

Satan was at highest dudgeon. It was now illegal to mention God at school but it was okay for kids to play occult games that invoked the name of fallen angels. That summed up the diabolical disorientation and it was leading to what the kids at LaSalette, Fatima, and now Medjugorje had warned about. Men simply could not discern good from evil and that meant chastisement. It had happened in the time of Moses. It had happened with plagues and hail and frogs sent when the Egyptians had been disobedient, the gnats, the darkness — the water like blood — the flies, the boils. Melanie had foreseen the destruction of several cities and the third secret of Fatima included the vision of *"a big city half in ruins."* Whether or not these prophecies had come already (for instance at Hiroshima) or remained in the future, they afforded an outline by which chastisement seemed first to befall particular areas, and then the globe — through both fire and water.

"The seasons will be altered, the earth will produce nothing but bad fruit, the stars will lose their regular motion, the moon will only reflect a faint reddish glow," Melanie had written (to partially repeat what she had said, as we approach what looked like further fulfillment). *"Water and fire will give the earth's globe convulsions and terrible earthquakes which will swallow up mountains, cities."*

Wars. Famines. Plagues. "Infectious disease." City-shaking thunderstorms. Fire that would *"consume three cities."*

Earthquakes that would *"swallow up countries."* She also mentioned *"a fearful hail of animals,"* and had re-emphasized that *"water and fire will purge the earth and consume all the works of men's pride and all will be renewed."*

Oddly enough, it had rained animals. Waterspouts had picked up fish and rained them on parts of England. But the entire prophecy had not yet occurred. Whole nations had not been destroyed from quakes, the stars had not lost their regular motion, the moon had not yet reflected a reddish glow, the seasons were only now altering, and while two cities had seen fire (Nagasaki as well as Hiroshima, unless one tossed in the burning of Dresden), the secret had predicted an event that consumed not two but three cities, as well as fire and water that gave the globe *"convulsions."*

The events foreseen involved a violent thrashing of water and did not limit the water to one event. In fact in using the plural *convulsions,* the prophecy from LaSalette implied a number of events, and one candidate was a "monster" hurricane. The question was: where? Would it be New Orleans — or something larger? Would Christ intercede again, stand as the obstacle to punishment — would His mother so beseech him, quenching chastisement as she was shown dousing the flames from the angel — or would the evil rank as so great as to bring a remarkable horror, wind that whipped sand as at Islamorada, piled water on flailing, gasping residents as the banners and t-shirts and beads from souvenir shops and Mardis Gras floated as rubble?

The idea that the "Big Easy," with its flourish of jazz and history and culinary splendor, could find itself under two stories of water, was not to be taken lightly. Something was going to hit here. It might not be the mega-storm and it might not send a surge to the feared extent, but something would materialize and gain strength in those warm Gulf waters if New Orleans didn't purge itself of an evil that was now engrained in the culture.

From New Orleans to Houston and on to Corpus Christi (which meant the "body of Christ") was great danger. God was going to send something this way if America did not repent. Jonah was once more calling to Nineveh. Would it listen? Would it pray and don sackcloth? Would leaders pay heed? Or would they choose to ignore the warnings, including those that had occurred recently by way of storms?

In 1999 the run of hurricanes that made landfall had included one which in fact had been expected to hit Corpus Christi but in a remarkable example of God's mercy had made landfall between Corpus Christi and Brownsville, in a county with less than 500 people.

How long would such mercy last? It had already gone on longer than many expected. From Texas to Florida were many good Christians — evangelicals, deliverance ministries, charismatics, pentecostals, Catholics, bible groups, and just plain faithful — who might yet forestall the huge disaster that was impending, but now was the time to hurry; now was the time to step up; now was the time to take the warnings public. Would people think this was nuts? Of *course* they would think it was nuts. Many could accept only certain parts, the pleasant parts, of Christ's teachings. When it came to admonitions, when it came to disaster (especially something that might interfere with a cushy lifestyle), when it came to warnings that immorality lead to ruin, this they classified as something embarrassing, as the "fringe," as notions that were to be avoided at all costs. The Bible was full of admonitions and leaders like Reagan and the Pope believed in divine retribution (in the case of John Paul, had earnestly implored the public to pray at a time he deemed as one of great darkness), yet now many who professed Christianity or at least registered it as their official religion relegated divine chastisement to the realm of superstition. God didn't send storms; the elements — the earth, the oceans, the air — did.

But in fact God did send storms or at least allowed them — allowed devils to scourge — and Texas too had to worry. While a seawall had been constructed in Galveston and land raised after the tragedy in 1900, there were still parts that were low or unprotected and the wall, 15 to 17 feet, would not keep out the surge from a storm that heaved twenty to thirty feet in the upper end of the bay — reaching all the way to the Johnson Space Flight Center. When I asked Tessa Duffy, an emergency manager at Galveston, what would happen if a category five came, she said simply, "It would be gone," and that was sobering because there were now 275,000 living in the county. From there the storm could sweep fifty miles west to attack Houston.

Chapter 42
Ground Zero

There were any number of scenarios but the most frightening was the most obvious and that was in Florida. For decades the state had been in a quiet cycle and in that time the population had exploded. Apartments, condos, boutiques, hotels, resorts, plazas, and gated communities — the richest of the rich — now stood along the shore like bowling pins. Less than 15 percent of the residents had experienced a strong storm, and the state was overwhelmed with newcomers. On average 770 were moving there each day, and most were locating on the coasts! The odds told the story; only God could prevent the kind of disaster that was being sown. A category five was expected within 75 miles of Miami every 32 years, and it had been twice that — nearly seventy years — since Islamorada. Andrew was a category four, and had it not missed Miami (which it did of course by a hair), it would have destroyed an estimated 100 hospitals, 125,000 businesses, 225,000 homes.

And as we have already seen, that was by no means the most powerful storm that could hit Florida. Where Andrew blustered with winds that may have gusted to 200 miles an hour, there were simple calculations that presented the ingredients for a much more terrifying storm. Scientists in England told me they expected a 25 percent increase in top winds with projected warming while at Princeton calculations called for an increase of up to 12 percent.

This was "conservative" data, numbers that erred on the low side because scientists did anything they could not to scare the public. Yet even figures like these were dramatic: Applied to top sustained winds, an increase of 12 percent would have given Labor Day sustained winds of up to 225 miles an hour, with gusts well over 250. There were those who claimed that the gusts at Islamorada already *had* been that high, so a 12 percent hike would have brought projections closer to 280. Moreover, according to the Hurricane Center, new technology now indicated that past wind speeds had been understated *by as much as twenty percent.* If we applied that to the increase in winds projected to occur with continued global warming, actual sustained winds would be at least 230 to 250 with gusts heading into the category of a major tornado.

At the same time, the mega-storm would be massive. Where Andrew's swath was only thirty miles, winds of hurricane force could extend more than a hundred miles from a major storm and possibly up to two or three times that. The eye alone could be larger than Andrew. There were hurricanes like Gilbert that had been just as powerful but many times larger and Tip had the gale-force winds with a radius of 600 miles. As for barometric pressure, Dr. Gray believed the limit was the 870 recorded with Tip, but Peterson argued that if temperatures continued to increase, it could go much lower. "Gilbert was the most potent (at 888) we've measured in the Atlantic, but I feel absolutely confident that it's not even close to the maximum that can be done," he said.

Could a storm plunge to 860? To 850?
Anything was possible in a climate that was swerving. It wasn't just a matter of heat; it was the flux. Energy was released when there was change. Even cooler periods had spawned major storms, and this indicated as much as anything the role of *instability.*

It depended on how volatile the air was, and by all signs it was swerving. Everyone (save those buried in statistics) noticed it, the way it would be totally dry somewhere and then that area would see nothing but rain. In the Northeast it might be a cool wet summer while in the West (as during 2000) fires raged. The only consistency was that events were growing extreme. Scientists tried to explain it as variations within a larger curve but simple observation told the story of increasingly radical behavior. The weather was erratic. Things were plunging or rising. There were no more middle areas. Commuters knew it; farmers knew it. The sun was either in hiding or *scorching*. There were no longer the intermediates of just a few years before, and that meant instability, which meant energy — which was what caused hurricanes. Sudden storms in Africa would send a pressure wave that tumbled into pressure systems over the Atlantic and began an undulation which caused great drafts of moisture, the commotion only enhanced as yet more moisture rose with air that was sent up yet faster — nucleating, tossing everything into motion, feeding on its own frenzy.

In a climate that was unsteady there was no reason why such a storm would not balloon into larger than Gilbert or Tip with winds of destructive force for several hundred miles. That meant the possibility of trauma for Florida. A new up-cycle was in place, would last a minimum of 15 years, and few were prepared for it. Florida had been "extremely lucky," said Gray, "just unbelievably spared," but was now a "recipe for disaster." At Cocoa Plum mansions were being erected on land that had been under whitecaps in 1965 during a hurricane called Betsy!

That had been a category three; what was coming now was a five; without prayer, no doubt about it. If not Florida, Virginia or the Carolinas. A five or a five-plus. And Dr. Gray was right: It was going to be a tragedy. There were now 6.7 million people in Florida who were susceptible to the effects of a category five, and even without further warming we were entering into what Gray deemed "a new hurricane era."

The big ones were coming, he warned. Maybe not next year, maybe not the year after, but they were coming. And it would deserve the term "mega," with Florida and specifically the "Gold Coast," the corridor between Miami and Palm Beach, the most inviting target, a candidate for the kind of event that would be heard by everyone everywhere. For a day or two it would be like the world stopped. The damage would be spectacular. This was a 60-mile stretch of luxury and honky-tonk and if decadence was the target, the area had more than its share of drug dealers, pornographers, discos, Santeria practitioners, gay bars, and among the country's most flagrant practitioners of materialism. There were yachts with helipads parked in canals in front yards!

Hundreds. Sitting there. Trying to turn earth into utopia. It was the old lie, that immortality was here, a fountain of youth, and this artificiality like the artificiality in the rest of the world was soon to be torn down. Would the faithful save it? Would the little cells of Christians who prayed here avert what was on the way — or was this where one of the events, one of the tragedies that would begin the grinding down of America, was destined to happen?

It was like Tyre. It was like the railing of the Lord against the city of great wealth and haughtiness and beauty and balm, threatening to "churn the abyss against you, and its mighty waters" (*Ezekiel* 26:19), striking it with the very heart of the sea. That was what would happen. 860 millibars? 850? It could be a storm larger than Tip and with greater intensity than any known hurricane. If it took this route, if it came from Africa, on the way it would erase islands. Barbados. St. Lucia. Martinique. There would be panic at the Hurricane Center. It would pound San Juan, crush the voodoo in Haiti. Entire islands would be uninhabitable for years after. And that would only be the beginning. So large would this one be that hurricane warnings would be posted from Norfolk to Key West. It would make Hugo look like a pittance. There would be traffic tie-ups from Miami to Orlando. Officials would urgently tell residents who had not evacuated to immediately move inland, where they'd be advised to seek shelter in cement or brick buildings. There would be a mandatory evacuation of a flock of barrier islands: Miami Beach, Key Biscayne. Soon they'd realize the entire eastern coast was in danger. All highway lanes would be turned northerly and bullhorns would rouse residents as far north as Georgia. No official liked to call for evacuation, but near its eye a mega-storm would not be survivable. There would be no refuge in a bathtub. Maximum concentric winds would be thousands of pounds per square foot. That's beyond catastrophic. Without God's grace that's what could happen. On radar the whirls would pulse, radiating like plasma. More air would be sucked in and as it was, more water would evaporate. The storm would feed on itself, spin faster. Total energy behind such a storm would more than equal five years of world energy consumption! It would be like a half a megaton — 33 Hiroshimas — every minute. If it hit this way at this angle it would send gusts of 150 miles an hour when it was still hundreds of miles off Florida.

Already, there would be tidal waves. They would rise steadily but quickly and break in such a way that some would see whitewater up their streets. What had started as overwash would rise into huge swells exploding with spray. The nation — the world — would watch as the storm-of-all-storms swept over the Bahamas like a giant cogwheel dealing hateful tongues of red and violet on the radar.

Panic. Could anyone survive within a hundred miles of this? Could the hurricane center — built with those ten-foot walls — itself survive?

There would be final communication from the Federal Emergency Management Agency and evacuees in some areas — in areas where surf was roaring over the roads — would be urged to leave their cars and seek the highest points. Networks would go to live coverage. Officials would scream at those who remained to seek cover. There would no longer be time for evacuation. It could happen anywhere. It could happen in Gulfport. It could happen in Virginia Beach. It could also be halted. Faith could do anything. It could move mountains (*Matthew* 17:20). And this would need such faith. If in Florida there'd be no leaving the Keys. There would be horror again at Islamorada. There would be great surges at Key West. It might not really be a category five; it might be more like a six. It would pound every beach it touched out of existence. Mountains of surge. That was how it would announce its approach. From Florida to Georgia coastal residents would suddenly see surf they never imagined. The *outer* reaches of this storm would be more damaging than Hugo. Those who stayed behind would be stunned as brooms and rakes became javelins and shingles flew like scythes. The wind would come from every which way as air was inhaled and exhaled from this monster that seemed now like the Aztecs had it right, that it was actually a spirit, a living breathing killing hurukan spirit that roared and groaned and hissed. There would be no hiding. The eye of this storm would see and destroy everything. Appliances and cars would be picked up. Trees would spin. There'd be a band of F-4, maybe F-5 tornadoes around sections of the storm, joined by tremendous downdrafts that would slash like a chainsaw. At the Weather Service officials would gasp at hook signals indicating several like those back at Xenia, twisters that were more than a mile wide, forming, dropping, rising back up. It would be a storm strong enough to lift brick houses off their foundations, to threaten the entire state, and as it swept over the Gulf Stream, as it sucked greedily at the warm currents running up Florida's east side, as it continued to surge in a way no one had foreseen — no one had *wanted* to foresee — it might keep dropping pressure. It might be a rapid intensifier. Its waves might push the wreckage of one home into another, and *then* it would hit — in the worst case, between Miami and Fort Lauderdale. And until the last minute forecasters wouldn't know it. "At 12 hours our error in forecasting where a storm is going to be is on the order of fifty miles," said Miles Lawrence of the National Hurricane Center. "Even as soon as six hours before it makes landfall you don't know precisely if it's going to hit Miami or Fort Lauderdale or farther south or north. And even minutes before it actually comes through you don't know where the swath of the very strongest winds are going to be."

The same could be said for Mobile or Charleston. They would not know until it happened and by then there could be thousands of cars blown from evacuation routes or under surges or turtle-side up in roadside gullies. There would be pandemonium on long stretches of highway. Stalled cars would block all routes and if the pressure dropped below 870 millibars, they'd be picked up. They'd roll like tumbleweed.

In the worst-case Florida scenario, at least 250,000 autos would be on the highway when the eye hits. And then there would be those in their homes, most of which were built to withstand winds of 120 miles an hour, *half* of a mega-storm's maximum potency. Horrid was the thought of the elderly watching as water came under the doors or cowering in a corner as drapes burst off, as lamps and mirrors and paintings winged, as furniture went tumbling, flying, dishes breaking into deadly shards as objects flew and walls and floors bowed and burst. In a landfall between Miami and Fort Lauderdale people would be affected from the Keys to Daytona. As the storm began to grind inland, floodwaters would rise with stunning speed. It would be America's first statewide disaster. As in the prophecy of LaSalette, it would annihilate several cities — Miami, Fort Lauderdale, and Palm Beach — before crossing to the west and destroying Naples, Fort Myers, or Tampa. In the right mix of warm unstable atmosphere the entire eyewall would resemble a tornadic system. There would be eighty percent residential destruction; glass would burst in one skyscraper after another; the rain would *lacerate*. "Although they can take very high wind velocities, once a window breaks — once you do get failure — the building gets pressurized and as the glass is stressed inward, the building fills up like a brown paper lunch bag and glass doesn't bend worth a darn, so you get sort of an outward explosion," explained Peterson. "If you have a hundred-mile-an-hour wind at ground level, 400 feet in the air you have over 150 miles an hour. We've discovered that the wind accelerates so violently around the corners that there was actually *erosion* in Andrew on the corners of concrete buildings. In downtown Miami where you have a whole series of skyscrapers, you'd have a domino effect. You'd have one building fail and everything downwind would fail due to the debris. So what would happen is that you'd have one of the buildings right on the water blow up and all the glass would go and shatter all the glass downwind of it. Many of the buildings would look like they'd been through a bomb. There'd be whole sides of buildings with no glass. There would be a point where this stuff would be literally raining out of the sky. It would be a terrible, terrible sort of a thing. There would be a threshold at which this would happen. It's highly unlikely that unless you go into a category five that you'd see it at all. But once you get into category five, all bets are off. The likelihood of exploding from pressure becomes very, very high and once it starts failing there would be a cascading effect."

What happened with Andrew would now happen to an area ten times larger and many of the deaths would be in Monroe County — the Keys, where there was only the one escape route and it was just above sea level. There was no way all or even most could get out — and there were 84,000. "If we ever got a category five," said one emergency manager, "we might as well kiss Monroe County good-bye."

CHAPTER 43

A Supervolcano?

This would be one of a number of major events and by all odds not the worst — not even one of the worst — but if it occurred as it seemed the elements were lining up for it to occur, it would be unforgettable. Whether the mega-storm struck Florida or urban areas in a state like North Carolina, Mississippi, Virginia, or even farther north, it would be an epic event. Anchormen would be on 24 hours a day. News coverage would rival that of the first moon landing. In Florida, thousands would drown, and the wind would claim thousands of others. It would be the first American catastrophe on the scale of those that have afflicted third-world countries. The carnage would dwarf Galveston. If the storm attacked several major centers, moving from one coast of Florida to the other, and then on to another state — and particularly if it made a second landfall in a city like New Orleans (as nearly happened with Andrew), the total damage would run between $80 and $225 billion (a quarter *trillion*), which was the exact sum a report issued by the National Science Foundation warned could be the range of a disaster America was approaching.

While Florida, which received forty percent of landfalls, had to be on special guard, the problem would be widespread. There was a chance there would be more than one mega-storm, and at the least a series of huge hurricanes that pounded the United States and helped push it into economic hemorrhage. We were in a situation where fifty million people lived within an hour's drive of the Gulf or Atlantic, with at least four trillion of insured property along the danger zone. The insurance industry barely survived Andrew; if it didn't prepare, it would not survive what this century had in store. With temperature flux there would be an explosion of powerful hurricanes, and even if the warming stopped or temperatures began to drop, the energy stored in our planet would sporadically burst into the open. The greatest vigilance had to be during what seemed like calm years, and though hurricanes were generated with greater frequency when there was heavy rainfall just south of the Sahara in what was known as the Sahel, even in drought years there will be heavy intermittent storms that could serve as a trigger for the mega-storm. All it took was one disruption and there was the seed of a hurricane that, feeding off instability, would act in ways that defy computer models.

We could expect oddities, a storm with something like two eyes (although meteorologists remained skeptical), or a tail of dense precipitation that caused massive flooding after the worst of the storm was through. If a mega-storm slammed into a mid-Atlantic state, and then hovered there, as Hurricane Mitch did in Central America and Floyd did over North Carolina, the inland flooding would be far more deadly than straight storm surge. Such a storm might then move south, drenching, revive itself over the Gulf or Caribbean, and wander north to join other systems and form another but much, much larger "perfect storm." We were entering a time when a single system could haunt us for exceptionally long times, affecting many states. In the Pacific a typhoon called John lasted 31 days in the northeast and northwest part of the ocean. They would act unpredictably, as did a storm in 1999 that suddenly reversed course and headed in a direction opposite of where it was projected. As it was shaping up hurricanes would move

A Supervolcano?

together and switch course in ways they had not previously while areas inland echoed with thunder. In the era that was upon us massive storm fronts would cover several midwestern states at a time. They would come with astonishing density and linger such that a strange darkness might reign for several days, with huge stabs of lightning. The type of storm described at LaSalette and implied in the hail that preceded the apparitions at Medjugorje would bear on us all. Thunderheads would spread over areas of up to 600 miles and hail visit places it had not previously visited; as occurred recently in Texas, it would be of such a size as to cause fatalities. It would rain with such intensity and over such protracted periods that it would seem as if the sun would never again brighten. A grayness would blanket large parts of the country. There would be fog worthy of purgatory. Ravines would run with flash floods in Arizona. There would be tornadoes, and they too would strike where they were not expected, including several major metropolitan areas. What hit Oklahoma City was a foretaste of what would happen to a larger city. Twisters with winds that reach 350 miles an hour would be recorded and there will be funnels with widths in excess of two miles. The area of intense tornadic activity that stretched from Kansas and Iowa to Oklahoma, Texas, and Mississippi would expand east, causing threats to St. Louis, Cincinnati, Chicago, southern Michigan, and northern Ohio. There would be increased activity in New York State, Pennsylvania, and Maryland. This might be another interpretation of LaSalette's claim that cities would be shaken by thunder. As things were shaping up, at some point a metropolis would see an F-5 rip through its skyscrapers and gut the downtown as had not yet happened but as was hinted through smaller tornadoes that materialized in places like Oklahoma City. One day news channels would be filled with images of a whirling black mass drilling through a major urban area, grinding into the cement, cutting like blades through tall buildings.

Tornadic outbreaks would no longer involve a flurry of small ones with just one or two large ones, but instead more of the higher scale. A wall of F-5s would roam the Great Plains. There would be twisters as far north as Montreal. With further warming or at least the continued disparity in temperatures (the tumble of warm and cold fronts), tornadoes would hit more in months like January that were previously devoid of such storms. Like hurricanes, it was only a matter of time before a large tornadic event captured more attention than any previous.

There would be updrafts and downdrafts and higher cumulonimbus and while there would be tortuously long periods of rain (days and weeks of it), when it stopped it would shut off like a spigot. Nothing would be gradual. From rain an area would leap into drought. Aridity would not only extend over vast reaches but in some areas last for decades. Scientists reported that between 1 A.D. and 1300 there were at least four mega-droughts that spanned the West, Southwest, and Great Plains for up to 240 years.

"*Suddenly, the persecutors of the Church of Jesus Christ and all those given over to sin will perish and the earth,*" said LaSalette, "*will become desert-like.*"

There would be drought over huge expanses of the United States and from all indications this would lead to great episodes of fire. The forerunners were seen in the wildfires that burned a million acres in 12 states in 2000. It was only a matter of time before one exploded into a major metropolitan area, the flames building a wall forty or fifty feet high, causing flashpoints before the flames themselves were visible, the air superheated and rolling like invisible hot coals, trapping hundreds in homes and offices.

Somewhere, a major metropolitan area would be threatened while gargantuan distant expanses of Brazil, Bolivia, Mexico, Indonesia, the Philippines, Malayasia, Borneo, New Guinea, Thailand, Cambodia, Vietnam, Russia, and

A Supervolcano?

southern Africa emitted a haze that fulfilled the prediction at LaSalette of the moon reflecting only a faint reddish glow. Some of these great fires would be spread over the course of entire decades while others would simultaneously erupt over great distances. These would correspond to biblical prophecy that the Lord would show Himself "like a whirlwind, to render His anger and fury, and His rebuke with flames of fire" (*Isaiah* 66:15). It would not spread and crackle; it would erupt. According to the U.S. Forest Service, nearly forty million acres in the United States were at risk of "catastrophic wildfire" and in California researchers at the Lawrence Berkeley National Laboratory calculated that the number of potentially catastrophic fires would dramatically increase, more than doubling losses. They would be events that complemented the great hurricane destruction. As LaSalette had said, "*water and fire will give the earth convulsions.*" And while the drama would be in flames that reached cities in states like Nevada, California, and New Mexico, the most far-reaching effects would be caused by the more remote ignition in Asia of millions of acres that caused carbon to be released from peat bogs in such quantities as to cause further changes in the weather.

There would be an hour of fire, a great hour, and it would show itself at a time when in other parts there were deluges equal or larger than what happened to the Mississippi and historic blizzards. Parts of the nation would be tormented by drastic cold spells, then sudden, spectacular melts. Snow would fall in late spring as the seasons shifted, with May more like April and April like March and March like February.

These changes would be joined and possibly greatly enhanced by something else that will at some point come onto the scene. While it was impossible to project the span of events, there was an excellent chance that a volcano — the explosive eruption of a mountain, or the creation of a

241

new portal from the netherworld — would be part of the convergence. When it would come was a mystery, but volcanoes had played a part in most convergences (in Minoa as the initial event), and may even have provoked some of the historic climate jolts. Mandelkehr assembled evidence of volcanoes in Hawaii, the West Indies, France, Alaska, and Iceland around 2450 B.C., and they also occurred during the Roman chastisements.

And so whether or not one served as a high point of the current episode, probabilities indicated that a significant volcano might also find its place in the coming parade of events. What "significant" meant was an eruption five to ten times that of Mount St. Helens, one that would further affect weather, causing it to gyrate downward. If this was part of the scenario it would probably occur somewhere in Indonesia, Japan, or the Philippines, all of which had shown signs of recent activity. If it was the size of Krakatau it would alter the weather for at least two years and drop the temperatures a full degree or more, adding to meteorological instability.

There were even dangers in Europe. One, a volcano called Campi Flegrei, lurked near Naples. Since 1969 there had been thousands of small earthquakes around Flegrei and the ground had risen more than six feet, indicating the build-up of pressure that in a sudden mass eruption could destroy a vicinity inhabited by a million people. The same was true of the vicinity near Vesuvius, which had also been greatly developed since ancient events. In Hawaii the fear was volcanic pressure that was pushing out a side of the big island at the Kilauea volcano, threatening to cause the collapse of a massive flank that on crashing into the Pacific would generate a tremendous tsunami. Some argued that the wave it would cause could rise to several hundred or even a *thousand* feet, washing over neighboring islands. Among them would be Oahu — where Honolulu sat but 18 feet above sea level.

It depended on how fast the flank fell. If it slid over a period of time instead of outright collapse, not much of a commotion would be generated. But a sudden disintegration would be the kind of catastrophe that, like a megastorm in Miami, Galveston, or New Orleans, would stun the world.

A wall of water would wrap itself around the big island and pour over neighboring islands.

It had happened any number of times in the past: whole sides of islands in the Hawaiian chain collapsing into the sea and causing massive waves to rise against neighboring islands. Some geologists believed that a wave as high as 1,000 feet had once washed up on the island of Lanai, and the debris from the various collapses was strewn on the Pacific's floor, rocks indicating past landslides that caused rubble to roll for phenomenal distances underwater. "North of Oahu the slide blocks — blocks that are at least a hundred meters [yards] across, the size of substantial buildings — are scattered out at least a hundred miles onto the sea floor," said one geologist, David Clague. "We have actually collected cores farther out and found sandy layers that are undoubtedly the finer material that was also traveling with those big blocks. They go out at least another 50 miles, and sandy materials maybe up to 300 miles, so these are very big events. There are 17 big deposits out on the sea floor [near the Hawaiian islands] and they represent the flanks and parts of islands. We know that some of these occurred very catastrophically, and that's because the blocks that slid down the slope went across the sea floor and then ran back *uphill* by several hundreds of meters. They had to have had a lot of momentum. They didn't just inch along twenty meters at a crack with every earthquake. Probably these occurred while the volcanoes were active because they have to have something that's pushing them. Probably the force is pressure from the magma system inside the volcano."

In 1975 a quake had caused the flank to move out by sixty feet and now it was creaking towards the sea within sight of thick streams of incandescent lava that flowed into the ocean from Kilauea, causing great billows of primordial steam at what seemed like the end of the world. Although odds were always against it occurring in any given century, if the flank fell it could affect coastal areas and certainly islands all around the Pacific, as far away as New Zealand. It was one of many scenarios that could play out with volcanoes. More troublesome was the prospect of an eruption in Antarctica that would cause the sudden meltdown of an ice sheet and raise sea levels around the world. There were 23 active volcanoes near the South Pole, including a new volcano, believed to be active, in the middle of the crucial West Antarctic Ice Sheet. "The finding of the volcano has great implications related to the melting of the ice sheets," wrote two geologists in a paper that was carried over the website for the University of California at Santa Barbara. "There is a hypothesis that says that the ice sheet covering West Antarctica is unstable and that it could melt causing the sea level to rise six meters all around the world. If this hypothesis is right, the presence of a line of active volcanoes along the boundary of West and East Antarctica could cause the splitting of the West Antarctic Ice Sheet."

There were at least 11 active volcanoes along what they called the Scotia Arc extending from the extremity of South America to Graham Land, and others associated with the fault patterns of Victoria Land and the Balleny Islands. The most famous Antarctic volcano was Mount Erebus, which rose to a height of 12,448 feet and at times presented small eruptions on a nearly daily basis. It stood as another warning in a world where few realized the extent of damage that could be caused by a gargantuan volcanic release, nor the sheer number. There were more than 1,500 active volcanoes around the world, with more to be discovered in the deep ocean ridges. They could erupt at any time and the simple fact was that supervolcanoes could alter life as we knew it, could kick up as much sun-blotting dust as an asteroid. Few were those who realized that the greatest known volcanic eruption had occurred 660,000 years ago at Yellowstone National Park — exploding with 2,500 times the force of Mount St. Helens and spewing pumice, gas, and hot ash across an area of 3,000 square miles.

SENT TO EARTH

CHAPTER 44

Tragedy in Waiting

Now, volcanoes were sending little signals. It wasn't like the indications from storms, but a crater had glowed near a refugee camp in Africa at the height of the hideous Rwandan holocaust and there was also the one that came to life during the great hurricane in Nicaragua.

Why would a volcano begin to erupt during a hurricane? Why would one come to life above a refugee camp at the height of a war?

They were God's way of underscoring something, and they were signs that as the tribulation unfolded, the weather would not be alone. There would be geological components. There was Thera and there were signals that a supervolcano may have led to the switch in weather that inhibited tree growth around the world in 540 A.D., and now there had to be concerns of the type of volcano that could alter global forces. The Yellowstone volcano was huge, the world's largest dormant one, and if we could believe the dates of scientists, it erupted every 600,000 to 700,000 years, the last, as I said, 660,000 years ago. During the past decade there had been signs of a substantial increase in what was often pre-eruption activity. The land there had risen from pressure, and the park's famous geyser activity had begun to change.

In Venezuela I had been told by a seer that the core of the earth was not in balance and I believed her. Deep below the surface, at levels no one could see, something was beginning to occur. There was a shift in the lithosphere — in the bulge of silicates — or below that deep in the molten flux that undergirded it. It was possible that something was beginning to move. In 1954 a mysterious and very deep quake had occurred at what was known as the Gorringe Ridge at the bottom of the Atlantic and in 1994 a powerful and highly unusual quake was felt from Bolivia to Canada and to repeat was an amazing 400 miles below the surface. Over a two-day period in 1998 a thousand little quakes had been recorded in an area southwest of Tokyo and 8,000 tremors occurred in a single month the year before. While most were small and Japan was prone to all kinds of earth movement (positioned as it was over zones of subduction and rife with the belches of volcanoes), its seismic activity was joining a cacophony that continued to stretch from Taiwan to the Near East and North America.

What had happened in 1906 — the flurry of quakes — was ready to burst into a global storm. Such was in accord with prophecy. Throughout the ages there had been a formula to chastisement and it had involved not just hail and thunder and mountains that trembled but quakes that LaSalette said would *"swallow up mountains, cities,"* indeed, whole *"countries."*

Few thought there was a quake powerful enough to destroy a sizeable country, but something big was in the fixing and although it was hard to see a large nation swallowed by the earth, a quake could certainly destroy a country's infrastructure, and no one had a *clue* as to the motion of massive slabs deep below the surface. Maybe there were forces that could wreak such surface effects, something that could cause the floor to drop from beneath us. From the crust to the center of the core it was a distance of about 4,000 miles, which was more than the distance between Los Angeles and New York. Geologists could not see below a few miles. But there were signals that in the deep something was stirring and they indicated that the prophetic formula in Scripture was right: that storms and fire would be accompanied by great earthquakes. A large block of foundation was about to drop.

And through the years, this would cause a series of major earthquakes, tremors larger than those to which we were accustomed; in some cases, much larger. God had long held back events that by now should have devastated humanity, but the calm geological period was about to end as so many calm periods related to other forces of nature were also about to end. It was the essence of chastisement and as in ancient times, when quakes accompanied whirlwinds, thunder, and fire (*Isaiah* 29:6), as in the tremor that shook Jerusalem during the Crucifixion (*Matthew* 27:54), earthquakes were going to provide the main conviction: Man had erred and God would reorient us with earth thunder. The words of Medjugorje again: something was coming "to shake up the world a little." More than bad weather there was something convincing about the earth shaking beneath our feet, and so it might be: Despite the assurances of geologists, a fundamental shift could occur in the deep out of notice and affect — bring alive — any number of faults. One quake would lead to another. There would be earthquakes, as Christ had said, "in many places" (*Matthew* 24:7). The time would come when one quake set off an immediate flurry of others, a sudden outbreak around the world, even where they did not usually happen — or that set off several gigantic ones. There would be periods of stepped-up activity that would last for years. I had received a prophecy that there would be a loud, globally-heard rumbling, something long and deep that would strangely murmur.

The planet was full of force and it would find an outlet. At some point there would be a cluster. This had been foreshadowed in 1906 when a quake in Japan was followed by the quakes I mentioned in Ecuador, California, Alaska, Chile, New Guinea, Australia, the Antilles, China, and Chile again the same year as the San Francisco quake. All were sizeable quakes (some over magnitude-8, one over *nine*), and as I mentioned the Alaskan event had been followed within an *hour* by the one in Chile — marking the precise amount of time it would have taken for seismic waves to radiate there and underscoring the fact that despite the skepticism of science, distant events bore a relationship. Faults "conversated." They were not isolated. They affected each other. And this was important because during a convergence they would group together. They would combine. A preview was seen in 1989 when the Loma-Prieta quake in San Francisco was followed by major tremors around Mount St. Helens and in Hawaii, which was 2,000 miles distant. There was also the example I cited of Landers, when a large quake of magnitude-7.6 in California was followed within hours by a significant step-up in seismicity across the entire West.

Clearly, quakes could and *would* set each other off. At some point (who knew the exact chronology?), there was going to be a geological storm — one that mimicked the meteorological variety — and along with other countries, along with Asia and South America, the United States was going to suffer. Few realized that in 1886, a decade after revelation of the LaSalette prophecy, a quake had caused extensive damage in Charleston, South Carolina, and before that, in 1811 and 1812, the center of America had been brutally shaken by a series of quakes that reached magnitude-7.5. Along the Mississippi dust, fog, and vapor filled the air with a smell that was described as like sulfur. At one point a short stretch of the Mississippi flowed *backwards*. Crevices opened and sucked the river into whirlpools. On land chunks of coal had flown from caverns. The earth split with electrical force, emitting flashes of lightning. There had been so much dust that the moon was swathed with gloom — and there was the appearance of a comet! Though originating near Missouri, the tremors were so strong they had been felt in Montreal and rang church bells in Boston.

A repetition of that was always possible (I myself had experienced a small quake while visiting the Midwest), but the greatest threat was in the West. There a huge quake was not just probable but inevitable. And among the concerns was Seattle. Throughout its past, shifts in the earth had raised and dropped this part of Washington like a length of lumber, and Indians had handed down legends of great tsunamis that had washed over the peninsula. Studying old sediments, geologists confirmed it. At various times tidal waves incited by quakes had plagued the coastline. This was because Seattle was near a spot where what was called the Juan de Fuca plate was subducting under the North American plate, the same set of circumstances that had led to eruption of Cascadian volcanoes like Mount St. Helens. There were great quakes; the sea floor dropped; the area was far more susceptible than most knew, on a par, nearly, with San Francisco. It didn't get big quakes as frequently as California, but the maximum it could attain, the magnitude, was higher. Though there had not been large earthquakes in the Pacific Northwest for at least 150 years, the Cascadian subduction zone seemed to be "storing strain energy to be released in future great earthquakes," wrote two government scientists, Thomas H. Heaton and Stephen H. Hatzell, who openly fretted about the possibility of "a sequence of several great earthquakes of magnitude-8" that would rumble on for years — what one geologist, George Carver of California State University, called a "decade of terror."

It would come in that fashion, or the stress where one continental plate was resisting and straining against another would release what Heaton and Hatzell called "a giant earthquake," a daunting magnitude-9. In other words, a quake greater than any known to have occurred in California, one the equal of the record quakes in Chile and Alaska, could occur in Seattle — one day, *would* occur. That would unleash a force hundreds of times greater than the quake that caused massive damage in Kobe, Japan, in 1995 (more than $70 billion in damage), and depending on terrain, tsunamis of thirty to a hundred feet would be generated.

It would affect Vancouver, Seattle, and Portland, and shaking that normally lasted for seconds might last for long endless *minutes*. That was an exceptional period. The great San Francisco quake was just 45 seconds. There would be tremendous destruction. There was a combined population in those three cities of more than 4.5 million (not to mention cities between), and it was guessed that the cycle of recurrence was 300 to 600 years — which was of major concern because the last had been in 1700.

It became clear once again that God had long held back overdue forces. But He would let them go. He would lift His hand if we offended Him. And that would spring things loose. They were overdue as just about everything was. As two other scientists phrased it, "it seems fair to say that we are now entering a broad time period within which the next earthquake will occur."

And while the greatest threat was the offshore subduction zone, there were also smaller faults that ran directly under Seattle. Geologists had located dead forests at the bottom of Lake Washington on Seattle's east side and had linked them to a huge quake that erupted on such a fault around 900 A.D., at the onset of the medieval chastisement. This was of intense concern because while a subduction quake had the capability of highest magnitude, it would be at more of a distance, out in the ocean, while an event right under the city would cause equally explosive damage at lower magnitude.

And the recurrence of this type of a quake was 1,000 to 1,500 years, meaning that a magnitude-7 or higher right there in the city, under homes, under the sprawl of computer companies, might also be imminent.

That was one place in need of prayer, the Northwest, and of course the other was San Francisco. Like Seattle, it too was riddled with a network of faults called "blind-thrusts" and "strike-slips," thrusting one chunk over another, or jolting by, and they hid in the mountains. While the largest fault was the San Andreas, which of course had caused the previous great quakes and which ran just west of the city (heading offshore until it continued on to Cape Mendocino), there was a flock of smaller faults that ran under the Bay Area. They were known as the Calaveras, San Gregorio, Hayward, and Concord faults, and most were east of the bay, a network caused by the stress of grinding plates. Of greatest concern was the Hayward, which coursed from Fremont (at the southern end of the bay) up through the Oakland area, El Cerrito, and Richmond, then out to San Pablo Bay before it turned into a crack called Rodger's Creek and made way towards Santa Rosa. Interestingly enough, it ran directly under the university at Berkeley — the nation's New Age mecca — and in fact right beneath the school's football stadium. A magnitude-7.5 was possible on the Hayward, and while that was far below what could occur in a Cascadian event, if it happened it would be close to many more people (the nation's fifth largest metro area), and the fear was a quake that would radiate in the northern part and rupture down thirty miles to Lake Chabot. It would take about 22 seconds to do that — directly under the roads, highways, and buildings. "Basically," said one sobering study, "the fault cuts through the most densely built-up section of the entire Bay Area." It had the potential of causing much more damage than the Loma-Prieta quake. It was described by a spokesperson for USGS as "the most dangerous fault in the United States." And it had a 32 percent chance of erupting in the next thirty years. The northern portion was the likeliest to go and was creeping at the surface. When it crossed roads and sidewalks it broke them. The movement at the surface was about five millimeters a year, and down eight miles below was a slip movement. Between the parts that were creeping and slipping was an area that had been locked since 1868. A northern section had not ruptured since the

Revolutionary War. These were going to have to give at some point soon. When one did, it was going to rupture at least thirty miles of fault and cause about six feet of slip when it moved. It would be comparable to what had happened in Kobe, Japan (Kobe meant "doorway to God"), and cause twice the duration of shaking as the 1989 quake. There were also the other faults and what one official estimated were at least a hundred hidden blind-thrusts that could cause untold damage. An eruption of the Hayward could trigger another large-magnitude earthquake on a neighboring fault. A series of quakes could lead up to the big one. "The East Bay's geological nightmare, the lurking seismic Grendel known prosaically as the Hayward Fault, may be an even bigger menace than last reported, which was only four months ago," said a local newspaper. "A geologist studying Strawberry Creek at the University of California at Berkeley has found that underground stress on the fault could be building even faster than previously thought." There were strainmeters and creep meters and it was getting edgy. On September 3, 2000, a magnitude-5.2 shook Napa Valley, and though causing relatively minor damage, it was in an area that startled experts because they had not even mapped it. It was an unknown fault. The known ones were hairy enough. "We're overdue for a large quake on the northern Hayward Fault," one USGS official said plainly. "People tend to forget," said another geologist. "These big earthquakes are close. They're going to happen, and they're going to be catastrophic." The Bay Area was characterized by extensive stretches of thick, soft soil overlain in spots by weak rocks that were susceptible to landslides. There were hundreds of places where hillsides could collapse as the ground cracked and liquefied.

This was Silicon Valley and one could only shudder at the potential damage. When a fault was locked as long as the Hayward had been, it was ready to go. They were waiting nervously at the USGS monitoring facility in Menlo Park and so great was the risk that one of the chief scientists had discouraged his daughter from attending Berkeley. There was a 70 percent chance of at least one major quake by 2030. Major quakes were "likely" in the next century on all four fault segments, said the USGS in an official statement, warning that "such an earthquake could strike at any time." If the Hayward went, it would cause *very* strong shaking in places like Palo Alto and San Jose — smack in computerland — and even in downtown San Francisco, not to mention the maximum effects that would occur in and around Oakland. And this was to say nothing of the San Andreas. That far more famous fault, which had been responsible, as I said, for the 1906 and 1989 events, was at a distance of just a few miles. While a major event on this particular stretch was not expected for a while, if it did occur — if there was a repeat of 1906 — it would cause about the same damage as a mega-hurricane: a quarter trillion in damage.

And remarkable though it seemed, neither San Francisco nor Seattle were in quite the danger of Los Angeles. It was close, but L.A. was the prime candidate for the really big one. The San Andreas ran by here too, and while not as close to the city as up near San Francisco, this segment was due for a quake. The recurrence of magnitude-8s at any one location was 130 years, and it had been more than 140 years since the last. Because it was an old subduction zone, and not one where plates were actively dipping below each other, but rather grinding past, the San Andreas was not thought to be capable of more than that, but that was quite enough and, once again, there was a bunch of smaller faults that resulted from the pressure at this great grinding point and many — dozens upon dozens of them — were hard by Los Angeles. Thrust faults with the capability of high magnitudes crisscrossed the sun-drenched basin and the latest estimate was similar to the Bay Area, at least a hundred capable of causing significant problems.

There was no way of comprehensively mapping the fault system, surprises could be expected, and if the Napa quake had startled geologists, much more jarring, much more alarming, had been the Northridge quake in 1994 — which had also occurred on a fault geologist did not even know existed. That was just about the only way blind-thrusts could be known: through quakes. They weren't discovered until it was too late, with occasional exceptions. One such exception had occurred in 1999 and made headlines. This was because of its danger. Scientists using information from oil drillers identified a major fault under the very heart of the downtown, and so high was the hazard to city hall from such tremors that it was being retrofitted for earthquake protection at enormous cost. Indications were that some of the faults could produce quakes strong enough to bring down a 20-story building and of those known, of those mapped, high on the list were the Whittier, San Jacinto, Chino, Malibu, Newport-Inglewood, and Elsinore faults. Most ran north to south, or east-west along the northern mountains, any capable of producing a major quake and in many instances aiming energy directly to the city (unlike the 1994 quake, which mercifully pointed its force in a sparsely-populated direction).

That was another measure of God's mercy but by odds — by where L.A. was heading spiritually — such mercy might not return. Next time there would be a direct shot. And it might be ten or twenty times the power. That was what Los Angeles faced. That was what would be wrought without God's continued forbearance. Only He could stop what was ready to occur here, only He could help San Francisco — where they had learned so little from the 1906 event — and only He could intervene for Seattle. These places had to realize this fast. They had all allowed the New Age in. They had all allowed remnants of old pagan gods to spring from the dust. They had spawned technology in a way that served themselves before others. They were drunk with "sophistication" (which meant worldliness), and now one worried for Los Angeles. The chief threat was a long band of faults along the San Gabriel

Mountains. They started with what was called the Cucamonga, turned into the Sierra Madre, and then there was the Raymond and the Hollywood — the latter running right where it said: below the film capital of the world, indeed directly under the famous HOLLYWOOD sign.

It was incredible: just as voodoo had placed itself in the way of a New Orleans hurricane, as consumerism had placed itself in harm's way in Palm Beach, as sodomy, satanism, and genetic manipulation were waiting for destruction in San Francisco (and as old paganism was on the very cusp of a Hawaii volcano), so had the film industry perched itself on the single most precarious intersection of urban faults, one that had to be seen to be believed and at points could be, rising behind Capital Records at Hollywood and Vine and running along the Walk of Fame not far from Paramount.

Tattoo parlors. Studios. Mann's Chinese.
All were under the nose of the fault, and I was fascinated by its course, the way it passed under Sunset Boulevard, edged the house that had belonged to Ozzie and Harriet, ran into Beverly Hills, formed a scarp in front of a huge Mormon Temple, and in general and in conjunction with a host of neighboring faults, including one that ran smack under Dodger Stadium, endangered most if not all of Los Angeles.
It was the most dramatic fault in the United States, and it was capable of a major quake, magnitude-6.5 or higher, if it ruptured along with others, which was a definite possibility. Faults in California set each other off. If a situation arose where several major faults ruptured at the same time, there would be trouble; there would be a cataclysm. A magnitude-6 that set off a seven that set off another seven or vice versa or higher, something unexpected — in short, a *storm,* perhaps including the huge San Andreas — was the singular seismologist's nightmare. There were now 34 million people in the state, and an additional 18 million ex-

pected by 2025 (which in the northern part was considered the deadline, as we just saw, for an occurrence). If in most situations they downplayed threats, not here; leading geologists, men who prided themselves on stoicism, described the situation to me as "tragic" and "scary."

There was no tornado, hurricane, blizzard, or hailstorm that could inflict the kind of destruction possible through simultaneous quakes and there was even the threat, both here and San Diego, of tidal waves: According to a geologist named Costas Synolakis, quakes from faults that were both offshore and on land could cause landslides in the steep ocean canyons — collapsing, gushing in, and pushing water to San Diego, Santa Monica, or L.A.-Long Beach Harbor. "We could have a fairly large local tsunami," said Dr. Synolakis. "We are at risk from tsunamis from Alaska or Peru or Japan, but historically those tsunamis have been fairly small by the time they reached us. If we have a tsunami that's coming in from Peru, we're going to have about ten hours warning. If a tsunami comes from Alaska, we're going to have 11 hours. But if we have a tsunami that's generated *offshore*, the travel time will be about ten minutes. There basically would be no warning. And what we're finding as more evidence comes in is that we do have the right geologic condition offshore for having the kind of tsunami that struck New Guinea. The continental shelf is such that there is evidence of massive landslides. Even if the earthquake is inland, there could be enough ground motion as in New Guinea to trigger a landslide."

The specter of a fifty-foot tsunami washing half a mile inland along a five or six-mile stretch of Santa Monica — or really anywhere in Southern California — was a disturbing vision: a crush of water and if at night the sparks of bioluminescence. But the main concern remained on land. When I spoke to Dr. Lucy Jones, chief of the USGS office in Los Angeles, she speculated that the frontal faulting at the base of the mountains northeast of the city could cause a magnitude-7.5 or even an eight or higher if it ruptured all the way from San Bernardino to Santa Barbara.

That was terrifically high in the midst of such a densely populated area, a risk only a step below that of Tokyo.

If the whole San Andreas went and there was a triggering of the faults closer to the city, then we were talking about a magnitude-8.5.

It had happened in Mongolia, where in 1957 a 160-mile fault had ruptured at the same time as one that was forty miles long.

And the height and lateral dimensions of the mountains where it occurred were comparable to those of the San Gabriel Mountains.

Some believed the greatest danger was a linking together of six or seven faults the size of the one in North-ridge, a setting off of half a dozen or more, a horrid convulsion.

SENT TO EARTH

Chapter 45

The Superquake

If that came, there would be no warning. It would come in a horrible instant. In a moment the shock would flatten buildings in a way that modern buildings had never been flattened. Wood would be splintered, glass turned to atoms, stone pulverized. There would be so many shocks coming from different directions that those caught in it wouldn't know where to flee. There would be no time to panic. There would only be the jolt. Seconds of it. A minute. One huge constant shake. Before it ended, another minute, and then another quake. It could be spread over days as one triggers a second and then a third or it could happen in hours, as one rapid devastating sequence.

An endless subterranean locomotive. And what followed the first would not be aftershocks. They would be separate quakes with their *own* aftershocks. There would be aftershocks occurring simultaneously. What survived the first would not survive the second. Nails would scream. Roofs would burst. Everything would be shattered. Those homes still intact would list like storm-tossed ships, the furniture heaving from one side of the room to the other, beds, sofas, huge dining room tables. There would be twisting, cracking, collapse. The frames around doors would contort like parallelograms before splintering.

The heart would stop. It did this in a quake. Run? Stay? Huge crevices would form. Cars would fall into holes. There would be sudden fountains of groundwater, bursting sewers. The landscape would shift as monolithic subterranean blocks thrust up hillsides. Fissures would rend mansions — would topple canyon lookouts — and palms would be shaken like pom-poms if they were left standing.

Miles of devastation. Miles of crushed and crashing and tilted buildings. That's what would happen in a large quake or a chain reaction. Smoke would rise and the priciest of cars, the sturdiest SUVs, would be crushed like cartons. No freeway or highway, if it is in the East or Seattle or the Midwest, would be left functioning. Natural gas lines would be ruptured and if it was a midwestern quake, a repeat of 1811, it could mean a shutdown of supplies to Chicago, Detroit, Buffalo, and New York, which would be a truly gruesome scene, a fairly inconceivable scene, if it happened during a cold snap in the dead of winter.

We weren't prepared for such a disaster, and such was the kind of occurrence we could expect: there would come a time when somehow the very foundations of modern living, of need, of convenience, food and water and gas, would be taken from us whether by quake or other means if we continued to stray from God. The storms that have knocked out power to places like Montreal and forced them to revert to primitive means (we recall the burning of wood from porches) would be repeated in some of America's major megalopolises. It would start with a bang but then unfold slowly, inexorably. The repercussions would span a region. This was what could happen in an earthquake. Gas could spew in the air and no matter the time of year it would ignite an inferno. Flames would move as in San Francisco in 1906 or in Chicago in 1871 — which had been right around the time Melanie was releasing her prophecy of cities and fire.

Somewhere, this will happen: huge rolling shocks, the land moving like an ocean's swell, in Seattle causing trees on the bottom of Lake Washington to shoot thirty or forty feet in the air, soil turning to pudding, liquefying, the lake spilling over its sides. In Los Angeles there would be all but total destruction from Malibu — from the ritzy beachfronts, from the film colony, from the old stomping grounds of Charles Manson — to Inglewood. Everything would be in motion. One epicenter might be the Hollywood fault. Another the Sierra Madre. And then faults downtown. On the West Coast a superquake involving Los Angeles or another region might go on for some time and according to a geologist at the California Institute of Technology one involving just several downtown thrusts or in the Wilshire district of magnitude-7.5 would be a half-a-trillion-dollar event — less than the ultimate superquake but double the economic loss of a mega-hurricane, sending a tsunami across the world economy. This, too, of course, would be something everyone everywhere would hear about. This too would dominate the media. It would fit the bill of making the world pause and think. If it was a regional event, if somehow the San Andreas were triggered or was the trigger to start with (and had a higher magnitude than currently guessed), the damage would also be seen in San Diego, Riverside, Santa Barbara, Monterey and if it was the whole fault, all the way north of San Francisco. The San Andreas was too shallow for the end to sever and fall into the ocean, but it might fracture along its entire length — setting off some of the smaller faults and if so throwing California's economy back into the 1950s (affecting all parts of the world because this state was not only the center of high-tech but the world's ninth largest economy).

I am talking about higher than magnitude-8. Perhaps a nine. Perhaps beyond what geologists know. I'm talking about an event somewhere in the world that will not be easy to measure. I'm talking about a time that will see a new paradigm of geology and will also see people cry out to God knowing now that the chastisements of the past —

the accounts of floods, the references to great shakings of the earth — were not myths.

Chasms would open. Mountains would heave — some would seem to be *"swallowed."* Whole valleys would drop. Such has happened over the course of geologic time and must happen again. It could start along the San Gabriel Mountains and spread from Pasadena to Glendale to Burbank. This was what we needed to pray about; this was the need for intercession. For it would take just an awful instant and the land would shift all over. If the Hollywood fault went, if it was above a magnitude-six, and if it was joined by neighboring crevices, the rubble would be chest-deep on the Walk of Fame. There would be a rumbling, a shattering, dust-belching rumbling — a leveling — from one town to another. If a thrust erupted in south-central, storefronts would burst into the streets, crash onto the pavement, send shards like a storm, and homes would fall into the canyons. There would be no functioning freeways. Some would split every quarter mile. Gas would spew and there'd be ignition — first a scattering of flames, then the united hellfire. The calm would be rudely broken by countless aftershocks. Survivors would be beyond the fatigue of battle. It would feel like an eternity. It would feel like the bowels of the earth had opened. It would be hard to *crawl*. Across the breadth of Los Angeles people would be on the floor or ground clinging to children and husbands or heads covered, in the fetal position, finally brought to prayer.

This would be no Northridge. This would be like nothing California had seen. This quake — these *quakes* — would go beyond expectation. There would be the sense of massive death. There would be the reviewing of one's life. There would be — as warned at Medjugorje — the pulling of hair, the burning desire for repentance, the cursing of one's life without God.

There would be the knowing that a new magnitude had been reached.

There would be the knowing that not just this or that neighborhood but an entire city — wherever the city was — had been put out of commission, had been severely damaged if not destroyed.

The Raymond. The Newport-Inglewood. The blind-thrusts. With a superquake it could take weeks to tally the dead. There would be no real magnitude, no way to measure the fact that several faults had slid or dropped.

Charlie Chaplin Studios. Staples Center. The Palladium.

Survivors would crawl over shards of chandelier.

L.A., if it was Los Angeles, would be a cloud of dust. A cloud that took days to dissipate. The HOLLYWOOD sign gone.

No matter how it had been retrofitted, no matter the engineering, city hall would crumble.

And across the street the emergency center would be rendered inoperative.

The sun would be red, darkened, and at night the moon would have lost its glow.

SENT TO EARTH

CHAPTER 46

The Last Secrets

It was only through love that such events would be averted, and especially love of God. It was not "doom and gloom" or any other cliche to point out the dangers. It was for the sake of urging love in the way that love could do all when it was focused away from the self and toward others. Otherwise, the disasters would come. No one could precisely predict what they would be. I could have painted similar scenarios for dozens of other earthquakes. Would they come together? A year apart? Before the hurricanes? There were endless variations and that was why, when finally it did come, its exact format would be unexpected no matter how much we tried to anticipate. God was like that. He arranged things with enough of a twist to cause surprise. No one ever really saw what was coming in the exact way it would come. Many scientists, anxious to believe that their knowledge was comprehensive, would deny the extent to which calamities could occur, and would dazzle us with numbers, but the fact was that darkness and sin could bring anything from the depths and would be quashed — sent back — only through goodness, charity, and care for one another.

It was love that would raise the protection which was otherwise slipping away and love that would cast out fear. It was those with guilty consciences who most tended to fret, and they could dispel it easily enough by confession, by partaking of Christ, and by heading for the refuge of the Gospels. With Christ there was moving forward and changing the world so these things — always under the ultimate control of God *Almighty*, Who did punish — would not come.

As time wore on, however, the dangers grew. There were only so many sinners that God would watch slouching toward hell before He took action. For there *was* hell. That had been clearly shown. It was not only in the Bible but had been shown during a vision at Fatima, and Lucia, in her waning years, still at a convent, had urged people to preach it, to warn about it (as was rarely done from the pulpit).

It was horrid and in comparison, alongside condemnation, no earthly chastisement — no fire, no storm, no quake — stood as comparable; these were earthly things. God had immortality in mind, and as Vicka said, those who followed the Ten Commandments had nothing to worry about; those who loved and cared for others had the Holy Spirit; those who were loyal would be shown ways around the danger that loomed.

Perfect love cast out all fear (*1 John* 4:18) except the holy fear of God. What did that say about those who dismissed the idea of calamity, who shunned reality, who fled from warnings? Over and again were those who said God was a God of mercy and that He was so full of forgiveness as to render warnings moot, yet at the same time the Bible was *filled* with chastisement (it was easier to find a chapter with it than without it), and according to the good book it came because of those who shunned God's admonitions, were lovers of self, were full of worldliness. That's what had gotten us into trouble: the skeptics and materialists and nonbelievers, devotees of their own inclinations, those who in *2 Timothy 3:2-8* were described as "proud, arrogant, abusive, disobedient to their parents, ungrateful, profane, inhuman, implacable, slanderous, licentious, brutal, hating the good," the "treacherous, reckless, pompous, lovers of pleasure rather than of God as they make pretense of religion but negate its power." They were the ones, skeptical of God Himself, who were "always learning but never able to reach a knowledge of the truth." That was the mindset of those who mocked the devout and it was seen in New York when newsmen cast God from any mention in their reports and in Hollywood when they thumbed their noses at every moral and in San Francisco when ministers and priests were afraid to wear their collars in public.

Good had been made to seem evil and evil as good and now trouble approached; it wasn't fun to talk about, but ignoring it, whitewashing it, would only invite what those who denied it didn't want: more disaster. Could a quake really be stopped? It could. There wasn't *anything* that couldn't be affected by prayer. At Medjugorje had been this remarkable quote: *"Prayers and fasting can prevent war and natural catastrophes."* That had been said on July 21, 1982, but few were those, rare indeed, who had heeded it. Instead of devotion and repentance there was partying as in the days of Noah (*Matthew* 24:38). People now thought that because the world was full of money and glamour and lust that it was being blessed! It was the deception of politics. It was the lure of the lucre. It was the deception of so-called prosperity ministry. It was the devil who bestowed extravagance; unless He had a mission in mind, God gave to those He loved only what they needed. He did not hand out jewels. He did not grant a Mercedes. His Son had come in the greatest of poverty and that itself had been a sign that life was a series of temptations to be avoided.

No one, however, believed that anymore. It was out of fashion. The New Age was in and with it the false compassion of those who told sinners not to worry about it, that God would never allow harm, that all was okay.

There was a disdain for purification at the same time that purification was increasingly imminent. Was a magnitude-8.5 really the limit when it came to quakes in California, or were there deep unknown mechanisms by which that state would see a magnitude-9? Could California encounter the kind of quake that Alaska had? Could the San Andreas set off a bunch of other major faults, and vice-versa? Could the quakes in California lead to major movements on the faults in Seattle or Portland or Vancouver, or vice-versa? Was there an obscure link by which reactions in California could connect to the huge subduction zone off Seattle or others that haunted us from Alaska to Chile? Could the faults near Japan cause a chain reaction?

These were urgent questions, and the fact was that no one knew the actual width and depth of every major crevice and didn't even know if we had a reckoning of the most dangerous. We were blind in a cave. The limits that scientists imposed on seismicity were arbitrary and even if we *had* seen the most powerful, this meant problems. Although there was almost certainly a quake in the future greater than any in the short history of seismographs, a simple repetition of the damaging but comparatively low-magnitude quake that had hit Tokyo in 1923 would in today's world with today's population amount to destruction estimated at 16 times that of Kobe, where damage had been assessed at between $70 and $147 billion. In total losses that would mean all Tokyo had to do was repeat the quake of 1923 to see $2.3 trillion in total losses — or more than 60 percent of Japan's gross domestic product.

That was only a magnitude-7.9 and it seemed presumptuous to believe that, just because there had been nothing larger in recent decades, the potential had been reached.
What about quakes that only came around every 2,000 or 4,000 years — not since the Bronze Age?
What about quakes that defied geological backtracking and had not occurred since the advent of Neanderthals?

No one had a good view of the past. There were almost surely quakes that took a pattern we could not fathom, and would perhaps cause a vibration underneath that would be heard and felt all over. Most likely was a series of major quakes that would occur for several decades as the geology went through a fundamental shift, breaking much of our artificiality down. In the midst of such destruction would also come events that were human. In any chastisement there was an element that was man-made — usually war — and so it would be in the one that now approached: There would be skirmishes, and in addition to the probability of a nuclear exchange (involving not just Russia, China, and the U.S., but also now third-world and Mideast nations), there was the shadow of terrorists who one day would devise a device small enough to smuggle in an attache or suitcase and detonate in the downtown of a major city.

It took no prophet; a device causing radiation would go off somewhere, perhaps more than one, perhaps in war but more likely through terrorism or regional conflict and however much we didn't want to think of it, there was also the prospect of bacterial, viral, and chemical agents. In the Soviet Union had been the capability of producing enough anthrax (a bacterial agent) to destroy the world several times, and we can imagine the sheer panic if an infection or toxic agent were unleashed in Tokyo, or if a bomb exploded with the flash of a Hiroshima, melting objects, blasting outward, the air whipped into a violent artificial wind that was scalding, that caused structures — skyscrapers — to implode, that felled something like the World Trade Center and left a legacy of radiation that would cause sickness (redness, boils, toothlessness) and cancer.

Was this in the Medjugorje secrets? Was there a mushroom cloud? The seers said only that the first two events would be announced beforehand as proof of the apparitions and the third secret involved a great sign as part of the third warning, some kind of manifestation that would be visible at Medjugorje for the world to see, as a final beacon. There were no real indications what this sign was but all six seers were told of it (the only secret we knew they mutually possessed), and in 1981, after hundreds of people, including Communist officers, had observed the strange fire burning at the very hillside where Mirjana and Ivanka had first seen Mary, the Virgin had explained that it was a *"forerunner of the great sign"* that was to come. The final secrets involved what the seers said were "grave, catastrophic chastisements" for the sins of the world.

"Father, I wish you only knew how I feel on some days!" Mirjana had said in her talk with the priest. "There are times when I feel that I could go mad. If Mary wasn't here, if she didn't fill me with strength, by now I would have surely gone mad. Could you imagine, knowing precisely everything that will occur in the future, just how enormously stressful that alone is to me? So then, when I see how people behave, especially in Sarajevo, how they use God and His name in their swearing, how thoughtless they are, how they curse God — these wretched ones have no idea what awaits them in the near future. It is then, as I observe them, that I will take pity on them. I feel so sorry for them and pray and cry and pray, pray so much for them. I pray to Mary to enlighten their minds because, as Jesus said: they truly do not know what they do."

The first secrets were "severe," said the seer, "but not as much as the remaining ones."

"What follows are the secrets which are *really* unpleasant," said Mirjana. "I would be happy if everyone would finally understand that. I cannot tell them [what is in the secrets], but once they begin to be fulfilled, then it will be too late." If people knew what was coming, she had warned, they would be shocked to their senses. She expressed relief that prayer had diminished the eighth secret confided by the Madonna, which was worse than the previous seven, "but then she told me the ninth secret and it was even worse. The tenth secret is totally bad." There could be diminishing with prayer — this was the urgent call — but it seemed unlikely (short of massive global conversion) that it could be averted. "The Madonna said people should prepare themselves spiritually, be ready, and not panic; be reconciled in their souls," Mirjana had told a priest. "They should be ready for the worst, to die tomorrow. They should accept God now so they will not be afraid. They should accept God, and everything else. No one accepts death easily, but they can be at peace in their souls if they are believers. If they are committed to God, He will accept them."

This sounded major. It did not sound like all the events were to be confined to regions. Something big was in the works. It wasn't the end of the world, but the intuition of something of great repercussion was given when a priest from Medjugorje said that after the secrets men would live more as in peasant times. It sounded like the modern way would be dismantled. Societies would be broken down. That was the implication, and while the seers dissuaded talk of the secrets and emphasized God's love over His retribution — did not focus on the evil — there was a time when that emphasis had to be made and Vicka had mentioned that it was our duty to do just this: to convert people, to "prepare them for the chastisement." With prayer and penance, said Vicka, the events could be substantially "lessened." "The Blessed Mother says that is why God is giving so much time for these apparitions, so that all may come to conversion," said the seer. "She wants to make certain that all people have this opportunity. She can't help anybody who doesn't want to change, who doesn't come back to God, who doesn't put God first. If you don't do this now, it will be too late."

It was said that the devil had been given special power for a century, and while there was confusion over this aspect, Mirjana said in an early interview that it had nothing to do with the year 2000 but, rather, that part of the satanic period was in the twentieth century, and that it would continue until the first secret — the first event — unfolded.

Somehow, in ways that were cryptic, suffering — a leveling of our artifices — broke the back of evil.

And wickedness there was. Although this too was not to be our focus, there were no bones about it in the early days of the apparitions, and it had to be exposed, brought into light, to be purged. "The world has become very evil," Mirjana had said (to reiterate). "It cares about faith very little. People have fallen into very evil ways, so that they *live* in evil routinely." According to Marija Pavlovic, the Blessed Mother said *"a cloud of darkness"* had enveloped *"the whole planet."* Few had faith, few believed, and this was what threatened the world, lamented Mirjana (mentioning Germany, Switzerland, and Austria in particular). The devil came and allured, said the seer, "by promising the beautiful things of the world. He always tries to turn a true believer away from the path to heaven. Satan is evil itself, but he always comes disguised. Usually, you can sense his presence when there is confusion or disorder or conflict. He particularly enjoys destroying family relationships. He is very powerful. He can distort memories; he can even distort what we think is reality." The answer was Christ. *"Pray to Jesus,"* said Mary. *"I intercede with Him, but say all your prayers to Jesus."* It was the last time that she would be speaking in such a manner on the earth, she informed them; at least in this fashion, it was the last such appearance. It meant, Ivanka said, "something momentous."

Were the ten secrets regional or global?

"I may not answer that question," said Mirjana.

Would it be global economic collapse?

This seemed likely. Somewhere in the future would be a great economic breakdown, a dearth of food, a running out of gas.

It was not, however, in Mirjana's secrets. "I don't know anything about that," Mirjana had responded to an interviewer named Jan Connell.

Were the secrets painful for Medjugorje or for the whole world?

"The whole world," she finally answered.

Although they were filled with peace and joy after most apparitions, there were times of deep anguish for the seers;

there were moments of distress. They were not to focus on this; they were not to obsess on the secrets. "Our Blessed Mother says we should pray more, and we should love God as our Father," said Mirjana. "We should accept the messages of prayer, fasting, conversion, and reconciliation that God is sending to the world through the Blessed Mother of Jesus. If we do this, we will not be afraid of anything, no matter what the future may hold."

But at the same time the moment had arrived for warning and it was a true shame that those who didn't share the Catholic religion so often dismissed such messages because they happened within the context of another religion. There were indeed times when such apparitions were a device of deception or a product of the imagination — as Protestants correctly pointed out — but there were also ones that had borne good fruit (*Matthew* 7:20), and so far Medjugorje was in that category. It was meant for all people. It was meant for Catholics and non-Catholics. There was time for prayer, a last time. There was no indication when the chastisements would come. Mirjana said only that she would live to see the first three secrets. The time between them could be quick or drawn-out, she hinted. *"Hurry to be converted,"* said the Virgin. *"Do not wait for the great sign. For the unbelievers it will be too late to be converted. For you who have the faith, this time constitutes a great opportunity for you to be converted, and to deepen your faith. Fast on bread and water before every feast, and prepare yourself through prayer."*

It was still a last moment. It had nothing to do with the year 2000. The apparitions had proceeded for twenty years, and while many had become discouraged that the secrets had not yet come to pass, the time-frame was similar to that of Fatima — where some of the predictions had taken decades to materialize. God's mercy was here. It never stopped. It was to be tapped. But one had to believe, pray, and do so firmly; any further skepticism or rejection because these messages were from one denomination instead of another was inviting peril. This was serious business. The time for parochialism was over. These were serious warnings. Those with ears would hear. There was every reason to believe from the absolutely consistent comportment of these seers that they had indeed been given a glimpse of the future and that despite the optimism and hope and faith we must always have, it was a future of upheaval. Vicka had cried in 1986 upon learning her ninth secret. *"Convert while there is time!"* was Mary's message. No wonder she came on the feast of John the Baptist. No wonder she came with thunder! *"I have always said, 'punishment will come about if the world is not converted. Call all mankind to conversion. Everything depends on your conversion."*

CHAPTER 47

Superwave

There would be a new evil that served as a test because of the prayers of the Virgin in putting off chastisements. How mankind responded to this new evil would determine the extent, length, and severity of the first chastisements. *"These chastisements will differ according to region, and like the great evil, will not always or usually be immediately noticeable for what they are,"* said a more obscure revelation. *"In the period also will be a warning that involves not fire from the sky but fear of fire from the sky, and strange loud rumblings. This, according to mankind's response, will then be followed by another chastisement."*

A series of scares.
What could cause such upset? What would shake up the world?

Out in the Atlantic was concern for a band of faults near an underwater range of mountains called the Gorringe Ridge, where the sea floor occasionally fell or rose. That could send devastating tsunamis across the shores of Western Europe and down to Africa with backwash in the U.S.
Located at 36.5 north latitude/11 west longitude about 300 miles west of the Strait of Gibraltar (between the Azores and Portugal), it was near the continental margin where the Messejana fault stretched along the St. Vincent Valley

and intersected what was known as the Azores-Gibraltar fault — joining in the very region of Gorringe, a bank that was separated from the divide between the Eurasian and African plates by a deep basin linking two plains. It was a part of the ocean that was as strange as it was dangerous. Those few who paid attention to this threat knew that a tsunami had originated here in 62 B.C. and again around 382 A.D. and that according to Roman historian Amiano Marcelino, the earthquake and corresponding tsunami sank two islets that were situated near St. Vincent Cape. The faulting was also responsible for a quake in 1755 that some believed was the most consequential in modern history. It had occurred on November 1 — All Saints Day — and as the tremors reached Lisbon they caused massive damage, the ground everywhere — in the markets, on the countryside — moving in actual horrifying waves. Birds had launched in alarm, horses were thrown, and in Lisbon — at the time one of the world's most powerful cities — destruction was such that thousands were killed in the first few minutes. So powerful was the event that it lifted the ocean floor more than thirty feet (tilting the 8,000 feet of water above it), which had caused a tidal wave that washed into Lisbon and smashed coastal fortresses with waves that crested to ninety feet near Algarve and pounded up the Guadalquivir River all the way to Seville.

In Lisbon, where 18,000 structures were felled, there had also been a fire that lasted for three days and caused an Egyptian darkness. The shocks as well as the tsunami (which had come thirty minutes after the initial shaking) also reached other countries. At the Strait of Gibraltar water suddenly rose. In Amsterdam ships were torn from their moorings. There were effects from Norway to Cairo. In Morocco water swept over ancient city walls and there was severe damage in the Azores.

Most peculiar was the effect inland. Across Europe "the agitation of the water of lakes, ponds, or bays, the swinging of chandeliers in the churches, the variation in the flow of springs or the muddying of their waters" was noted.

In England the water in several canals was visibly disturbed; in Bohemia a major spring overflowed. "About half an hour before this vast increase of the water the spring grew turbid, and flowed muddy; and having stopped entirely near a minute, broke forth again with prodigious violence, driving before it a considerable quantity of reddish ocher," wrote a priest named Father Joseph Steplin. Water rose and fell on the shores of the Lake Stora Leed in Scandinavia while on Gottland Island several large trees were knocked down. There were even reports of effects in Antigua, Martinique, and Barbados, with waves up to 22 feet high. "According to a notice from Boston, several strong shocks were felt there at 12:30 p.m.," wrote a scientist named Harry F. Reid of the magnitude-8.9 undersea quake. "All Pennsylvania was disturbed by a light shaking. In the neighborhood of Lake Ontario movements of the ground were already noticed in the last days of October; but on November 1 the lake rose with great violence five and a half feet, three times within half an hour."

Scientists estimated that nearly eight percent of the earth had been shaken in a way that could be felt, which meant millions of square miles. "Before the shock it was not suspected that the effects of an earthquake could be observed at such very great distances," said Reid. "Many of the inland waters of southern, middle, and northern Europe were set in oscillation; the most distant place reporting such a disturbance was Abo in Finland, 3,500 kilometers from the assumed origin. The sea waves were very marked in the Antilles."

As an English merchant who survived it said in a letter, "On a sudden, I heard a general outcry: 'The sea is coming in, we are lost!' Turning my eyes toward the river, which at this place is nearly four miles broad, I could perceive it heaving and swelling in a most unaccountable manner, as no wind was stirring. In an instant there appeared, at some small distance, a large body of water, rising, as it were, like a mountain. It came on foaming and roaring, and rushed toward the shore with such impetuosity, that we all immediately ran for our lives, as fast as possible; many were actually swept away, and the rest were above their waists in water, at a good distance from the bank. I had the narrowest escape...."

Waves washed up to the Celtic Sea and even entered the western end of the Mediterranean. At a pond called Eaton-Bridge in England witnesses reported the water open in the middle so that they could see the post and rail a good way down, almost to the bottom, and the water dashing up over a bank about two feet high, and perpendicular to the pond.

It was estimated that the tidal wave swept along the entire length of Europe and though hardly noted by colonists, caused water to rise in some fashion along America's coast too.

And so the question now came: Could this happen again? Could there be a bigger event? Might this be part of the chastisement? Could the water go farther and higher?

There had been quakes near Gorringe in 1936 and 1941, and while they had not caused catastrophic tsunamis, it was a matter of time. Ten events with a magnitude of more than six had occurred along this boundary since 1931 and this was where mysterious deep quakes had happened in the 1950s and 1969. The latter event didn't persist to the surface (causing, therefore, no significant tsunami), but it had been as though a slab or blob of lithosphere had fallen as one part dropped and another rose into a range of mountains.

Now if one went, if another slab, a larger one, fell, there would be a great catastrophe. That was the only word for it. It would exceed the word "event." There would be the immediate blaring of alarms and men would spring to attention at a hundred seismic stations and it could reach magnitude-9.5. Maybe — if cataclysmic — higher.

At first, no one would be able to tell what was going on. It would be the most serious scenario we have yet considered. No one would know how far the damage would go. They would know only that the readings were higher than in 1755. A magnitude higher.

That would mean a massive shift in water.

Seismologists would stare at each other. An entire region of the ocean would be set in motion, radiating eastward. There would also be the quakes. They would hit the coast. Bilbao. Nantes. Whole inland ranges would tremble. Whole stands of pines would be upturned. Portugal, Spain. France. Within minutes there would be pockets of mass destruction. Whole villages would fall to rubble for hundreds of miles.

Experts would stab at computers and learn that the first tsunami would hit in thirty minutes and that would reduce them to hysteria. There would be calls to the Portuguese Institute of Geophysics and USGS and governments everywhere, presidents everywhere, militaries everywhere, if something like this hit in any ocean, here or in the Indian or the Arctic or the Pacific.

All the while the tsunamis would be moving at the speed of a jet, a mere ripple in the open ocean but waiting to pile. When they reached the continental shelf, they would form towers.

There would be a roar and coastal towns would disappear and if there was some kind of larger drop we can't currently conceive, something down in the asthenosphere, the water might go farther inland than thought possible. The waves might reach phenomenally inland. There would be a series of them, and at the shore they would be mammoth.

Cars and homes and factories would be swept. Barns would swirl. It would be far worse than the surge from the largest cyclone. Homes would be flung into woodland. A surge would break through the Strait of Gibraltar. At

Algarve waves would crest at 150 feet or more. The water would carry trains. It would carry boulders. Waves like a wall of mud. No longer water. A bulldozer.

There would be massive coastal destruction as well as terrific damage inland from Africa to England. The terror for the U.S.: word that there was a backwash. Something was heading this way too. How high would it be? A couple feet? A monster? Where would it strike?

No one would know. There would be a scrambling of pilots. Ships would attempt to make port. From Maine to Virginia to Florida there would be evacuation.

CHAPTER 48

A Sinister Disease?

It was the kind of event that would fit the bill of what the seers called "catastrophic." The earth would convulse. Somewhere, a huge chasm would open. The commotion of the earth would blend with the commotion in the weather, causing a time of great chaos. There would be other disasters and possibly a war with or between China and Russia. In the midst of such commotion would come new evil and one might be in the form of a personage who through direct or indirect means took the reins of a new world order based on a structure that evolved from the United Nations and took advantage not only of the overall global breakdown (including great economic strife), but also the dehumanization of societies that now were so artificial — that had replaced spirit with logic, thinking with software, had corrupted their young, and sought to create their own life forms.

This God would purge. Fire would erupt. Dust would rise. As the ground shook, as oceans stirred, there would be an almost primordial atmosphere. The natural order would break down. There might be increased meteorite activity as well as increased magnetic solar flux, which would not only further affect the weather by influencing upper-level clouds, but also lead to another powerful display of the aurora borealis. A precursor has been noted in Colorado, where curtains of red, green, and blue seemed to pour out of mountain peaks. The lights were fueled by a shock wave from the sun that came at the same time that officials on earth announced they had cloned pigs (as a first step towards using such animals to grow spare human organs) and planned to introduce legislation in Britain to allow the cloning of human embryos.

In the West, pinkish nocturnal clouds usually seen in the Arctic had been spotted, and strange lights glowed from a large crater on the moon.

Scientists explained it as escaping gas, but there were other lights that could not be as readily explained — strange formations seen over Phoenix and Upstate New York and other cities as there had been the strange lights over Paris, Florence, and Avignon in the 14th century.

There were flares of light, discs, balls, flecks.

There were also comets, small for now, but multiplying. Streaking fireballs and meteors were seen over San Francisco, Las Vegas, Florida, Pennsylvania, Halifax, Alaska, Spain. In Finland meteorologists reported five comets that had crossed the southern skies and in Greenland the sky near Qaquortoq was lit by a "blinding flash."

As astronomical phenomena increased, as a cycle of meteorites began to give way to larger debris, this, like the "black comets" of the 1300s, might show the way to epidemics, which were so often a part of chastisement. I was given a chilling prophecy by a seer who claimed the Lord had warned him in apparition (not just a voice or dreams) that there could be *"two much more vicious sexually transmitted diseases"* (than AIDS), which I had also heard from the seer in Venezuela: disease that would kill quicker, in weeks, in a month, that could be stopped only by conversion. There was every reason to believe that such a threat or another kind of illness would join in an onslaught. Between 1980 and 1992 deaths due to infectious disorders had increased in the U.S. by 58 percent (with increasing problems with drug-resistant bacteria), and in 1997 Brazil alone reported 240,587 cases of virulent dengue fever (which by 2000 was also killing in Bangladesh). There was "mad cow" disease. There was "flesh-eating" bacteria. Delaware, California, Washington, Michigan, Florida, New York. All had seen that, and there would be more with a breakdown in infrastructure. Whether the shift was to warmer or cooler weather, a topsy-turvy, unstable environment would cause holes in our resistance and through those holes would come microbes, sometimes vicious microbes, outbreaks as rain and warmth spawned mosquitos.

There would be plagues, LaSalette had said, and already mosquitoes carrying malaria were a threat in Azerbaijan, Tajikistan, and Turkey, and were tracked with greater frequency in the U.S. Already extreme weather had set the stage for cholera in Central America. As ice melted at the polar caps, scientists feared that deadly prehistoric viruses might be unleashed. They had already found a plant virus in the Greenland icepack. Systems like El Niño were spawning blooms of plankton and those blooms carried cholera. There was Lyme disease. There were rats. In Washington they owned the alleys at night, hissing at humans, clawing their way up stairwells, partaking in broad daylight at bird feeders. Some were described as the size of cats, and there was also a problem with rabid bats. From Africa to Texas, huge swarms of locusts, swarms with as many as fifty billion members, were stripping crops and flying like frenzied malevolent clouds. They were in China. They were in India. They were cropping up here and there, fantastic sudden swarms that devoured entire stretches of corn, sorghum, right out of the Book of Exodus: "They shall cover the ground, so that the ground itself will not be visible. They shall eat up the remnant you saved unhurt from the hail, as well as all the foliage that has since sprouted in your fields" (10:5).

It wasn't the end-game yet, but there were dangerous germs, staph infections that were even spread in hospitals. At the CDC I was taken to the famous level-four biocontainment unit, a laboratory so dangerous that it was entered only by scientists wearing what looked like spacesuits, a lab that contained samples of ebola, which had created such a panic at a hospital in Kikwit, Zaire, recently that not even the staff wanted to take care of the patients. And that wasn't even the major concern. According to Dr. McDade, the great threat to the world was from an epidemic of influenza. In Hong Kong a strain found in chickens had jumped to humans, causing international alarm. "If that virus ever acquired the ability for rapid transmission from person to person — and it mutates very fast — if that virus had taken off, there was absolutely no underlying immunity anywhere in the world because nobody had ever been exposed to the particular virus strain and there was no vaccine available," he told me. "It had the potential for a pandemic much like the 1918 influenza that killed 20 to 30 million people worldwide."

CHAPTER 49

"Evil Star"

In the flow of natural events would be pockets of sickness. How many would die? There were already 170 million people with hepatitis C, another eighty million were expected to contract malaria, and there were thirty million with HIV — which had so stunningly fulfilled the Kibeho prediction, and which had first jumped from primates to humans around the time of the northern lights in the 1930s.

Now the lights were back, and the fact that they were coming with meteorites brought us to the last and most dramatic part of the LaSalette secret. *"Pagan Rome will disappear,"* Mary had said. *"The fire of heaven will fall and consume three cities. All the universe will be struck with terror and many will let themselves be led astray because they have not worshipped the true Christ who lives among them. It is time,"* Melanie claimed the Virgin said. *"The sun is darkening; only faith will survive."*

Fire. Three cities. Was it nuclear?
Or a comet?
There were indications that in the mix — as we grappled with other events — would be phenomena that were astronomical. There were any number of ways they might figure in. Every so often the sun exploded with gas in what were known as coronal mass ejections, and these

sent highly charged particles that played havoc with earth's magnetic field — not only leading to brilliant displays of the aurora, but also causing currents that blew out electrical plants. Would there be an extraordinary coronal ejection that destroyed our computer network?

Theoretically, I was told by experts at the government's space weather bureau, a solar storm could knock out the nation's entire electrical grid.

And then there were other stars. They too sent out magnetism. They too could affect us. One, called Eta Carinae, was ready to burst (or so said astronomers), and mysterious observations were made. Scientists were baffled by a point deep in the sky that was emitting a vague, unidentified light, and also by long dark streaks that had marked the sky before a solar eclipse.

What else was out there? What other threats?

The greatest threat we knew of was asteroids. Of all the hazards, this was the most frightening. An asteroid could cause all the effects of other disasters — fire, tidal waves, dust clouds, quakes, wind storms, shock waves, darkness, and change in climate — in one package. There were millions of them out there — literally millions — and while most were tiny, all it took was one the size of a garage to take out a city.

The latest estimate was that there were 700 such objects larger than half a mile that came within five million miles of the orbit of the earth. That was crucial because half a mile, which was about eight times the size of the object that exploded over Tunguska, was the size that could cause serious global effects. Other tallies had it at more like 2,000 such objects. Of those, at least 268 were of a proximity and size that even unfazed scientists deemed "potentially hazardous" (read: very dangerous), and whether hazardous or not, there were months that saw up to 24 new discoveries. In most cases the asteroids, chunks of debris left over from the formation of planets, were on long orbits that stretched out to a belt between Mars and

Jupiter, which meant more than 140 million miles, but there were some whose orbits were within the earth's own, between us and the sun, and they were the ones, I was told by Eleanor Helin of NASA's Jet Propulsion Lab (who had discovered the first), "that are most likely to really whomp us."

They were called Aten or Eros (for ancient gods) and eventually, over the course of eons, over millions of years, many were destined to hit earth, and others farther away were also a hazard. All it took was a tug from the gravity of Saturn, Mars, or Jupiter, or a collision with another chunk of debris, to take one out of its regular orbit and send it towards us. They were now suspected of having caused far more effects through history than had been realized (including an ice age), and while there were no recent calamities, the close calls were building. Helin told me that there had been a number of quiet, unpublicized scares. "You put the phone down and say, 'what do I do now?'" she said. In 1998 an asteroid known as XF-11 was calculated to come dangerously close to earth in 2028 until Helin found an old photograph of it and a recalculation indicated that it would not be so near. The next year there was a scare over asteroid AN10, which was projected to come within 25,000 miles of earth in 2027 — or a tenth of the distance to the moon. Although it was decided that it could not hit at that time, there was a "slight" possibility of a collision in 2044 or 2046. How many other objects there were that could come far closer and hit much sooner was not known. Although the general public was under the impression that every inch of the sky was watched, the reality was that a mere fraction was monitored. According to one of the foremost experts, Clark R. Chapman, a mountain-sized space rock big enough to disrupt global climate, "could hit tomorrow and we wouldn't even know it was coming."

The most likely warning time, said David Morrison of NASA, "would be zero."

What we did know was that every twenty-five years a rock 500 yards or larger came within lunar distance and this concerned me because there was a plethora of prophecies to do with such objects. I didn't know how many to believe but as I traveled the world speaking with seers I had been repeatedly warned of what would come from space, and for centuries there had been prophecies of a scourge from heaven. It was the *fear* of fire from the sky. That was what the one prediction said. There would be a great terror.

Something was coming "at great speed," an Irish seer told me, and great speed indeed: objects from space could travel up to 150,000 miles an hour! And they had hit before. During the Great Mesopotamian events at least 13 asteroids or comets (a comet was an asteroid that still flared with gas) struck Australia, where aboriginal legend included what was known as "Devil Rock," and it was suspected that during Incan times a 200-yard rock had entered the atmosphere at a shallow angle in Argentina and skipped across the surface causing a wall of fire. In 1770 a comet had appeared in the sky with a coma that was larger than the diameter of the moon. Some believed that the crossbars of the swastika were a rendition of what a comet looked like to ancients, how it flared, as it was approaching head on.

Would we see this? Would it be part of the chastisement? Would it be one of the warnings? Was it in the secrets?

"Yes, I do think we are going to experience something, a smaller size, not necessarily something that's going to be a kilometer or so," Helin told me, "but we simply don't know that for sure."

She spoke with aggravation about those who downplayed the threat.

"I know I've been at the telescope more than anyone else I know in my lifetime, and I think you've got to have a hands-on sense and my feeling is that we *are* going to see an event."

It was also the opinion of a Harvard astronomer named Brian Marsden. "It seems to me quite likely that in the next five to ten years, given the surveys going on, that we will discover a small object not too far away that in a matter of days is going to come into the earth's atmosphere," he told me. "We can say that it will be too small to do any damage, but the fact is that it would be a first and I don't know how the public would take that. I'm not sure how NASA would take that."

We were in for a scare. The likeliest situation was that we were going to know something was headed our way, and have to wait to see if it missed and if not where it would hit. There were 100,000 asteroids twice the size of the one that blew down all those trees in Siberia, according to Morrison, and one didn't have to hit a populated area to cause mayhem; it had only to strike the ocean. If it hit a hundred miles offshore, it would cause a wash over all the major East Coast cities. "In the absence of wave dispersion, even an asteroid 200 meters in diameter impacting in mid-Atlantic would produce tsunami several meters high on either side of the ocean," wrote scientists from Los Alamos National Laboratory in 1998.

What about one larger?
Now we were in the realm of a disaster larger than any that could be visited by a quake. So great would the speed be that as it smashed into the sea, water would not be a significant source of resistance. The asteroid would go all the way to the bottom and cause a crater on the floor of the ocean. And as the water parted, walls of it would rise several miles high in the immediate vicinity. Close to shore this would cause a disaster greater than any since Noah, and even if it hit in the middle of the ocean, an asteroid just half a mile in size would cause a 35-foot wave to wash on the coastlines. And it could be yet bigger. One of the scientists, Jack Hills, told me that an asteroid three miles in size would send up a wall of water that was more than

twenty miles high at the point of impact. While that would diminish as it traveled, by the time it got to the United States (a distance of 1,800 miles), it would still be enough to wash all the way to the Appalachian foothills. Delaware, Maryland, Virginia, and lower New York would be flooded. All coastal cities would be history.

And there were asteroids that size. There were asteroids larger. The biggest known to cross the orbit of the earth, Ivar and Betulia, were each about five miles in diameter (slightly smaller than the object thought to have caused extinction of the dinosaurs), but way, way out there beyond Mars were asteroids the size of small planets. One, Ceres, was 600 miles in width, and it wasn't even worth discussing what that would do; there would be no semblance of *anything* left.

It was unlikely that an object approaching that size would threaten for millions of years, but all it took was one a thousandth that size to enter the realm of cataclysmic. And it had happened. Helin cited the legends from islanders as well as accounts in the Bible that hinted at impacts. "For a long time we pooh-poohed and discouraged this sort of speculation because we would have just a little bit of information here and there, just a trace, and we would just push it off the table," she told me. "But the more I see, the more I think there's an awful lot out there that we've ignored for an awful long time."

It had been during the medieval chastisement that islanders fled from one island to another, that there were the accounts from New Zealand of fire from the sky, and right there in *Revelation* 8:8 it predicted "something like a huge mountain all in flames" that would be "cast into the sea."

There were millions of comets — *millions*. They were out in the Kuiper Belt past Neptune or way beyond Pluto in the Oort Belt, which was estimated to be up to 200,000 times the distance of the sun. These belts served as gargantuan reservoirs for comets that were "short-term" if they made their orbits around the sun within 200 years and "long-term" if more. It was here that the greatest danger, the terror, resided. Although most comets were small, there were also huge ones that were invisible until they approached the sun and that even then might arrive with less than three months of notice. So infrequent were their passes that we had no idea of their existence. And they would come at speeds greater than those of asteroids. They were at the root of the very word "disaster," which meant "evil star" (etymologically dis-evil; aster-star). They were what Helin called the "stealth bombers in the solar system, the ones that give no warning, that leave no calling card, that are just there in our face," and as she added, "These long-period comets are always being found and just thank God they haven't come that close. Some are earth-crossers, and so you've got to be concerned."

CHAPTER 50

Floods, a Flash, Darkness

The numbers were jarring. Although no one had an actual count, there were estimates as high as a million comets within the orbit of Neptune, and in total 200 million in the Kuiper. Out there beyond Pluto there was no telling how much debris was circling, and it wasn't just a direct hit that was dangerous. If earth passed through a comet's dust veil, there would be a rain of fire.

Clearly, space was not an empty vacuum, and there was no way to know when a comet or asteroid would be bumped by some kind of cosmic vibration and head for earth; there was no telling how many already *were* heading in such a direction. They moved in all sorts of formations — as dust, as chunks, as loners, in small couplings, in clusters, and in long trails of large and small debris that made periodic passes.

Wherever it had originated, it now seemed clear that extraterrestrial debris had affected the earth at least five times in the last 6,000 years and researchers were beginning to blame it for everything from the falling fire at Sodom to the climate jolt at the end of the Roman period (if that event had not been caused by a volcano). At Queen's University in Northern Ireland Professor Mike Baillie said it was very clear from the narrowness of growth rings in the bog oaks and archeological timber, which of course indicated how good a growing season there had been, that a great catastrophe struck the earth around 540 A.D., cooling the climate, ostensibly with dust. "The trees are unequivocal that something quite terrible happened," he told the British Association's Festival of Science. "It was a catastrophic downturn that shows up all over the world." Traditional myths recorded in 13th-century texts referred to a comet in Gaul around 540 when the sky *seemed to be on fire*.

Floods. Darkness. There was no question that objects traveling with such velocity could produce apocalyptical effects, clouds of dust that would obscure the sun and circle the earth for years. That would drive down temperatures, leading to famine and epidemics. The impact could cause great earthquakes and might even trigger the activity of volcanoes, not to mention tidal surge, which was why an increasing number of scientists looking at past episodes of cold, drought, floods, and seismic damage were beginning to blame asteroids. The periodic rendezvous with a trail of debris could mean decades or centuries of such effects — dust, darkness, meteors, small asteroids, temperature downturns, and tidal waves — as the earth traveled through a particularly dense part of the stream, and might explain not only the length of certain episodes, but also their suddenness. There were the glassy spherules found in Mesopotamia from the 2300 B.C. event — spherules from something hot — and such had also been detected during the 1600 and 1000 B.C. upheavals. "The spherules found, which are the only hard evidence from these events, could be of volcanic origin, but according to the literature available they could not be associated with any known major volcanism," wrote Franzen and Larsson. "Their heterogeneous composition points to another formation mechanism, maybe comet or asteroid impacts in ocean shelf sediments. Hence we take the liberty to suggest that relatively large extraterrestrial bodies hit somewhere in the eastern North Atlantic, probably on the shelf of the Atlantic coast of North Africa or southern Europe, around 1600-1400 B.C.

and 1000-950 B.C." They said the object was probably half a kilometer and had affected southeastern and central Europe, the British Isles, the Near and Far East, and the Mediterranean parts of Africa, with global repercussions. They also suggested that such occurrences returned every 570 years in some cases and just over 1,100 years in others, raising the possibility that asteroids or comets had at least contributed — had at least *punctuated* — the events of 2300 B.C., 1600 B.C., 1100 B.C., and 540 A.D., along with causing the migrations of islanders, the strange strike on the moon in the 12th century, and the black comets that had announced plague.

It was speculated that streams of debris made the rounds and that in some were thousands of objects: asteroids, mountain or island-sized boulders, smaller meteoroids, assorted celestial fragments, dust, and in one case the remnant of what had once been the Encke Comet, which some believed was all the result of a break-up that occurred in the inner solar system long ago. In Armagh, at the same observatory where I was shown the old weather diaries, several of the world's leading asteroid experts maintained that there indeed had been such periodic bombardments and estimated that there could be 5,000 to 10,000 dormant comets which could cause gigantic problems, what they called "dark-Halleys." The fact that they could come without detection until three to six months before impact meant there would be no means of defense; the comfortable margin for preparation, Dr. Marsden told me, would be ten to twenty *years*. And if one arrived from behind the sun, we would be all but blind to its arrival. "They can take you by surprise in a matter of weeks," said Donald Yeoman at the Jet Propulsion Lab. "If it's a smaller object and it doesn't start vaporizing very quickly and it's in the daylight sky, coming from the general direction of the sun, it can run into us before we have a chance to observe it in the night sky." It could also be large. Halley's was nine miles wide, Hale-Bopp more than 25; which meant cataclysmic. Could

Hale-Bopp have hit? Yes, I was told, if it had been captured by Jupiter and changed to a small orbit in the solar system. Every 3,000 to 5,000 years astronomers expected an object that was at least 600 feet in diameter. That was several times the size of an asteroid that, if it hit London Hill, would kill an estimated ten million people.

Clearly, streams of debris hit the earth on a regular basis, and without the shielding of God, without the Holy Spirit, would do so again. These were matters, said Dr. Clube, that required "urgent attention." Estimations varied but some claimed the last event involving a dense part of the Taurids had occurred from 500 B.C. until the birth of Christ, and if, as others thought, the periodicity was on the order of 1,500 to 2,000 years, this too was "overdue" or close to it. It had become "fashionable to assume that the world is safe," said the Oxford scientist, "when in fact multiple-Tunguska bombardments, releasing around 5,000 megatons, the equivalent of a full-scale nuclear war, may happen at intervals of about 1,500 years, producing a Dark Age."

It's what may have occurred during the Mesopotamian Chastisement — a series of asteroids that struck near the Dead Sea but also elsewhere — and it was what was most likely to happen if a global asteroid event was in the works now. Multiple strikes. A 100-yarder here, a 200-yarder there. It would be a point of punctuation.

Strike. Another strike. A third. There would be overpressure, a pulse of infrared, a flash of heat. It would be incredibly bright, much brighter than the sun. Anyone looking at it would be blinded. The shock would roll large objects. It would pulverize. It would suck upward. Debris would be ejected into the stratosphere. Near the crater the air itself would be on fire. Flames would be ignited at a distance of a hundred miles. What amounted to a magnitude-8 earthquake would be felt by those living 300 miles away. There would be dust all around, more debris than a hydrogen bomb. It would look like the ground was heaving. Then the storm of dust would halt, stop for an eerie moment, reverse, and sweep back to the direction of the impact, as air was taken up in the vacuum. At just 600-yards wide a comet or asteroid would cause total destruction over an area the size of Connecticut; if it hit in the Midwest rocks would be falling on both coasts within ten minutes. At half-a-mile in size, it would reach cataclysmic levels. And at just twice that size — a mile to a mile-and a half — it would blast a crater the size of Washington, D.C. to a depth of twenty Washington Monuments.

There would be no agriculture for years. The ground would be atomized. Millions or even a billion would die. If it hit Washington the blast zone would reach north to Maine, south to Atlanta. A hole would be punched through the atmosphere and debris thrown into space would cause massive fires when it returned.

If it hit the ocean, if it struck between Hawaii and California, the water would superheat and there would be hyper-wind and the wave would be 160-feet as it came ashore, flooding violently inland for twenty miles.

Chapter 51

"Return to My embrace"

"The intensity (of chastisements) can be diminished or be lost forever," I was told by an obscure seer in South America, but if not, she quoted Mary as saying, *"the great trial will come."*

So far, there were few indications that society was awakening. Despite the prophecies and despite the signs of danger, despite what nature was telling us, there was still no mass conversion. There were some good signs: thousands protesting the exclusion of public prayer in North Carolina during the summer of 2000, or gathering as believers in Portland, and two million — five times the number at Woodstock — flooding to see the Pope on Youth Day (the greatest assembly of people in the history of the Eternal City).

But humanity was still falling short.

If at LaSalette a famine had been caused by swearing with the name of Jesus, and if at Fatima there had been a warning that many went to hell for sins of the flesh, what was the outcome for a society that didn't even consider such things sin any longer?

A line had been crossed, and there was darkness. Society had allowed the seed of anti-spirit and now something was coming. At Medjugorje the Virgin had made it plain that she didn't want those who were converted to obsess on it; they were to recognize the danger and now pray to avert it. That was the call. The attitude of the Christian was hope. It was salvation! God did not have a hard heart. He was only love. He wished the best. Obsession with the negative, Mary wanted everyone to know, was not the message. *"Those who think only of wars, evils, and punishment do not do well,"* she had advised. *"For a Christian, there is only one attitude toward the future. It is hope of salvation. Your responsibility is to accept divine peace, live it, and spread it. Definitely eliminate all anguish. Whoever abandons himself to God does not have room in his heart for anguish. Love your enemies. Banish from your heart hatred, bitterness, preconceived judgments. Pray for your enemies and call the divine blessing over them. Pray to the Holy Spirit. Place yourselves permanently in a state of spirit bathed in prayer."*

It was the call of the Bible: If there was enough prayer, if there was repentance, heaven could be felt on earth. Natural laws could be suspended! *"Be converted,"* said the Madonna. *"It will be too late when the sign comes. Beforehand, several warnings will be given to the world. Hurry to be converted. I need your prayers and your penance. I will pray to my Son to spare you the punishment. Be converted without delay. You do not know the plans of God; you will not be able to know them. You will not know what God will send, nor what He will do."*

There was not to be an obsession with gloom but it was time to issue strong warnings. While scientists believed a strike by a series of small asteroids would be the likeliest extraterrestrial event, there was always the chance for the terror of a comet. One day mankind might awaken to news that astronomers had spotted a small comet coming very suddenly from behind the sun, only days away, or a giant that would sweep by in several months, a comet the size of Hale-Bopp, but this time one that would come much closer, with the distinct possibility that it would make a direct hit or break up and shower earth.

"Return to My embrace"

No one wanted that — the trial of waiting as the approaching object grew from a speck to a distinct celestial dot and then to an orb that was there each time we looked out the window. All day, all night, in fitful sleep, a world facing the possibility of mass cataclysmic destruction might repent of its errors, might finally perceive God's attempt at drawing its attention. Such a close call might be the final warning before the worst of punishment.

In all likelihood that chastisement would include war and epidemics. Except for astronomical events, or a sudden, cataclysmic change in temperature (perhaps through a tilt in the earth's axis), there were no known earthly events that could cause quite the carnage that these could. Judging from what was in both the LaSalette and Fatima secrets, war was also a player in the Medjugorje secrets, and we are all well acquainted with the capability of nuclear bombs, which in an all-out conflict would erase the majority of people through residual radiation if not the initial blasts. It took only a few detonations to create a global ecological crisis if radiation was carried in the wind and contaminated rivers, lakes, and farms to the point of no return.

That was "wormwood" (the Bible said a third of the waters would one day be poisoned, which could readily happen), and then there was disease: the prospect that millions would die from influenza or as a more exotic illness attacked the organs — causing massive convulsions and hemorrhage as have been glimpsed with ebola in Africa. A new plague, a mutated microbe, could begin there or in China or in the southern hinterlands of what had been the Soviet Union, perhaps from old leaking depots of germ warfare agents or in the West due to the transference of virus from animals cloned to provide human organs. It could come from wildlife, or farm animals, and with jet travel, reach anywhere in the world in less than a hundred hours. It could spread through the air or by touch or water or food, by sex. It could torment areas instantly, completely, with a speed that would first amaze and then appall. It could be a strain never before seen that attacked like ebola but let the person live long enough to spread it. It could be a Frankenstein virus (as they called it at CDC), with new spikes of protein that eluded a cure or vaccination, that allowed it to rage through schools, through work, through the supermarkets, that allowed it to come into entire regions at once, to arrive in a major city by way of a single tourist or postman or businessman.

It would be like a curtain dropping. Fever. Violent coughing. These were things that could occur on a global scale at any time and if one came with the same proportion as the Black Death, which had taken a third of those in Europe, the global numbers according to current demographics would be two billion.
That was more than seven times the U.S. population and close to the combined populations of China and India and the sort of event that once again would cause people to pull their hair, to curse the lives they had lived without God. And it was possible; it was at the point of nearly being probable. When the world became a staging area for hell, when it sought to destroy God's plan, when it made the bold attempt to circumvent His rule — when there was coldness, haughtiness, and killing, when science sought to rule all — God broke it down. It was that or let all the more fall into hell, the abyss that had been described by Lucia as "a great sea of fire which seemed to be under the earth. Plunged in this fire were demons and souls in human form, like transparent embers, all blackened or burnished bronze, floating about in the conflagration, now raised into the air by the flames that issued from within themselves together with great clouds of smoke, now falling back on every side like sparks in a huge fire, without weight or equilibrium, and amid shrieks and groans of pain and despair, which horrified us and made us tremble with fear. The demons could be distinguished by their terrifying and repellent likeness to frightful and unknown animals, all black and transparent."

"There are many people there," added Marija of Medjugorje, who had a similar vision. "I particularly noticed a beautiful young girl. But when she came near the fire, she was no longer beautiful. She came out of the fire like an animal; she was no longer human. The Blessed Mother told me that God gives us all choices. Everyone responds to these choices. Everyone can choose if he wants to go to hell or not. At the moment of death, God gives everyone the grace to see his whole life, to see what he has done, to recognize the results of his choices on earth. And each person, when he sees himself in the divine light of reality, chooses for himself where he belongs. Every individual chooses for himself what he personally deserves for all eternity."

It was God in His mercy Who broke down the constructs of wrong choices and while there were many who attempted to portray Him as too gentle and kind to chastise, to purify — and while there was no doubt that He was the essence of love — He was also a God Who reprimanded, Who rebuked, Who called the Pharisees "hypocrites" (*Matthew* 23:14), Who termed a disciple "satan" (*Mark* 8:33), Who warned of Gehenna and the gnashing of teeth in the "outer darkness" (*Matthew* 8:12).

God knew what awaited sin and in His mercy would reorient us, would purge evil. If the devil was not stopped there would be diseases and they would not be diseases that science could eradicate. *"Did you not taste enough of his deceptions and slavery in his viciousness through the ages?"* asked the Lord in a reputed Canadian apparition. *"Never have My children delighted in sin as now. In Noah's age I cleansed the world of sins much lesser than these in which My children now take delight. I call each of you to return to My embrace, to seek shelter in Me through your sincere prayer and in My living gifts, but My children remain oblivious to the signs. Babylon has been rebuilt. It stands again. Soon in your midst and in full view will also stand a grand image of a false god. The symbol of this image will be worshipped by many, in almost every land."*

If it was true that sins were now greater than in the time of Noah, then the last secrets of Medjugorje were a larger catastrophe than those I have described. And Noah was again in the news. In 2000, archaeologists found remains of a man-made structure more than 300 feet below the surface of the Black Sea, providing what even the secular media reported was "dramatic new evidence of an apocalyptic flood 7,500 years ago that may have inspired the biblical story of Noah." A team of explorers had found the outlines of an ancient coast below the current water line, the first visual evidence that a flood had occurred in the region eons ago, followed by subsequent disasters such as those in Egyptian, Minoan, Greek, Medieval, and Roman times.

"*Out of my love for you, these now are the times of My special graces,*" said the Lord. "*Return to My embrace. Bring to Me your tired and sick bodies, consecrate your wounded hearts to Me, allow the splendor of My love into your souls and you shall be healed, nourished, crowned, and freed by My love. I caution you to soberly and courageously examine the paths of your lives, those from the ages past and these of today.*"

We had to stamp out sin. We had to conquer hate. There was a central commandment, and that was to love. When men loved there was no murder; there was no deception. It was the force — along with faith! — that would thwart chastisement.

"*The disturbances which, in these times, will be brought to you by the heavens are intended to exile the malefactor from your souls,*" said the Lord during the alleged Canadian revelation. "*He seduces you with false emotions and beliefs. He is the infection which you, in My love, shall eradicate. The Shining Darkness knows that the time of his evil is approaching the end. My children,* be vigilant, for the Shining Darkness will multiply his evil powers, especially where he recognizes the divine heavenly presence. Each of you, convert totally and, through My gifts, you shall be the victors over the malefactor. Convert and your prayers will be granted. Through your faith and love for me and for one another you shall receive My gift back, your human dignity. Because of your conversion the Shining Darkness shall lose this battle. But the victims among you shall be many. In these special times you will soon be witnesses of My graces. Many among you who were tortured, disgraced, banished, exiled, and persecuted will soon take their place among those who are first. Convert and through My love you shall be the victors. The tragedies which the Shining Darkness is preparing as his 'gift' to you My children will be thwarted by your faith."

I knew nothing of the end of the world but I knew that something would happen, that God would act in some manner and that He — we — would win. Through a simple turning to Him, happiness awaited. No suffering on earth was much in the light of eternity, and all we had to do was ask God to come into our lives and to remember each waking moment that every moment was a test. We had been given whole and pure souls but we had forgotten that there was one and only one Truth and that the "gifts" of the devil led to damnation. He was the "shining darkness" because he glittered in a way that lured us into something that was blacker than black. *"Every one of My children whom the Shining Darkness seduces, accuses Me and complains that I am the one punishing you,"* said the revelation. *"Even in the moment which you call the time of judgment, each soul is asked what it brings to the eternal paradise with its earthly life. Deep is My pain whenever I cannot open the doors of paradise to a soul which has not accepted My gifts and My infinite love. I tell you that by far more souls proceed to eternal damnation than into the peace, tranquility, and joy of paradise."*

My heart leapt at the descriptions of heaven. I heard from visionaries and those who had near-death experiences that it was a place of incomparable beauty, with colors like no earthly colors, with a consuming peace. They described the rolling hills and buildings made as from precious stones — buildings that were somehow defined and yet without walls — and flowers that emanated light and swayed as they praised Him.

People in heaven were happy because they were in God's presence. There was a feeling of total well-being. They had found their true home. That was what God intended and what He fought to save for us — what we now had to fight to win back. The lesson was Christ and if He was not honored there would be chastisement. The Lord had terrific devices at His disposal. We have only glanced at them. If man did not return to God and also return to God His *authority* — His full dominion over nature, especially over the creation of life — then He would cleanse the earth, break down our technology, reduce us to the simplicity of the Dark Ages (if not worse). There would not be another Flood as in the time of Noah (*Genesis* 9:11-16), but endless other things could happen. Only with God and through God could we stop it. If we proceeded without Him, we would see tragedy in short order, and in this regard, the greatest danger was cloning. If we began to synthesize humans, it would bring certain destruction. *"I am the Creator, the Redeemer, and the Truth,"* God had said and when we tried to circumvent Him, when we sought to immortalize the flesh and alter Creation — when we tried to reverse the judgment of Eden — we were aspiring to the Throne. *"Out of My love, for the justice of My children who consecrate their lives to Me, I wipe away their tears and pain,"* said the Lord. *"I am with you for all times. By your return into My embrace, I gift to you the power to thwart all of those intentions of the malefactor against which I warn you. Satan knows that he does not have much time left. Resist him tirelessly, evict Satan from your lives, never allow him any place among you."*

We did not have to repeat the tragedies of the past but so far that's what we were doing and a battle raged around us. Make no mistake: a battle raged. Arrogance. Suicide. Abortion. I must admit to deep concerns about the entire culture, the very premise of what we have erected, the way we have now glorified science far beyond what it deserves and in so doing have repeated the sin of idolatry. As evil grows there is the danger of the personage of evil and I must also admit concern that he will act through science and a governing body such as the United Nations, to whom no one should surrender sovereignty. It was my fear: that a man who used science and the media would rise, a man more of influence than raw political power, but one who would try to affect a new world order. Was that in the future? Did LaSalette still have warnings for us? God would win but we were in for real disasters and real war! *"Here is the King of kings of darkness, here is the beast with his subjects, calling himself the savior of the world,"* Melanie had concluded in her secret. *"He will rise proudly into the air to go to heaven. He will be smothered by the breath of the Archangel Michael. He will fall, and the earth, which will have been in a continuous series of evolutions for three days, will open up its fiery bowels; and he will have plunged for eternity with all his followers into the everlasting chasms of hell. And then water and fire will purge the earth and consume all the works of human pride and all will be renewed. God will be served and glorified."*

Notes

Chapters 1 & 2: I use a number of different bibles, and so at times chapter and verse numbers may differ. For the main part I use The New American and King James. The study sponsored by the National Science Foundation was "Disasters By Design, A Reassessment of Natural Hazards in the United States," by Dennis S. Mileti of the University of Colorado. It says a quake in Los Angeles could cost $250 billion in direct economic loss. M. M. Mandelkehr's quote is from "An Integrated Model for an Earthwide Event at 2300 BC, Part I: The Archeological Evidence," in *S.I.S. Review*, volume five. I also use two follow-up papers, "An Integrated Model for an Earthwide Event at 2300 B.B., Part II, the Climatological Evidence," in *Chronology and Catastrophism Review* and "An Integrated Model for an Earthwide Event at 2300 B.C., Part III, the Geological Evidence," in *C & C Review*, volume X. For the Bronze Age event see also "Comparative Analysis of Late Holocene Environmental and Social Upheaval" by Benny J. Peiser in a report called "Natural Catastrophes During Bronze Age Civilisations" published by Archaeopress in Oxford, England, in 1998. The Weiss quote is from *Third Millennium B.C. Climate Change and Old World Collapse* (Springer). For the images of destruction in Egypt see the Leiden Papyrus and R. O. Faulkner, "Notes on the Admonitions of an Egyptian Sage," *Journal of Egyptian Archeology* 50 (1964). The Courty quote is from "The Soil Record of an Exceptional Event at 4000 B.P. in the Middle East," in *Natural Catastrophes During Bronze Age Civilisations,* published by Archaeopress in Oxford, England, in 1998. The quote from Herodotus on depravity in ancient times comes from *Sexual Life in Ancient Egypt* by Lise Manniche (London: KPI).

Chapters 3 & 4: For the Minoan event see *Thera — Pompeii of the Ancient Aegean* by Christos G. Doumas. The Pellegrino quote is from *Unearthing Atlantis*. For destruction in Greece see *The Greek Dark Ages*, published by Ernest Benn Ltd., London: 1972. See also remarks on this period from J. M. Roberts in *The Penguin History of the World* (Penguin Books, New York: 1995). For Lars Franzen and Thomas B. Larsson see "Landscape Analysis and Stratigraphical and Geochemical Investigations of Playa and Alluvial Fan Sediments in Tunisia and Raised Bog Deposits in Sweden" in *Natural Catastrophes During Bronze Age Civilizations* (Archaeopress, 1998). For destruction in Hungary at this time see R. Carpenter in *Discontinuity in Greek Civilization* (Cambridge University Press).

Chapters 5 & 6: For historical asteroids see William Napier's article, "Comets, Dragons & Prophets of Doom," in *Frontiers*, published by the Particle Physics and Astronomy Research Council in England. For another example of climate change (this time around 850 B.C.) see "Dating Raised Bogs: New Aspects of AMS 14C Wiggle Matching, A Reservoir Effect and Climatic Change" in *Quaternary Science Reviews*, volume 14. For morality in the Roman Empire see *Sexual Life in Ancient Rome* by Otto Kiefer (George Routledge & Sons, 1934). The Etienne quote is from *Pompeii: the Day a City Died* (Harry N. Abrams Inc., 1992) and for Caligula I use *Caligula* by Arthur Ferrill (Thames and Hudson, 1991) and *Caligula, The Corruption of Power* by Anthony A. Barrett (B.T. Batsford Ltd., 1989) among other sources.

Chapters 7 & 8: The Brion quotes are from *Pompeii and Herculaneum* (Crown Publishers, 1960). The Wellesley quote is from *The Long Year 69* (Paul Elek Ltd., 1975). See also *Pompeii, Its Life and Art* by August Mau (The MacMillan Company, 1904). Information on the Huns comes from *The World of the Huns* by Otto J. Maenchen-Helfen (University of California Press, 1973), and *A History of Attila and the Huns* by E. A. Thompson (Oxford, 1948). For more on ancient drought see "2000 Years of Drought Variability in the Central United States" published by the Bulletin of the American Meteorological Society in December 1998, volume 79, number 12. The quote from David Keys is from his well-researched book, *Catastrophe* (Ballantine, 1999), which was the source for much of the climate material.

Chapters 9 & 10: For background I use *A.D. 1000* by Richard Erdoes (Harper & Row, 1988). I also use Barbara Tuchman's thoroughly researched *A Distant Mirror* (Knopf, 1978) for some of the history of the Middle Ages. Similarly, I use Thomas Bokenkotter's *A Concise History of the Catholic Church* (Image Books, 1979). The quote from Lamb is from his book *Climate History and the Modern World*, second edition (Routledge, London: 1995). The Pacific migrations and phenomena come from mathematician Emilio Spedicato's speculations in "Evidence of Tunguska-Type Impacts Over the Pacific Basin Around the Year 1178," issued by the Department of Mathematics at the University of Bergamo in 1997. The impact in the Bald Mountains was reported in the September 4, 2000, CCNet on the internet by E.P. Grondine. Deaux's account is in *The Black Death* (Weybright and Talley). The description of the disease itself comes from *The Black Death* by Philip Ziegler (The John Day Company, 1969). See also *The Black Death, The Impact of the Fourteenth-Century Plague*, a chapter in there "Al-Manbiji's 'Report of the Plague:' A Treatise on the Plague of 764-65/1362-64 in the Middle East," by Michael Dols (Center for Medieval and Early Renaissance Studies, Binghamton, New York, 1982). For the light in Paris see *Exodus To Arthur* by Mike Baillie (B.T. Batsford, 1999), page 161.

Chapters 11, 12, & 13: The quotes from Dumanoir and Rousselot come from Sandra Zimdars-Swartz's excellent, *Encountering Mary* (Princeton University Press, 1991), which I use for much of the background on LaSalette. Another major source was *A Woman Clothed with the Sun*, edited by John J. Delaney (Image Books, 1961). I also visited the mountain. The University of Michigan study that had to do with church attendance was released by the school's Institute for Social research on December 19, 1997.

Chapters 14 & 15: For historical events I often use Bernard Grun's *The Timetables of History* (Touchstone, 1963). Much on the Nazis and Hitler, including the magician planting bottles as an incantation, comes from an excellent book, *The Twisted Cross*, by Joseph J. Carr (Harvest House, 1985). The remark on wave height and other background hurricane information comes from *Florida's Hurricane History* by Jay Barnes (The University of North Carolina Press, 1998), which is also the source for the quote from Elisee Reclus, who had originally written this in a book called *The Ocean*, and Lieutenant Colonel W. Reid, whose book was *Law of Storms*. The quote from the ship captain comes from *Isaac's Storm* by Erik Larson (Crown, 1999), page 121. The quote on Chartres is from William Thomas Walsh in *Shrine's of Heaven's Bright Queen* (London: Burns & Oates, 1904). For Marx see Richard Wurmbrand's fascinating book *Marx and Satan* (Crossway Books).

Chapters 16 & 17: For background I used *The Timetables of History* by Bernard Grun, based on Werner Stein's *Kulturfahrplan* (Simon & Schuster, 1991). I use the Larson book for the description of the Galveston flood and the formation and onset of that storm. I also use "The Virtual Tour of Galveston Island" by Todd A. Guillory from Galveston's website. The description of the 1926 hurricane, including the quote on the Rheims cathedral, comes in part from *The Florida Hurricane and Disaster* by L. F. Reardon (Arva Parks and Company, 1986). His quote is on page 44. The millibar readings come from NOAA. The information on aerial lights comes from *The UFO Encyclopedia*, edited by John Spencer (Avon). For the quake in San Francisco I again refer to *Darkest Hours* by Jay Robert Nash. The quote from the local newspaper was from an edition put out jointly by the San Francisco *Call, Chronicle,* and *Examiner,* who pooled their resources after much of their individual operations were destroyed. The quote from Walsh comes from his terrific book, *Our Lady of Fatima* (Image Books, 1954). Other material on Fatima comes from a personal journey there as well as books such as *The Third Secret* by Frere Michel de la Sainte Trinite (Immaculate Heart Publications, 1985); *Fatima — Tragedy and Triumph,* by Frere Francois Marie de Agnes (Immaculate Heart Publications, 1994); and especially an erudite book called *The Secret of Fatima, Fact and Legend,* by Joaquin Maria Alonso (The Ravengate Press, 1979). For Lenin see *The Young Lenin* by Leon Trotsky and *Lenin: the Compulsive Revolutionary.* The Cladwell quote is from an article called "The Dead Zone" in *The New Yorker,* September 29, 1997. The information on Fort Riley comes from Dr. W. David Parsons and an article made available through the University of Kansas website called "The Spanish Lady and the Newfoundland Regiment." The quote from Lucia is from her book, *Fatima in Lucia's Own Words* (Postulation Centre, Fatima, Portugal, 1989).

Chapters 18 & 19: For Margaret Sanger see *Birth Control Review* volume II, number 10 (October 1918). See also *Birth Control in America* by David Kennedy (Yale University Press, 1970); *Margaret Sanger* by Madeline Gray (Richard Marek Publishers), and *Pioneer of the Future: Margaret Sanger,* by Emily Taft Douglas (Holt, Rinehart, and Winston). Some of the information on famine comes from the files of Congress (Report to Congress: U.S. Commission on Ukrainian Famine — 1988). See also *The Black Deeds of the Kremlin — A White Book.* For the Chinese floods see *Darkest Hours* by Jay Robert Nash (Pocketbooks, 1977).

Chapters 20, 21, & 22: For Ukraine see my books *Witness* and *The Final Hour* (Queenship Publishing, Santa Barbara). Again I use *Florida's Hurricane History* (University of North Carolina Press, 1998). For details on the third secret see again *The Third Secret* by Frere Michel de la Sainte Trinite (Immaculate Heart Publications, 1985). For a background on evil in Europe, including witchcraft, see *Witch Hunting in Southwestern Germany 1562-1684*, by H. C. Erik Midelfort (Stanford University Press).

Chapters 23–28: In addition to my interview with her, the quotes from the teacher in Hilo come from a first-person account, "Carried to Sea by a Tidal Wave," that she published in the March 1959 *Reader's Digest*. The quote from Mieko Browne was from *World Magazine*, October 1996, an article entitled "I Survived a Tsunami." The Nash quote is from *Darkest Hours* (previously cited). I also draw information from The Tornado Project website in St. Johnsbury, Vermont. The quote on the fog and other information on Tangshan is from *The Great Tangshan Earthquake of 1976* edited by Chen Yong, Kam-ling Tsoi, Chen Feibi, Gao Zhenhuan, Zou Qijia, and Chen Zhangli (Pergamon Press, 1988). For abortion and witchcraft see "The Massacre of Innocence" by Eric Holmberg and Jay Rogers posted on the internet, and "Abortion, Cancer, and Baal Worship" on the website run by Spiritual Warfare News. For the attempt on the Pope see *Pope John Paul II* by Tad Szulc (Scribner, 1995). The photograph that shows Christ and the Virgin in a mushroom cloud was circulated by a news-photography agency called Black Star and appeared in *Newsweek*. The quotes from Medjugorje seers come in several places from *Queen of the Cosmos* by Jan Connell (Paraclete Press, 1990), or her book *Visions of the Children* (St. Martin's, 1992). In addition to the private interview, Mirjana's quotes come from *The Apparitions of Our Lady at Medjugorje* by Svetozar Kraljevic (Franciscan Herald Press, 1984). I may note here that Billy Graham commented on natural disasters as a response to evil in his book *Storm Warning* published in 1992 by Word Publishing.

Chapters 29–33: For the sun and its effects see "Lunar and Solar Cycles in Earthquakes of the American West," by Martin Kokus with Darren Ritter in *Cycles*, November 1988. For volcanoes and tides see, "On the Triggering of Volcanic Eruptions by Earth Tides," by F.J. Mauk and M.J.S. Johnston in the *Journal of Geophysical Research*, volume 78, number 17, which also contained an article called "Tidal Cycles of Volcanic Eruptions: Fortnightly to 19 Yearly Periods," by Wayne L. Hamilton on Hawaiian eruptions. See also "Tide-Forming Forces and Earthquakes" by G.P. Tamrazyan in *Icarus*, volume 7. The quote from Sister Lucia is from a pamphlet called "Two Hours With Sister Lucia" by Carlos Evaristo (St. Anne's Oratory, P.O. Box 133, 2496 Fatima Codex, Portugal). The Kleinberg quote is from *The Florida Hurricane Disaster* (Centennial Books, 1992). For typhoon intensity see a paper called "FAQ: Hurricanes, Typhoons and Tropical Cyclones" issued by Chris Landsea of NOAA, available on the internet. For ancient Peruvian storms see M. M. Mandelkehr's paper, "An Integrated Model for an Earthwide Event at 2300 B.C. in *C.& C. Review*, volume X. For the Mississippi see "The Summer of 1993, Flooding in the Midwest and Drought in the Southeast," by Neal Lott of the National Climatic Data Center. The *Reader's Digest* story was in the December 1993 issue. For Ebola I used *The Hot Zone* by Richard Preston (Random House, 1994) and *The Coming Plague* by Laurie Garrett (Penguin, 1995). The quote from the Marshall Islands was in *The New York Times* on December 1, 1997, an article called "Global Warming" by Nicholas D. Kristof. For asteroid impacts see "Tsunami From Asteroid and Comet Impacts: the Vulnerability of Europe" by Jack G. Hills and M. Patrick Goda in the International Journal of the Tsunami Society (volume 16, number 1). For NASA and asteroids see its report "The Spaceguard Survey," issued on January 25, 1992, and its

"Memorandum for the Record" during Congressional hearings on May 21, 1998.

Chapters 34–39: The mention of the invisible "assailant" in India comes from *The Times of India*, July 7, 2000. For a compendium of Marian apparitions around the world see *A Guide to Apparitions of Our Blessed Virgin Mary* by Peter Heintz (Gabriel Press in Sacramento). For the earth's core and the fact that it may be out of balance see, "Earth's Rapidly Spinning Core Is a Planet Within the Planet" in *The New York Times*, December 17, 1996. *The Los Angeles Times* story on the crows was on August 10, 2000, and was headlined, "Tokyo's Feathered Terrorists." For Hokkaido see "Extreme Inundation Flows During the Hokkaido-Nansei-Oki Tsunami," by Vasily V. Titov and Costas Emmanuel Synolakis in NOAA's website. For expected increase in storms and especially lightning see, "Possible Implications of Global Climate Change on Global Lightning Distributions and Frequencies" by Colin Price and David Rind in the *Journal of Geophysical Research*, volume 99, number D5, May 20, 1994. They are also authors of a study entitled, "The Effect of Global Warming on Lightning Frequencies," which was provided to me by the National Meteorological Library and Archive in England. For drought see, "2000 Years of Drought Variability in the Central United States," by Connie A. Woodhouse and Jonathan T. Overpeck, *Bulletin of the American Meteorology Society*, volume 79, number 12, December 1998. The *USA Today* quote comes from its January 17, 1996, edition.

Chapters 40–51: Father Amorth made his warning in a book called *An Exorcist Tells His Story* (Ignatius Press). In addition to press clips and personal interviews, one Gray quote came from the December 1999 issue of *GQ* Magazine. The Princeton study on wind speed was done at the government's Geophysical Fluid Dynamics Laboratory and was published in the February 13, 1998, issue of

Science by Thomas Knutson, Robert Tuleya, and Yoshio Kurihara. The estimate of damages in Miami comes from interviews with Dr. Robert Sheets, Dr. Chris Landsea, and Dr. Roger Pielke, as well as Pielke's and Landsea's joint paper, "Normalized Hurricane Damages in the United States: 1925-1995." The figures on return rates were provided to me by the National Hurricane Center. Data on wildfires come from the Lawrence Berkeley National Laboratory and a paper entitled "Will Climate Change Spark More Wildfire Damage?" by Margaret S. Torn, Evan Mills, and Jeremy Fried for the U.S. Environmental Protection Agency (LBNL Report Number 42592). For volcanoes and global warming see, "Blowing Hot and Cold" in *New Scientist* (volume 156, issue 2103). For the Seattle events see, "Tree Ring Correlation Between Prehistoric Landslides and Abrupt Tectonic Events in Seattle, Washington," by Gordon C. Jacoby, Patrick L. Williams, and Brendan M. Buckley in *Science*, volume 258, December 4, 1992, and "The calm before the quake?" in *Nature*, volume 343, February 8, 1990. The study I quote on the Hayward Fault was entitled, "Scenario for a Magnitude 7.0 Earthquake on the Hayward Fault," put out by the Earthquake Engineering Research Institute in 1996. See also *The Earth in Turmoil* by Kerry Sieh and Simon LeVay (W. H. Freeman and Company). The new fault in Los Angeles was reported in an article called "Scientists Identify a Major Fault Under Los Angeles That Could Produce Quake" in the March 5, 1999, *New York Times*. See also, "Wilshire fault: Earthquakes in Hollywood?" in *Geology*, volume 22, April 1994. For 200-year periodicity see, "Prospects for Larger or More Frequent Earthquakes in the Los Angeles Metropolitan Region" in *Science*, volume 267, January 13, 1995. The figures on a Tokyo quake come from an assessment from Risk Inc. For anthrax see a dispatch from Reuters on August 14, 2000, called, "Biological Weapons: Major Menace of the Future?" The quotes from Mirjana and Vicka come from *The Apparitions of Our Lady at Medjugorje* and *Queen of the Cosmos,* both of which I cited previously, along with *Visions of the Children*. I also use *Messages and Teachings of Mary at Medjugorje* by Rene Laurentin and Rene Lejeune (Faith Publishing Company). For the Gorringe threat see an article by Harry Fielding Reid in the *Bulletin of the Seismological Society of America*, volume IV, number two, June, 1914. Other information comes from Victor Sousa Moreira and his paper, "Seismicity of the Portuguese Continental Margin" in *Earthquakes at North-Atlantic Margins*, edited by S. Gregersen and P. W. Basham (Kluwer Academic Publishers, 1989). For viruses in polar ice see, "Scientists fear epidemics from frozen viruses" in a Reuters dispatch on September 1, 1998. For the strange small light see, "Rarely Bested Astronomers Are Stumped by a Tiny Light," in *The New York Times* August 17, 1999. For the XF-11 scare see *The New York Times* on March 12, 1998. The Franzen and Larsson quotes were cited previously. The Clube quote came from *The Times of London*, May 24, 1990. The last Marija quote was from *Queen of the Cosmos*. The quote on Noah and what archaeologists found was from MSNBC. The seer in Canada, Jim Singer, published his messages in a booklet, *"Use My Gifts,"* Ave Maria Centre of Peace, Toronto.

About the Author

Michael H. Brown is the author of 17 nonfiction books. This is his eleventh spiritual one. He has traveled to hundreds of cities here and in other nations, speaking and conducting research. He also has a website with daily spiritual news from around the world and it is accessed at WWW.SPIRITDAILY.COM.

Other Books by Michael H. Brown

The Trumpet of Gabriel
Society is currently fascinated with angels and other spiritual/supernatural phenomena. What does it mean? Many denominations report this as God's call for mankind to reform. Includes insights from Pat Robertson, Billy Graham, Fr. Stefano Gobbi, and Pope John Paul II. 320pp.
Order #7714 — $11.00   **ISBN: 1-880033-16-X**

Witness - Josyp Terelya
Autobiography of Josyp Terelya
Co-Authored By: Michael Brown
The dynamic autobiography of a contemporary mystic, suffering servant, and victim of Communism. Published before dramatic changes in Europe and the Soviet Union, it is a story of supernatural events and accurate predictions. 344pp.
Order #7715 — $12.00   **ISBN: 1-877678-17-1**

Final Hour
Akita, Betania, Fatima, Garabandal, Knock--all are obscure places on maps, or are they? Has the mother of Jesus appeared at these and other international locations? Why? Investigative journalist Michael H. Brown provides compelling information about our extraordinary century. This all time best seller includes a fascinating look at secular history and Biblical prophesies! Excellent photos. 368pp.
Order #7716 — $12.50   **ISBN: 1-57918-133-3**

Secrets of the Eucharist
The continuous True Prensence of Christ with us in the Blessed Sacrament is good news worth sharing! This book of heart-felt reflections on the Holy Eucharist demonstrates that devotion to this profound Sacrament is fundamental to our Faith. 96pp.
Order #7712 — $6.50   **ISBN: 1-880033-25-9**

Prayer of the Warrior
Spiritual warfare is at an all-time high! In whose army are you a member? A riveting account of front line action in the eternal battle between good and evil as experienced by best-selling author Michael H. Brown. Parapsychology, a brush with the Mafia, and fascinating encounters with the supernatural make Michael's story something you will not want to miss and inspires all to join in this spiritual war. 256pp.
Order #7711 — $11.00   **ISBN: 1-880033-10-0**

Seven Days with Mary
This is a book of devotion based on the most ancient and solid of Mary's historic apparitions. Mr. Brown takes one of Mary's approved appearances for each day of the week and explains its often hidden aspects and offers prayers and meditations to accompany it. 112pp.
Order #7713 — $6.50   **ISBN: 1-880033-26-7**